STRESS

the PSYCHOLOGY
of MANAGING PRESSURE

STRESS
the PSYCHOLOGY of MANAGING PRESSURE

DIANE McINTOSH, MD, FRCPC
AND JONATHAN HOROWITZ, PhD
WITH MEGAN KAYE

Penguin
Random
House

Senior Editor Camilla Hallinan
Senior Art Editors Emma Forge, Karen Constanti
Designer Tom Forge
Editorial Assistant Alice Horne
Jacket Art Editor Harriet Yeomans
Producer, Pre-Production Rebecca Fallowfield
Print Producer Poppy Werder-Harris
Creative Technical Support Sonia Charbonnier
Managing Editor Dawn Henderson
Managing Art Editor Marianne Markham
Art Director Maxine Pedliham
Publisher Mary-Clare Jerram

Written by Megan Kaye
Illustrations Keith Hagan

First published in Great Britain in 2018
by Dorling Kindersley Limited
80 Strand, London WC2R 0RL,
A Penguin Random House Company

A CIP catalogue record for this book is
available from the British Library
ISBN 978-0-2412-8627-2

Printed and bound in China

All images © Dorling Kindersley Limited
For further information see: www.dkimages.com

A WORLD OF IDEAS:
SEE ALL THERE IS TO KNOW

www.dk.com

CONSULTANT PSYCHIATRIST

Diane McIntosh, MD, FRCPC

Dr McIntosh is a clinical assistant professor in the
Department of Psychiatry at the University of British
Columbia, Canada. She has a busy private practice and
is extensively involved in providing continuing medical
education programs for colleagues nationally and
internationally, with a focus on rational pharmacology.
She has a particular interest in the neurobiology of
mood and anxiety disorders, and sits on the Board of
Directors of CANMAT (Canadian Network For Mood
and Anxiety Treatments). She also blogs about mental
health issues for *The Huffington Post*.

CONSULTANT PSYCHOLOGIST

Jonathan Horowitz, PhD

Clinical psychologist and certified cognitive therapist,
Dr Horowitz specializes in the clinical treatment of
stress and anxiety disorders. As a researcher, he has
contributed to federally funded research projects in the
areas of stress and anxiety, substance abuse, and
organizational behaviour. As a clinician, he has over ten
years of experience providing treatment to individuals
suffering from anxiety disorders. He is the founder and
director of the San Francisco Stress and Anxiety Center,
which provides stress and anxiety management
services to individuals, couples, and organizations.

ACKNOWLEDGMENTS

The publisher would like to thank:
Toby Mann for editorial assistance; Corinne Masciocchi
for proofreading; Margaret McCormack for the index;
and US editor Kayla Dugger.

CONTENTS

CHAPTER 3
STRESS IN THE MOMENT
TROUBLE-SHOOTING TACTICS FOR SHORT-TERM STRESS

FOREWORD

Age, race, gender, money – nothing can shield us from having to face stressful situations that might feel difficult, even impossible, to overcome. Nor should they, because stress is an essential part of life. Any experience or situation that makes you feel threatened or overwhelmed is a "stressor". Good stress helps you to focus on your goals and complete important tasks. Without stress we would fail to achieve our greatest accomplishments because the ones we value most are usually stressful and require a great deal of effort. Bad stress isn't productive and can halt your advancement and dampen your spirits. This book will help you master life's stressors, good or bad, with greater ease – not by eliminating stress, but by building on your strengths and encouraging the development of new coping skills.

The five chapters that follow are based on a careful review of the most recent and important scientific research, which has been translated to be relevant and helpful for anyone who wants to feel better able to manage their stress. When you're trying to overcome life's challenges, particularly the more stressful or unpleasant ones, understanding how your body and your brain react, and how you can influence that reaction, can help you to feel a greater sense of control. Chapter 1 focuses on just that, by defining stress and explaining how your body reacts physically and emotionally to scary situations. These pages will help you determine why you feel stressed, which is the first step towards taking control.

We all have our own ways of dealing with stress, but there are some simple yet powerful, proven coping techniques – and by understanding their pros and cons, you will be able to choose the strategy that's right for you. How you manage stress must work for you, so that you can develop a realistic, practical plan that fits your own needs.

In Chapter 2, you'll see that you are not alone in feeling stressed when you're coping with the ongoing pressures of day-to-day life. It can sometimes feel like we're juggling many balls and struggling to keep them all in the air. Whether that's in our work or home life, all of us can feel under pressure sometimes, but there are many useful approaches to dealing with stress that can help us lead a more peaceful life, even during busy times and in stressful situations.

We also face the stress of difficult, even life-altering events at some point, such as caring for a loved one during illness, dealing with a painful loss, or living through a difficult divorce. In Chapter 3, you'll learn that feeling overwhelmed, sad, or frightened is a completely normal reaction to a major stress, but it is possible to learn skills that will help you to endure and build strength as you weather the storms.

Chapter 4 is all about de-stressing your life, with a review of how to manage your stress in the long term. Close friends, pets, or activities you might turn to when you need to feel calm and comforted – all these and more have science to back up their powerful stress-relieving properties. Finally, Chapter 5 discusses the importance of knowing when stress has become so serious that you need to ask for help. While this book aims to help you manage your stress before you're feeling completely overwhelmed, it's good to know there is help available and that you are not alone.

Most importantly, this book is about building resilience – the ability to bounce back after a very stressful period. If you think of resilience as being your "emotional muscles", you might feel that those are a little weak right now. The stress management tools you will learn about in this book will help you to build those muscles by using your existing strengths and further develop them to become a more powerful resource, so in future when stress happens – and it will – you'll be able to recover rapidly and without lasting harm. Some people are naturally more resilient than others, but these are skills that anyone can learn throughout life.

While we are both clinicians and educators with many years of experience, we never stop learning, especially from our clients. We share these lessons throughout this book because they are key foundations of happiness. This book is not about living a stress-free life; it's about living a happier life because you are better equipped to manage your stress.

Diane McIntosh, MD, FRCPC   **Jonathan Horowitz, PhD**

CHAPTER 1

STRESS IN PERSPECTIVE

HOW STRESS AFFECTS YOUR BODY AND MIND

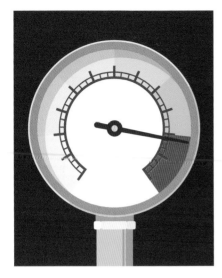

WHAT IS STRESS?
WHAT IT IS, AND WHAT IT ISN'T

Stress feels uncomfortable, but not every uncomfortable feeling is stress – and being confused about what you feel is stressful in itself. Let's begin by gaining some clarity in understanding our own emotions.

People use the word "stress" interchangeably with other terms such as worry, anxiety, and fear, but stress is, at its heart, our conviction that we won't be able to cope with the challenges we're facing.

It's always easier to deal with difficult emotions if we understand them better. Stress can provoke fear, anxiety, and worry but each represents a different emotional reaction. By appreciating the differences and the relationships between these emotions, we can put our problems in perspective.

Is worry the same as stress?
Put simply, worry is an attempt to avoid unpleasant consequences by adopting repetitive thought patterns – for example, "What if" questions such as "What if I fall

sick? What if I lose my job?" – which we describe with words such as "fretting" and "brooding". We don't need or want those thoughts to pop into our minds over and over, but it can be hard to stop them.

It might feel like worrying or "thinking about" our problems is helpful, but that is not the same as

> ## It's not stress that kills us,
> it is **our reaction** to it.
>
> **Hans Selye**
> Hungarian physician and father of stress research
> (1907–1982)

"thinking through" our problems – in other words, confronting a situation and trying to address it. By actively problem-solving, we gain a greater sense of control.

Fear and anxiety
Where worry is a mental habit, fear is an instinctive reaction – usually in the face of a perceived threat. Fear is a survival trait, and there are good evolutionary reasons why we're capable of feeling it. Our reactions to fear are grouped into four categories:

- **Escape** (flight) or avoidance (preflight). We run away from a threat if we can.
- **Aggressive defence** (the "fight" part of "fight or flight"). If we can't escape or we don't stand a good chance of victory, we may attack.
- **Freezing/immobility.** A valuable reaction if we're trying to hide, or if we don't want to antagonize someone who is unpredictable.

■ **Submission/appeasement.**
When the threat comes from within our own "herd", the best option is sometimes to suppress our anger to avoid being rejected.

If fear is a normal reaction to a scary event, what is anxiety? When fear becomes excessive or unwarranted and starts to affect our quality of life and prevents us from doing what we need or want to do, it is best described as anxiety. The stress-management techniques described in this book will give you more confidence and security, which will help reduce your anxiety.

Learning from our feelings

Throughout this book we'll focus on building your stress resilience through growing your understanding of how stress can impact your life. Recognizing that stress can provoke worry and heighten anxiety (see below) can be empowering. Facing our fears head-on makes them less threatening and helps make us stronger and more resilient.

❓ TELLING OUR FEELINGS APART

If we're feeling nervous or tense, are we necessarily experiencing stress? Actually, it's helpful to consider four different categories so we can be clear how we feel – and hence what we need to do to feel better.

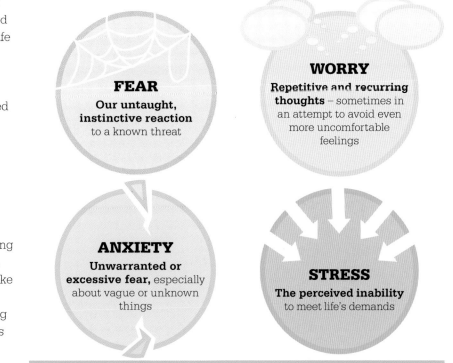

FEAR
Our untaught, instinctive reaction to a known threat

WORRY
Repetitive and recurring thoughts – sometimes in an attempt to avoid even more uncomfortable feelings

ANXIETY
Unwarranted or excessive fear, especially about vague or unknown things

STRESS
The perceived inability to meet life's demands

🔍 MAKING FRIENDS WITH FEAR

We shouldn't fear fear, as it can be a good motivator to make positive changes. Anxiety and worry, though, can fuel stress. As this book will show, we can reduce our stress by managing our anxiety and worries better.

ANXIETY
"I can't work properly, I'm too anxious to concentrate."

STRESS
"I can't handle my workload."

Stress and worry feed into each other

WORRY
"What if I can't cope and I lose my job?"

Anxiety makes worry worse

Fear can prompt constructive behaviour change, reducing worry

FEAR
"I'm afraid of falling behind, so I'll take some work home."

NATURALLY STRESSED
A NECESSARY PART OF LIFE

It's a popular belief that stress is bad, to be avoided at all costs. In fact, though, stress is a normal part of being alive – and the less we fear it, the more we can lead a happy and healthy existence.

Undoubtedly many of us could do with more peace of mind, but stress is a natural part of being human. It motivates us, provokes change, and encourages learning. Sometimes it's healthy to embrace what stress has to offer.

How dangerous is stress?

There are many studies showing that stress is bad for the body. High stress levels are found to increase the risk of cardiovascular disease, diabetes, cancer, and high blood pressure. The mere thought of that is enough to make anyone nervous.

Stanford psychologist Kelly McGonigal argues that our problem isn't exactly stress itself, but a "toxic relationship to stress". If we see stress as an enemy against which we are helpless, then science does show that we suffer ill effects. A 2006 American study found that a stressed attitude to our emotions – feeling we'll be harmed by, or unable to cope with them – makes us more vulnerable to panic attacks and anxiety disorders. If we get stressed about being stressed, that's when we suffer the worst effects.

A healthier approach

We can certainly change aspects of our lives to make them less stressful, and this book offers ideas for how to

> Pain is inevitable. **Suffering is optional**.
>
> **Haruki Murakami**
> Japanese novelist

ONLY CONNECT

Worrying about stressful situations tends to make us feel more isolated – we feel as if no-one else understands what we're going through. American psychologist Kelly McGonigal advises that we ask ourselves how our stress is connected to something that is meaningful to us (see pp.44–45), and to view ourselves in a broader context – all of humanity. By placing ourselves in the bigger picture, we can put our stress in proportion as part of a meaningful life.

Situation	Ask yourself	How does this tie to something meaningful?	How does this make me like other people?
I've got exams coming up and I'm not sure I'll pass.	Do I want to give up? Or is this qualification worth struggling for?	This subject is something I really want to know about and will help in my career.	Everyone feels tense when they take an exam.
My baby has been crying on and off all night.	Do I really want to turn over and sleep? Or comfort him so he knows he can count on me?	Everyone needs a loving start in life. I want to give him that.	Babies are hard work. I'm sure all parents have to cope with this sometimes.
Our annual employee reviews are coming up.	Do I have to depend on my boss for self-esteem? Or do I see myself as a valuable person?	I might be able to learn something useful from the feedback.	Workplaces aren't easy. Coping with criticism is a challenge we all face.
My mother-in-law is elderly and wants to move in with us.	Would I rather she was in a nursing home, or does her wellbeing matter more to me?	She was always good to me, and I want to support my family.	It might be difficult at times, but many people care for their elderly loved ones.

do that. However, we can also view stress as what McGonigal calls "a signal of meaning". We don't stress out about things that don't matter to us; stress is a sign there's something going on that we care about.

When we're facing a situation that has consequences that matter to us, we may experience some natural fear at the thought of things going wrong. This feeling of fear is what provokes us to react to the situation, and it might mean we need to change our approach or create a new strategy to cope. Facing these uncomfortable feelings is healthy, and helps us adapt to the changing

circumstances that are a normal part of life. Rather than avoiding the stress, we can make good use of it.

Stress is, fundamentally, an adaptive response to high-pressure situations. By "adaptive", scientists mean a process that helps us adapt to a situation and create a positive outcome. We adapt faster and better by learning not to be overwhelmed. We can face stress and take back our sense of control by learning and adapting strategies over time. As you go through this book, we'll discuss the tools and tactics you can use to ride your stress like a wave, rather than sinking under it.

IS IT JUST ME?

In 2017, the American Psychological Association's annual "Stress in America" survey reported that…

20% … around 1 in 5 Americans experience a **chronic level of stress** …

36% … and around 1 in 3 say **reducing their stress** is a priority.

CAN STRESS BE GOOD FOR US?

A BOOST TO THE SYSTEM

If believing stress is bad for us is a self-fulfilling prophecy, then how can we convince ourselves to believe the opposite? Well, there's a lot of good science suggesting that some stress can be healthy.

According to American psychologist Kelly McGonigal, our beliefs about stress have as much to do with its impact on our health as the stress itself. It's good for both body and mind if we understand how a moderate level of stress can actually be a beneficial experience.

Staying sharp

A key concept is "neuroplasticity". Our brains are malleable, and rewire themselves in response to new experiences. At the University of California, Berkeley, stress researchers Daniela Kaufer and Elizabeth Kirby point out that this means moderately stressful events can actually be good for us: they force our brains to keep learning.

In 2013, Kaufer and Kirby exposed lab rats to a few hours of moderate stress. At first, the stress appeared to have little effect on the rats – but two weeks later, after repeated exposure, their brains had

> **Intermittent stressful events** are probably what **keep the brain more alert**, and you perform better when you are alert.
>
> **Elizabeth Kirby**
> neuroscientist, University of California, Berkeley

developed new neural connections that improved their performance on memory tests. The same applies to humans, Kaufer and Kirby believe: as long as it doesn't reach the point of serious misery or trauma, exposure to intermittent bursts of moderate stress helps our nerve cells to proliferate. Put simply, stress challenges our brains, and our brains respond to challenges by adapting and growing.

Boosting the immune system

According to a 2012 American study, rats subjected to various kinds of stress also showed more infection-fighting white cells in their bloodstream. In terms of survival, we cannot afford to get sick if we're in a potentially dangerous situation, so when we are facing danger – anything from witnessing a car crash to tackling a difficult project – we release more of the cells that guard us against infections. Chronic, long-term stress can be bad for our health (see pp.196–197), but a moderate amount may help protect us from disease.

The power of belief

Does it do any good to reflect on these benefits? In 2013, American researcher Alia Crum and her colleagues split 400 employees of an international financial institution into two groups, and showed each group a different series of videos about stress – one series described stress as debilitating, and another described it as life-enhancing. The workers shown the "enhancing" videos reported that, as a result, their productivity and their

? BREAKING THE ASSOCIATION

Facing a challenge can be either a frightening or an exciting experience. According to a 2012 American study, it depends on how we appraise the situation – that is, how we interpret it and what we tell ourselves.

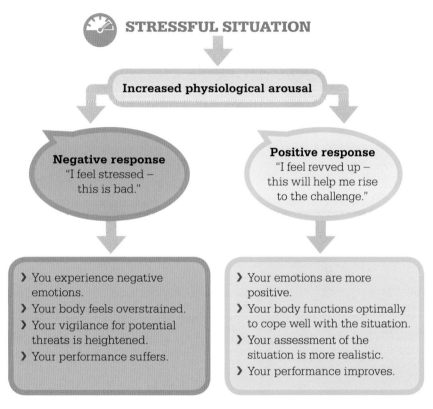

STRESSFUL SITUATION

Increased physiological arousal

Negative response
"I feel stressed – this is bad."

Positive response
"I feel revved up – this will help me rise to the challenge."

> You experience negative emotions.
> Your body feels overstrained.
> Your vigilance for potential threats is heightened.
> Your performance suffers.

> Your emotions are more positive.
> Your body functions optimally to cope well with the situation.
> Your assessment of the situation is more realistic.
> Your performance improves.

wellbeing had increased as a result of watching the videos. Stress can give us the stimulation we need to develop and perform at our best – as long as we're able to see the stress as a worthwhile challenge.

Severe or chronic, long-term stress is not good for us, but moderate, short-term stress can make us more alert, observant, and healthy – and the more aware we are of these benefits, the more likely we are to experience them.

3.8/10

In the American Psychological Association's 2015 stress survey, on a scale of 1–10, people saw 3.8 as a **healthy level of stress**, but ranked their own stress at 5.1.

ACQUIRING RESILIENCE
BEND BUT DON'T BREAK

Nobody likes feeling stressed, but some people are particularly skilled at coping with upsetting events and carrying on. What is the secret to building resilience, and how can we develop it in ourselves?

What is resilience? The word comes from a Latin verb, *resilire*, meaning "to leap back". A resilient person is not someone who never suffers, but one who can suffer and spring back again. It's a quality that can help us to successfully endure stressful times: studies have confirmed that resilient individuals show a smaller increase of the "stress hormone" cortisol (see pp.20–21) when under pressure. We can all benefit from a more resilient attitude.

A resilient personality?

If some people cope with stress particularly well, does that mean they were simply lucky to have a resilient personality – and if we weren't born resilient, should we simply resign ourselves to unhappiness? In fact, the opposite is true. Resilience is not a personality trait, and no one is immune to the challenges of life. It is, rather, as a European team of psychologists put it in 2013, "a dynamic and adaptive process". Essentially, we can learn to be resilient. How we choose to *react* to adversity can make a big difference.

> Resilience is not invulnerability to stress, but, rather, the **ability to recover** from negative events.
>
> **Rachel Dias**
> Brazilian psychologist

✓ THE POWER OF SELF-EFFICACY

A major pillar of resiliency is what psychologists call "self-efficacy": the belief that our actions have the power to affect our circumstances. There are four key ways we build self-efficacy, so be alert to opportunities that can increase your sense of confidence and control in the face of stress:

Persevering through failures
"I've survived worse than this, I'll manage."

Finding good role models
"Mum raised me all by herself. People can be strong."

Interpreting our feelings positively
"I'm feeling so nervous. Let's call it an exciting challenge."

Social persuasion
"My best friend says I'm resourceful. Maybe he's right."

Unexpected tactics

An influential set of studies in the 1990s by American psychologist George Bonanno examined the coping methods of people who had endured significant stress and loss but maintained good mental health. Their resilience was admirable, but how they were able to maintain wellbeing was surprising. Bonanno described it as "coping ugly" – and yet it worked. Strategies included:

- **Exaggerating** how well they had behaved under stress. It could seem vain, or even narcissistic, but it helped them to avoid self-blame.

- **Refusing** to entertain negative thoughts. Some people simply declared they could handle things – and this seemed to be a self-fulfilling prophecy.
- **Laughing it off.** While some psychologists might have called this denial, and the jokes weren't always in good taste, humour could lessen the pain of a stressful event.

As ugly coping demonstrates, when you're under stress, don't feel guilty about using unconventional means to cope. Build up your buffers (see right) and be confident. Use the tools that work for you.

🔍 CREATING A BUFFER

When we face the stressors that are an inevitable part of life, resilience can limit its impact. A 2015 Brazilian study of people caring for family members with dementia – an unquestionably stressful role – identified a strong collection of traits, resources, and attitudes that built resilience and heightened the caregivers' sense of wellbeing.

STRESSFUL LIFE EVENTS

BUILD UP YOUR RESOURCES

- **Good coping strategies** (pp.26–29)
- **Focusing on the positive** (pp.52–53, 180–181)
- **Self-efficacy** (above left)
- **An internal locus of control** that is, a "master of my own fate" attitude (pp.46–47)
- **Being fully engaged in daily activities** (pp.174–175)
- **Seeking and embracing a challenge** (pp.16–17, 174–175)
- **Strong social support** (pp.176–179)

GAIN RESILIENCE
and enjoy lower stress, more confidence, and better mental health.

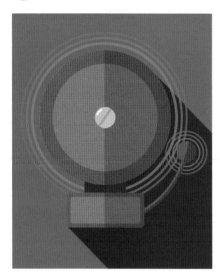

THE BODY'S ALARM SYSTEM
THE PHYSIOLOGY OF STRESS

Science has traditionally used the term "fight or flight" to describe the body's reaction to stress, but recent research paints a more complicated picture. Being aware of this can help us manage stress more effectively.

What actually happens to us when we're stressed? The experience begins as a physical reaction, which can be extremely powerful.

The stress chemicals

Stress is a complex biological process that involves the entire body, led by two chemicals: the steroid hormone cortisol and the neurotransmitter noradrenaline –

> The **changes in the body** [make it] more **efficient in the struggle**.
>
> **Walter Bradford Cannon**
> American neurologist, on the fight-or-flight response

one of the chemical messengers that sends signals through the nervous system.

Noradrenaline is the "fight-or-flight" messenger that is responsible for our immediate reaction when we are faced with a threat. For example, if a barking dog suddenly and unexpectedly lunges towards you, you jump back and either you brace yourself to fight it off or you run away. Noradrenaline causes the body to:

■ Increase the heart rate.
■ Elevate blood pressure.
■ Boost energy.
■ Heighten vigilance.
■ Send more blood to the muscles, allowing the brain and body to react quickly in the face of a threat.

Cortisol, the "stress hormone", works more slowly (minutes) than noradrenaline (a fraction of a second). Cortisol:

■ Stimulates glucose production, which gives you energy.
■ Enhances the brain's ability to use glucose, allowing you to think more quickly.
■ Regulates other systems, such as appetite, sex drive, and digestion. In times of stress, cortisol directs the body's resources away from these systems, so the body can focus on more immediate actions necessary for survival.

Cortisol also helps us to recover from stress, restoring calm to the brain and to the rest of the body.

Noradrenaline and cortisol are essential to our survival, playing key roles in our stress response – but if the amount of either one is too high for too long, that can lead to negative consequences. Moderating our stress by learning good coping strategies protects our mental and physical health.

Q TWIN SYSTEMS

Rather than having a single nervous system, there are two systems that complement one another: the sympathetic and the parasympathetic nervous systems. When we talk about the stress response, we're talking about the activation of the sympathetic nervous system.

SYMPATHETIC NERVOUS SYSTEM The fight-or-flight neural pathways, quick to react	**PARASYMPATHETIC NERVOUS SYSTEM** The rest-and-digest neural pathways, slow to react
⬇	⬇
Dilates pupils Dries mouth Opens airways in lungs Quickens heart rate Inhibits digestive activity Contracts bladder Tenses muscles	Contracts pupils Stimulates saliva Constricts airways Slows heart rate Promotes digestion Relaxes bladder Relaxes muscles

The sympathetic nervous system allows us to take immediate action in response to a threat. However, when it is time to rest, eat, and recover, activities that stimulate our parasympathetic nervous system – such as relaxation (see pp.150–151) and meditation (pp.132–135) – can help.

THE STRESS CURVE

Is stress good or bad for performance? In fact there's a "sweet spot", which differs for each of us. In 1908, American psychologists Robert Yerkes and John Dodson created an inverted-U model for the ideal amount of pressure, a model that's still used today. They were describing the effect of the stress hormones secreted by the body's hypothalamic-pituitary-adrenal (HPA) axis. With too little pressure, we aren't engaged; with too much, we become flustered and unable to concentrate. In between these two extremes, we experience a state of flow – we're alert, focused, and ready to give our best.

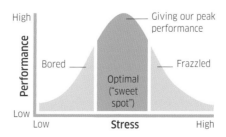

⬤ ACTIVATING OUR ALARM SYSTEM

In producing a stress response to a real or potential threat, the body assesses external circumstances and internal resources.

Our senses (eyes, ears, etc) detect a **threat.**

⬇

The message passes straight to a part of the brain called the amygdala.

⬇

The amygdala immediately provokes a **fear response.**

⬇

Instantly, noradrenaline increases heart rate and blood pressure, so we can **react quickly** and **fight or flee.**

⬇

Cortisol increases the blood sugar level and diverts resources so the body has the **energy** it needs to respond to the threat.

If the threat is not imminent, giving us time to think, the brain's hippocampus reminds us of past experiences that might reduce our fear, and the cerebral cortex allows us to take stock and plan a response.

WHEN YOU CHOOSE TO VIEW STRESS AS HELPFUL, YOU CREATE THE BIOLOGY OF COURAGE

KELLY MCGONIGAL, HEALTH PSYCHOLOGIST AT STANFORD UNIVERSITY

IDENTIFY YOUR STRESSORS
FINDING THE TROUBLE SPOTS

Any experience, problem, or situation that makes us feel threatened or overwhelmed is a "stressor". As a first step in making your life more manageable, see if you can get a good overview of your own stressors.

A stressor is an event that disrupts our homeostasis. That's the state where the body's internal environment is in balance, and factors such as body temperature, blood sugar, blood pressure, and hormone levels are relatively stable. These can all be affected by both physical and psychological threats, and unless they return to their usual level, the body will start to suffer ill effects.

Real or perceived threats

Any threat to our physical wellbeing is a stressor – a fall or a car accident will provoke some degree of stress. A stressor can also be something we merely perceive as dangerous. If you get a poor evaluation at work, you aren't in bodily danger, but you may worry about losing your job and being unable to pay your bills. Your body processes the experience as dangerous, and responds with symptoms such as elevated blood pressure, even though no direct physical confrontation took place.

Stress can result from a wide range of experiences. Try the self-assessment on the facing page and see how many questions you tick: every individual has their own stressors, but this list covers the experiences that are stressful for almost anyone. While few of us could experience such problems and not feel some degree of stress, exactly how much you suffer can be, at least partly, in your hands. This book discusses a wide variety of techniques you can use, both to reduce the number of stressors in your life and to cope better with the ones you can't eliminate completely.

? RELATIONSHIP STRESSORS

- Have you recently separated or divorced?
- Are you having marital problems?
- Have you recently been widowed?
- Have you recently lost a close relative or friend?
- Are you single?
- Are you having problems in your sex life?
- Are you planning a wedding?
- Are you pregnant?
- Have you recently had a baby?
- If you have recently had a baby, did you have a difficult birth?
- Has your son or daughter recently left home?
- Has your partner recently changed their job or retired?
- Are you caring for someone who is disabled or in poor health?
- Are you having trouble with your in-laws?
- Are you seeing more or less of your family than usual?
- Has your social life changed recently, becoming more demanding or emptier?

? PERSONAL STRESSORS

- Are you in poor health or injured?
- Have you, in the past, been in combat or done other dangerous or frightening work?
- Have you experienced a traumatic event, such as an accident or mugging?
- Are you trying to break a habit, such as smoking or junk food?
- Have you recently achieved anything major that you now have to measure up to?
- Are you just starting or finishing an educational stage?
- Are you moving house?
- Do you live somewhere unpleasantly noisy?
- Are you having trouble sleeping?
- Are you in trouble with the law?
- Do you face discrimination, based on your race, your sexuality, or any other reason?
- Is someone bullying you or abusing you?
- Do you have problems with substance abuse, such as alcohol, medications, or caffeine?
- Are you lonely?

? JOB AND MONEY STRESSORS

- Are you unemployed?
- Have you recently been promoted or demoted?
- Are you having problems with your boss?
- Do you have more work than you feel you can manage?
- Does your work involve long hours, presentations, physical dangers, or a hostile environment?
- Are you changing your line of work?
- Do you have a tough commute?
- Have you taken on a mortgage or other loan?
- Are you struggling to pay bills?
- Have your financial circumstances recently undergone any drastic changes?
- Are you approaching retirement, or have you recently retired?

Q THE TOP FIVE

The Holmes-Rahe Stress Inventory, a questionnaire the medical community considers an authoritative measure of stress, lists the top five stressors in life as: **1** the death of a spouse; **2** divorce; **3** separating from a spouse; **4** imprisonment; **5** the death of a close relative.

COPING MECHANISMS
GETTING SOME CONTROL

We all have our own ways of dealing with stress, but some methods are more productive than others. A clear understanding of the pros and cons can help you choose the right strategy.

Coping is a broad concept, covering all the thoughts and actions we use to make a threatening situation more manageable. Psychology sorts coping methods into two basic types – "problem-focused" and "emotion-focused". Which of these responses is best for you can depend a great deal on your circumstances.

Problem-focused coping

Where we have the power to change things, problem-focused coping is generally the better tactic. Methods include:

- **Improving time management,** allowing us time to make necessary changes.
- **Analyzing** the situation and what we can or cannot take on.
- **Working extra hours** to get through a crisis. (This is only a solution to a short-term problem; if long hours become routine, the problem is the routine itself.)
- **Talking** to someone who can help change the situation.

If you can change the situation, the stressor may go away, or at least become less burdensome.

> Make the best use of **what is in your power**, and take the rest as it happens.
>
> **Epictetus**
> Stoic philosopher
> 55–135 CE

HOW TO MAKE THE RIGHT CHOICE

Problem-focused coping is excellent if we can manage it, but there are situations in which emotion-focused coping is the only option. Base your choice of coping style on how much control you have over a situation.

Ways of coping	A situation you can change	A situation outside your control
Problem-focused coping	✓ Helps reduce stressors	✗ Liable to increase your frustration
Emotion-focused coping	✗ Leaves problems unresolved (such as a health problem) and possibly deteriorating	✓ Helps reduce your internal stress level

Emotion-focused coping

Emotion-focused tactics involve trying to control your response to a stressor. This is sensible if you have no control over your circumstances; if you cannot change a situation, changing your reaction can limit its negative impact. That said, some emotion-focused methods can lead to more problems:

* ✖ **Alcohol or drugs.** These may offer a brief respite from stress, but can lead to health problems, and sometimes dependency.
* ✖ **Comfort eating.** Junk food or too much food is unhealthy, as is weight gain, which can also hurt our self-esteem.
* ✖ **Brooding.** Dwelling on a bad situation tends to make it feel even worse.
* ✖ **Fantasizing.** Indulging in wishful thinking can make reality feel less satisfying.

* ✖ **Avoidance.** If we deny there's a problem, we don't fix it.
* ✖ **Blame.** Self-blame increases our risk of depression, while blaming others can alienate people.

More effective emotion-focused methods include:

* ✔ **Getting social support.** Studies confirm that the comfort of friends and family lowers our stress levels (pp.176–179).
* ✔ **Meditation and/or prayer.** For people comfortable with these methods, they can be an effective way of improving our emotional stability (pp.132–135).
* ✔ **Writing** – for instance, keeping a gratitude diary can help to improve our moods (pp.40–41 and 108–109).
* ✔ **Seeking out a therapist.** The right treatment can be extremely helpful (pp.208–209).

? CURE OR ENDURE?

Does your situation call for problem-focused or emotion-focused coping? To help you decide, ask yourself some simple questions:

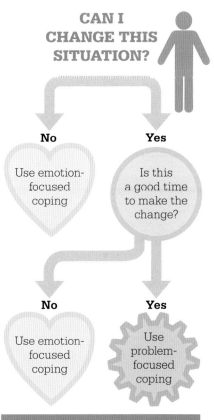

CAN I CHANGE THIS SITUATION?

No — Use emotion-focused coping

Yes — Is this a good time to make the change?

No — Use emotion-focused coping

Yes — Use problem-focused coping

Psychologists agree there are situations where emotion-focused coping may be the right choice in the short-term, provided we choose a strategy that actively addresses our feelings rather than trying to avoid them.

Which method you choose is likely to vary from stressor to stressor, so use your best judgment and pick a coping strategy that fits your needs.

»

> [**Coping** consists of] efforts to **prevent or diminish threat**, harm, and loss or to **reduce associated distress**.

Charles S. Carver and Jennifer Connor-Smith
American psychologists

⟫ The power of re-framing

One of the most constructive coping mechanisms is a technique known as "cognitive re-framing". Since stress is the feeling that we are unable to cope with a challenge, one way to reduce the stress is to consider how our thinking can cause us to believe we can't cope.

Half full or half empty?

Cognitive Behavioural Therapy (see pp.52–53), is based on the principle of re-framing. CBT is a well-researched, effective approach for managing both short-term and chronic stress. It helps you to be aware of how you talk to yourself about stressful situations. If you tend to interpret events negatively – viewing the glass as half empty rather than half full – see whether trying a different perspective gives you more confidence.

A 2014 American study asked volunteers to sing karaoke in front of the experimenters. Those who were asked to say "I am excited"

⊙ PROCESSING LIFE'S DEMANDS

American psychologists Richard Lazarus and Susan Folkman see stress as a combination of our external circumstances and how we react to them. Lazarus defines our reaction as "cognitive appraisal" – how we present the situation to ourselves – and notes that we go through primary and secondary appraisal stages. If you're under pressure, be aware that your secondary appraisal is as important as your first in managing your stress.

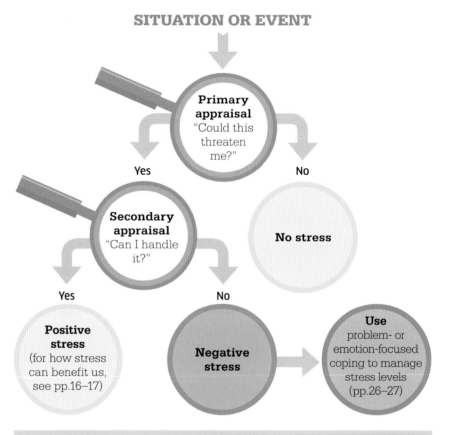

SITUATION OR EVENT

Primary appraisal
"Could this threaten me?"

Yes   No

Secondary appraisal
"Can I handle it?"

No stress

Yes   No

Positive stress
(for how stress can benefit us, see pp.16–17)

Negative stress

Use problem- or emotion-focused coping to manage stress levels (pp.26–27)

before they sang made fewer mistakes and reported feeling greater confidence in their abilities, than those who had been asked to say "I am nervous". By re-framing the situation and their reaction to it, the excited singers were able to turn their stress into a sense of energy that helped both their

objective performance and their subjective feelings.

Sometimes we need to tackle stress with problem-solving, and sometimes with emotion management. Either way, try to re-frame the situation to yourself more positively: it is likely to give you a better outcome.

? THE SCALE OF MATURITY

Psychodynamic theory focuses on a person's thought processes as opposed to actions, and argues that in the face of stress, we employ defence mechanisms – some of which are more mature and thus more useful than others. More primitive (childish) responses tend to be emotion-focused, while the most mature include both problem-solving and more positive emotion-focused solutions. Under extreme stress, we are more likely to revert to immature coping strategies. If you're feeling extremely stressed, stop and ask yourself: if you're using any of these more primitive tactics, could a more mature approach help?

| PRIMITIVE | LESS PRIMITIVE, MORE MATURE | MATURE |

PRIMITIVE

- **Acting out.** Tantrums, self-harm, and other dangerous behaviour: *"How dare that driver overtake me!" (Accelerates)*

- **Compartmentalization.** Acting as if one part of your life has no connection to another: *"I don't feel guilty for the unethical things my boss makes me do – that's work, that's not me."*

- **Denial.** Refusing to accept reality: *"That breast lump is probabaly nothing."*

- **Dissociation.** Checking out mentally so as to numb yourself from noticing or feeling anything: *"I can't think about this right now, I'll just watch TV."*

- **Projection.** Attributing your own thoughts and impulses to someone else: *"That guy I don't like clearly thinks I'm an idiot."*

- **Reaction formation.** Changing an undesired thought into its opposite: *"I don't trust Martha? Of course I do."*

LESS PRIMITIVE, MORE MATURE

- **Displacement.** Taking anger out on someone who isn't the cause of the problem: *"I've got enough to deal with without you messing up as well!"*

- **Intellectualization.** Focusing on thoughts to avoid feelings: *"No point in me crying about Mum's stroke – I'm going to research it instead."*

- **Rationalization.** Coming up with an explanation for an unwanted reality: *"Nina says she's thinking of leaving me, but she doesn't really mean it – she's just testing my commitment."*

- **Repression.** Squashing down unacceptable thoughts: *"Nice people don't get angry."*

- **Undoing.** Compensating for a regretted action by going to the other extreme – for instance, lavishly praising someone you accidentally insulted: *"Oh dear, Frank is offended. I'll tell everyone how smart and talented he is."*

MATURE

- **Assertiveness.** Respectful, clear, and firm communication of your needs: *"Darling, if I'm going to collect the kids from their swimming club after school today, I need you to get dinner ready."*

- **Compensation.** Counter-balancing perceived weaknesses in one area with strengths in another: *"Yes, my boss is always picking on me, but I'm lucky to have good workmates."*

- **Sublimation.** Channelling unacceptable impulses into more acceptable ones, such as joking, distraction, or altruism: *"I'm so frustrated with my sister right now, but I'll feel better about myself if I offer to help."*

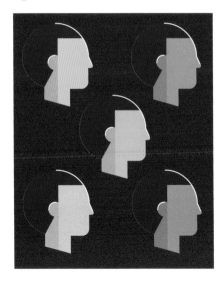

STRESSED BY NATURE?
PERSONALITY AND PRESSURE

Our personalities affect every aspect of stress, from what sort of situations we get into, to how we respond and cope. A classic psychological model can help us assess how vulnerable we are.

In 1981, after decades of testing and refinement, the "Five Factor Model" was finally designated the "Big Five" by American researcher Lewis Goldberg. The Big Five is one of the most authoritative and widely accepted means of measuring personality. The Big Five traits are extroversion/introversion, agreeableness, conscientiousness, openness, and neuroticism.

Openness
Conscientiousness
Extroversion
Agreeableness
Neuroticism

A "Big Five" acronym

Neuroticism

The term "neuroticism" sounds harsh, but it simply implies that someone is more vulnerable to stress and finds it more difficult to shrug off negative feelings and experiences.

If your neuroticism is relatively high, it's all the more important to practise ongoing, effective self-care. Neuroticism can be managed or reduced if you work on your coping skills (see pp.26–29), and so with good stress management, having a "neurotic" personality trait does not mean you cannot have a happy life.

Other traits

Even people with low neuroticism are prone to stress in certain situations. To help maintain your wellbeing, consider these points:

- **Arrange your social diary** to suit you. Extroverts become stressed when lonely; introverts when socially overloaded.
- **Choose the right friends.** Agreeable people – who prefer to cooperate, not confront – are more troubled by conflict than less agreeable types, who may feel stressed if they're expected to defer to social expectations.
- **Plan your work realistically.** Conscientious people are more likely to take on heavy loads and become stressed, while the less conscientious can find themselves in stressful situations if they neglect essential responsibilities.
- **Know your comfort zone.** People open to new experiences can become stressed if feeling bored or confined. Less open people are stressed by change and having to think in new ways.

Be aware of your own needs and remember that there is no "right" personality, just individuals who find their own effective means of coping.

? TEST YOURSELF

Where do you fit within the Big Five model? If you agree with most of one section, you score highly on that trait. As different traits mean different comfort zones, the results can be a guide to which ways of living will be least stressful for your personality.

1
- I enjoy socialising with big groups of people.
- People see me as talkative and energetic.
- I find it easy to assert myself.
- I can sometimes be a bit interfering or nosy.

2
- I find it easy to sympathize with people.
- I'd rather let something go than seek retribution.
- I like to give others the benefit of the doubt.
- I'm not a competitive person.

3
- It's important to me to be organized.
- I take my responsibilities and duties seriously.
- You couldn't call me a rebel.
- I like to be consistent.

4
- I love discussing new ideas.
- Creativity and imagination matter a lot to me.
- It's good to get outside your comfort zone sometimes.
- I'm not particularly conventional.

5
- It's easy to upset me.
- My self-confidence isn't very high.
- When stressed, I find it hard to calm down.
- I can be hard on myself.

1=Extroversion: you are outgoing rather than introverted.
2=Agreeableness: you cooperate rather than challenge.
3=Conscientiousness: you're more dutiful than impulsive.
4=Openness: you enjoy new experiences and ideas rather than preferring the familiar.
5=Neuroticism: you are particularly vulnerable to stress.

? THE BIG FIVE SCALE

Each of the Big Five traits is a sliding scale – you can place anywhere from an extreme end to right in the middle. Using the test (left), see where you place on your trait; it can help you to understand why some people and situations are easier to deal with than others.

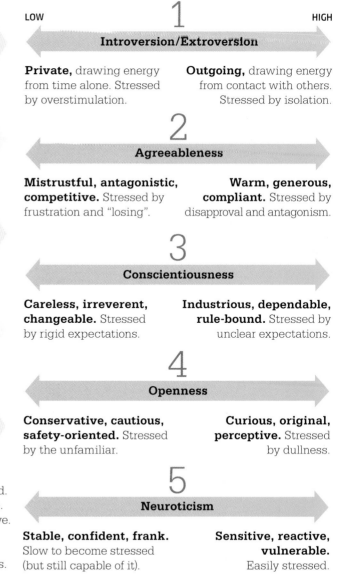

1
LOW ———————————————— HIGH
Introversion/Extroversion

Private, drawing energy from time alone. Stressed by overstimulation.

Outgoing, drawing energy from contact with others. Stressed by isolation.

2
Agreeableness

Mistrustful, antagonistic, competitive. Stressed by frustration and "losing".

Warm, generous, compliant. Stressed by disapproval and antagonism.

3
Conscientiousness

Careless, irreverent, changeable. Stressed by rigid expectations.

Industrious, dependable, rule-bound. Stressed by unclear expectations.

4
Openness

Conservative, cautious, safety-oriented. Stressed by the unfamiliar.

Curious, original, perceptive. Stressed by dullness.

5
Neuroticism

Stable, confident, frank. Slow to become stressed (but still capable of it).

Sensitive, reactive, vulnerable. Easily stressed.

TAKING IT LIKE A MAN?

MEN, WOMEN, AND STRESS

It may be a stereotype that men are competitive and women nurturing, but as far as stress goes, research appears to bear the stereotype out.

In 2000, the journal *Psychological Review* published an influential American study reporting that men may respond to stress by going into "fight or flight" mode, either seeking to escape the situation or becoming aggressive. Women, however, are more likely to respond with "tend and befriend" – that is, reaching out to other people to foster supportive relationships.

A 2014 study at the University of Vienna tested this gender gap and found that the results echoed. The researchers predicted that people would become more egocentric under stress – that is, less able to see past their own feelings and consider other people's. They were right about men, but not about women: under strain, women grew better at "reading" other people's emotions.

Q ALL IN THE BRAIN

A 2013 American study scanned male and female brains to see if they were wired differently. The results: male brains showed more connections between perception and action, while female brains showed more connections between analytic and intuitive processing modes. Under stress, male brains are generally more inclined to look for active solutions, while female brains tend to scan the social environment and try to understand everyone's motivations.

While every individual is unique, the evidence suggests that there do seem to be typically "male" and "female" ways of handling pressure. Sometimes both men and women can learn from each other

Is our biology our destiny?

At a biological level, men and women experience stress in the same way and produce similar levels of the stress hormone cortisol. However, the evidence suggests that men and women choose different coping methods in response to the same basic feeling of stress.

Exactly why is not clear. Part of the reason may be hormonal: women in the 2014 study were found to have higher oxytocin levels than men: oxytocin is the "cuddle hormone", most associated with social bonding. It's also possible that "tend and befriend" is learned behaviour: as the research speculates, women "may have internalized the experience that they receive more external support when they are able to interact better with others", whereas men have found this useful lesson more difficult to learn.

Whether the explanation is "nature" or "nurture", men and women do exhibit different behaviours in response to stress.

The lessons of gender

Whatever your gender, there are some useful lessons in these findings. As the researchers observed, being able to "tend and befriend" under stress is a valuable skill: most of the stresses of contemporary life are slow-burn and rather complicated. "Fight or flight" is useful if we're hunting or chasing off a rival, but in modern life, social support is more likely to help us with our problems (see pp.176–179).

WHO'S MORE STRESSED?

According to a 2015 stress survey by the American Psychological Association, there's a gender gap in how men and women view their stress levels:

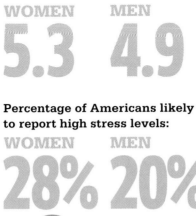

Average reported stress levels on a scale of 1–10:

WOMEN 5.3 MEN 4.9

Percentage of Americans likely to report high stress levels:

WOMEN 28% MEN 20%

If you're male, it may be useful to remind yourself that reaching out to others may be the most helpful choice you can make under pressure. Women, on the other hand, may sometimes "tend and befriend" too much for their own good. As Carl Pickhardt, spokesman of the American Psychological Association, remarks, "Self-sacrifice in relationships is how many women enter stress" – sometimes a little more self-interest might help you to protect your own needs. A balance between "male" and "female" means of coping is probably best for everyone.

⑦ HOW DOES STRESS COME OUT?

A 2010 survey by the American Psychological Association found a variety of symptoms of stress that affect us to different degrees – if you experience some of these, don't judge yourself too harshly.

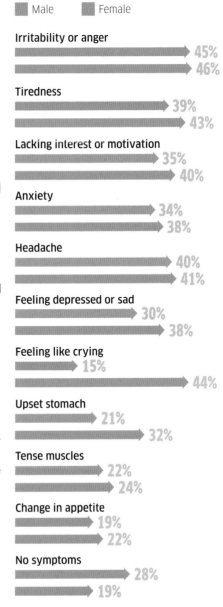

■ Male ■ Female

Irritability or anger
45%
46%

Tiredness
39%
43%

Lacking interest or motivation
35%
40%

Anxiety
34%
38%

Headache
40%
41%

Feeling depressed or sad
30%
38%

Feeling like crying
15%
44%

Upset stomach
21%
32%

Tense muscles
22%
24%

Change in appetite
19%
22%

No symptoms
28%
19%

PERFECTLY IMPERFECT
THE RELIEF OF REALISTIC STANDARDS

Is your best never good enough? The demanding standards of perfectionism can drain the joy out of your life and keep your stress levels high. Is it time to give yourself a break?

Perfectionism might sound like a good trait – after all, people who care about high standards in any walk of life are likely to be achievers. However, holding ourselves to excessive standards can become highly stressful.

The perfectionism debate

Is perfectionism always bad for us, or only in certain cases? A 2003 study by American psychologist Kenneth Rice made a distinction between "adaptive" and "maladaptive" perfectionism in people with high standards. An adaptive trait helps us fit into our environment in a positive way – in this case, having high standards but also being able to cope when we fall short. Maladaptive traits cause problems, such as being highly distressed by a perceived failure.

Canadian psychologist Paul Hewitt doesn't think perfectionism is in any way adaptive, pointing out that it increases our risk of mental illnesses, including anorexia and depression, and can heighten our risk of suicide.

Meanwhile, a 2003 British study found that the people most at risk of hopelessness and distress were those who combined perfectionism with "avoidance coping" – that is, dealing with problems by ignoring rather than confronting them The combination of impossible standards and avoidant behaviour caused stress and depression.

Psychologists' opinions differ as to whether perfectionism can ever be a positive attribute. Taken together, the evidence suggests perfectionism has a tendency to make it harder to cope with the stresses of life.

What can I do?

When others are pressuring us to be perfect, our best protection is to create appropriate boundaries and to be assertive (see pp.92–95). If the perfectionism is coming from within, take some tips from Jeff Szymanski of America's International OCD (Obsessive Compulsive Disorder) Foundation:

- **Prioritize** based on your values. Trying to do everything perfectly is hugely stressful. Save your high standards for the things that matter to you most.

> Understanding the difference between **healthy striving** and **perfectionism** is critical.
>
> **Brené Brown**
> American therapist and researcher

STRESS-SAVING CUE CARDS

The Anxiety Disorders Association of British Columbia recommends that we write some positive, realistic statements on cue cards, and carry them with us to serve as a reality check when perfectionism is making us too stressed.

"I'm only human."

"Nobody's perfect."

"Having an off day doesn't make me a failure."

"It's okay to make mistakes – everyone does."

"If I've done my best, that's the best I can do."

- **Get comfortable** with the idea of experimenting. Taking risks and making mistakes needn't be a disaster and can be a positive learning experience.
- **Be process-smart.** The majority of the payoff for your efforts tends to happen fairly early in the process; after that, the benefit-to-effort ratio starts to decline – and at some point it stops being worthwhile.
- **Reward yourself** for imperfect achievements. For instance, it may be better to meet a deadline with a slightly less-than-perfect product than spend so long getting it right that you don't deliver at all.
- **Find role models.** Who do you know who has similar goals, but seems to struggle less? When facing a challenge, ask yourself – or them – how they'd tackle it.

We all have to learn to tolerate a level of imperfection. Your life can be far less stressful if you can allow yourself to be human and fallible.

? HOW PERFECTIONIST ARE YOU?

Perfectionism has more than one face.
See which of these statements you agree with:

A I really want the people I care about to succeed.

B The more I succeed, the more people around me expect.

C I can't relax until I've got something perfect.

A I can't be bothered with people who won't do their best.

B It's difficult to measure up to people's expectations of me.

C It makes me uncomfortable when I find I've made a mistake.

A I don't tolerate people who let me down.

B People don't say it, but my mistakes really upset them.

C I must always work to my full potential.

"A" statements indicate "other-oriented" perfectionism: you expect perfection in others.
✔ You can make your social relationships less stressful by developing your forgiveness skills (pp.106–107).

"B" statements indicate "socially prescribed" perfectionism: other people expect perfection from you.
✔ You can draw some healthier boundaries by improving your assertiveness skills (pp.92–95).

"C" statements indicate "self-oriented" perfectionism: you set yourself perfect standards.
✔ You can de-stress by being more tolerant of yourself – nobody is perfect.

OUR IMPERFECTIONS ARE WHAT MAKE US CARD-CARRYING MEMBERS OF THE HUMAN RACE

KRISTIN NEFF, PSYCHOLOGIST AND COMPASSION EXPERT

SELF-COMPASSION
BECOMING YOUR OWN COMFORTER

Sometimes we're our own worst enemies: it's difficult not to feel stressed if we berate ourselves for every mistake or failing. A series of exercises to help you treat yourself compassionately may be the answer.

When you feel stressed, you need comfort, and the first person who can comfort you is yourself. A 2005 British study found that self-compassion – having the same forgiving attitude towards ourselves that a kind person would show to others – deactivates the body's alarm system. Giving yourself some compassion is key to de-stressing.

Three routes

American psychologist Kristin Neff identifies three components we can use to keep our stress levels down:

1 **Self-kindness.** We value showing kindness to others, but often say things to ourselves that we'd never say to anyone else, like "You idiot!" If we treat ourselves with the compassion we extend to others, we're likely to feel much better.

2 **Common humanity.** Everyone faces challenges in life. Rather than feeling isolated by our errors and problems, see them as a sign that we share a great deal with other people – an insight that can comfort by making us feel more connected.

3 **Mindfulness.** We don't always recognize how hard we're being on ourselves; some of us even find it hard to notice how upset we're feeling. Take a moment to acknowledge feelings with the respect they deserve.

Gentleness and awareness of our own feelings can help us feel better able to cope – and that feeling is the foundation of managing stress.

Compassion-focused therapy

Developed by British psychologist Paul Gilbert and influenced by Buddhism, compassion-focused therapy posits that some people find it particularly difficult to manage their stress levels because they have an over-active threat-detection system – they identify stressors more quickly than the average person. A 2000 paper by Gilbert recommends the following methods to become more relaxed:

- **Compassionate attention.** Focus on memories of giving or receiving kindness, or times when your positive qualities shone. Direct your attention to thoughts that make you feel warm and safe.
- **Compassionate reasoning.** Avoid dwelling on feelings of shame and self-criticism: instead, use logic to find more compassionate interpretations of your situation and actions (see pp.52–53).

- **Compassionate behaviour.** When you have to do something stressful, give yourself plenty of private encouragement. In particular, focus on the process rather than the task – that is, appreciate the efforts you make, no matter what the result.
- **Compassionate imagery.** Picture a compassionate figure that gives you the support you need, be it human, animal, or divine – whichever feels meaningful to you.
- **Compassionate feeling.** Work on cultivating compassionate emotions, for yourself and others.
- **Compassionate sensation.** Become more aware of how your body feels when you're feeling compassion. For instance, do your shoulders drop? Do your facial muscles relax? By recognizing the physical experience, you'll be better able to understand your emotions, which makes it easier to develop your compassion skills.

✓ PICTURE THIS...

A 2008 British study found that a simple visualization exercise helped reduce stress. If you're feeling tense, try this:

1 **Picture a figure that represents ideal compassion,** be it human or non-human (see "Compassionate imagery", left).

2 **As the researchers put it,** "Allow yourself to feel the loving-kindness that is there for you".

Subjects reported feeling safer afterwards, and their levels of the stress hormone cortisol dropped significantly. When we're feeling stressed, the more kindness we can show ourselves, the easier it is to manage feelings and face life's challenges with confidence.

✓ SELF-COMPASSION EXERCISE

American psychologist Kristin Neff recommends the following "self-compassion break" when you find yourself stressed:

Identify the feeling you are suffering. Use a phrase such as "This is stress" or "This is painful".

Remind yourself of common humanity. Tell yourself, "Suffering is part of life" or "Everyone feels this way sometimes".

Rest your hands on your heart or adopt another comforting pose, and say, "May I be compassionate to myself" or "May I have patience and strength", or another affirmation.

WRITING IT OUT
KEEPING A STRESS DIARY

You may not be Shakespeare, but with a pen in your hand you can become your own best listener. Writing can be an excellent tool for coping with stress, helping you to understand and manage your own feelings.

Therapeutic writing helps to calm both the body and the mind. Pen and paper might turn out to be your most useful tools during stressful times.

Good for our health

Extensive research published in 1998 by American psychologist Joshua Smyth confirmed that writing boosts the immune systems of patients with distressing medical conditions such as arthritis and asthma. A 2004 study in New Zealand found similar benefits for patients suffering from HIV/AIDS. Writing about their emotions made the patients feel better.

However, as Smyth noted, it's not enough just to vent your feelings, which can make us feel more negative (see pp.180–181). Writing is most useful when it helps us gain insight about what causes us stress and how we react to that stress.

The importance of meaning

It's useful to begin with a clear idea of how you want your writing to help you. A 2002 study by American researcher Susan Lutgendorf found that volunteers who kept a diary to help them find meaning in their health problems experienced improved health, while those who simply wrote about their negative feelings felt worse – not just worse than the meaning-oriented writers, but worse than the control group as well. As Lutgendorf observed, "You need focused thought as well as emotions."

Simply grumbling, whether verbally or in writing, may make you feel more stressed. It's best if you use your diary to reflect on:

- How you feel you're coping with your stress.
- Whether you might try other coping methods.
- What you are learning from the experience.
- What currently gives you a sense of meaning in your life – or, if nothing does, what would.

If you can use writing to find meaning in your situation (see pp.44–45), you may start to feel better emotionally and physically.

> By writing, you put some **structure and organization** to those anxious feelings. It helps you to get past them.
>
> **James Pennebaker**
> University of Texas at Austin

A DAILY STRESS DIARY

Feeling stressed, but not sure why? A daily diary can help to pinpoint your stressors and track your reactions. This can show you whether your response to a stressor actually helps to improve a problem or makes it worse. Try keeping a log with two sections, hourly and daily. Draw a grid with headings and questions for the day ahead, so it's easy to fill in even when you're busy.

The hourly section
Draw up a grid for the whole day, write in it once an hour, and keep it brief.

Time	10am	11am
What am I doing?	Arranging boss's files	Gone on an errand
How enjoyable is it?	2/10	6/10
How efficient am I being?	8/10	8/10
How do I feel physically?	Restless, fidgety	Relaxed - good to be out in the daylight
How stressed am I?	7/10	2/10

The daily section, when a stressful event happens
Find a quiet moment to add this section and answer these questions:

When and where?	Saturday, 3pm at home
What happened?	Neighbour playing loud music again
What did I do about that?	Banged on the wall
Was this problem-focused or emotion-focused? (pp.26–29)	Problem-focused, but it didn't solve much
What was most stressful?	Feeling like I can't get privacy in my own home
Did it help?	He turned the music down, but only a bit and I'm still angry
Would could I do next time?	Ask him to listen to his music from our side of the wall, so he realizes how loud it is for us

THE PENNEBAKER PARADIGM

In the 1980s, American social psychologist James Pennebaker created a technique for what he called "expressive writing" – a way of becoming your own therapist when you're dealing with a specific, identifiable stressor. He offers some simple guidelines:

1 **For at least four consecutive days,** write for at least 20 minutes solidly.

2 **Choose a topic** that is personal and important – for instance, the stress you're experiencing about a family crisis.

3 **Write continuously.** Spelling mistakes, punctuation, ink blots, bad handwriting – these things don't matter. Just keep your pen on the page and your hand moving.

4 **Write for your eyes only.** When you're finished, you might even destroy the pages. This is writing for the experience, not for an audience.

5 **Don't push yourself over the edge.** If you come to a point where you feel that writing about a certain subject will make you too upset, then stop.

6 **Expect to feel a little sad** or tired after you finish writing. The feeling should pass in an hour or two.

AM I WORTH IT?
STRESS AND SELF-ESTEEM

It can be hard to feel good about yourself when you're overwhelmed. Sometimes a healthy self-esteem is helpful: believing you deserve to feel better is a powerful motivator for improving stress management.

Feeling that you're unable to cope with everything that life throws at you can erode your sense of ability and worth. If your self-image isn't healthy to begin with, you might question whether you even deserve to overcome your stress and feel better. We all strive to feel calm and self-assured, so let's consider the techniques that can bolster your self-esteem.

Avoid comparisons

A key element of secure self-esteem is liking yourself *as yourself*. Comparing yourself with others often increases stress levels: there will always be somebody who can do something we can't, or who has something we don't – even if we have plenty of achievements.

Psychologists contrast "secure" high self-esteem with "fragile" high self-esteem. Secure high self-esteem is the sense that we are basically likeable and worthwhile. If we have fragile high self-esteem, we define ourselves by our successes and ignore our failures – but by doing this, we don't learn from our

> High self-esteem individuals are people who like, value, and accept themselves, **imperfections and all**.
>
> **Michael Kernis**
> American psychologist

? THE SELF-ESTEEM SPECTRUM

Isn't it good to be modest? Perhaps, but too little self-esteem is unhealthy. Chronic stress can make us feel bad about ourselves, which can lead us to neglect our self-care, feel worse, and think we don't deserve better. Recognizing this pattern can start us on the road to an improved sense of worth. It's helpful to think of self-esteem as a spectrum, and aim for the moderately high end rather than the extremes. See where you place on the spectrum below, and whether you'd benefit from a more secure sense of mastery (see "Build yourself up", below).

Very low	Low	Healthily high	Over-inflated
❯ Feeling worthless ❯ Self-neglecting ❯ Depressive ❯ Experiencing chronic (long-term) stress	❯ Uncertain ❯ Vulnerable ❯ Unassertive ❯ Frequently stressed	❯ Confident ❯ Realistic ❯ Deserving happiness ❯ Managing stress	❯ Self-aggrandizing ❯ Defensive ❯ Hostile ❯ Stressed by any perceived slight

mistakes. We then become easily agitated by any suggestion that our self-image might be questionable. When building your self-esteem, appreciate your accomplishments but focus most on those that are meaningful to you, whether or not they're impressive to others. This approach engenders self-esteem and greater emotional stability.

Build yourself up

A 2011 Swiss study found that a key factor is a sense of mastery – feeling competent and able to manage your life. American psychologist Guy Winch advises some practical steps to increase this sense:

1 **Forget generic affirmations.** If you don't truly believe it, saying "I'm a great person" will only make you feel worse by reminding you that you don't actually feel that way.

2 **Identify your authentic strengths.** Being good at anything, however small, is a solid reason to feel confident.

3 **Engage your abilities.** If you can do something well, do it more: you are demonstrating your competence to yourself.

4 **Accept compliments.** If you are uncomfortable with praise, simply say "thank you" and allow yourself to hear good things.

5 **Affirm yourself** – it's healthy, not vain, to be pleased by doing something well.

Rather than comparing yourself to others, work on appreciating your best attributes. With time, this will heighten your self-esteem and improve how you manage stress.

✓ DESERVING A NICE SPACE

A run-down and dirty home is dispiriting: when you look around your personal space, you're getting the message that you aren't worth much, further eroding your self-esteem and your ability to cope with stress. British psychiatrist Neel Burton advises creating a setting that feels comfortable (see pp.166–167). By displaying photos, souvenirs, and reminders of special times and people, you will see evidence of your own value.

FINDING MEANING
MAKING STRESS WORTHWHILE

Do we need to be stress-free in order to be happy? Far from it: a healthy level of stress helps us to develop emotionally and attain our goals. The challenge is to identify what makes that stress feel worthwhile.

Stress can make us unhappy – but happiness isn't the only measure of wellbeing. It's also important to have a sense of meaning in our lives.

Three routes to happiness

American psychologist Martin Seligman is a pioneer of the positive psychology movement, which focuses on studying how and why people thrive. He argues that it is a mistake to assume we should measure our lives purely on whether they're pleasant. Instead, Seligman describes three routes to happiness:

- **The Pleasant Life** (also known as the "hedonic" life): having many pleasures and the skills to make the best use of them.
- **The Good Life:** knowing your strengths and building your work, family life, leisure, and friendships around being able to use those strengths to be more fully engaged (see pp.174–175).
- **The Meaningful Life:** using your strengths in the service of something bigger than yourself – a cause you truly believe in.

A 2008 Australian study surveyed more than 12,000 adults and found that all three types of happiness predicted wellbeing, but that engagement (or "Good Life" experiences) and meaning were more powerful predictors than hedonism. Pleasurable experiences aren't antithetical to our wellbeing, but meaning is more fundamental to it – and while stress certainly isn't pleasurable, it is compatible with living a meaningful life.

How to create meaning?

Viktor Frankl was an Austrian psychiatrist who survived the Holocaust. He spent his career studying the psychology of meaning – and suggested that we can discern meaning through three separate paths:

1 **Meaning through creative values.** Making or accomplishing something we feel is worthwhile.

2 **Meaning through experiential values.** Frankl gives the example of a mountain-climber who is uplifted at the sight of an alpine sunset.

> He who has a **"why"** to live for can bear almost any **"how"**.
>
> **Viktor Frankl**
> Austrian psychiatrist, quoting German philosopher Friedrich Nietzsche

Q THE FULL LIFE

Stress undermines positive emotions – but meaning can be another way to feel your life is positive. Positive psychology identifies five elements to a well-rounded existence, summed up in the acronym PERMA:

P Positive emotions	Happiness, pleasure, delight
E Engagement	Interest and "flow" (see pp.174–175)
R Relationships	Loving connections with other people
M Meaning	Feeling part of something worthwhile
A Accomplishments	Meeting challenges and taking pride in yourself

3 Meaning through attitudinal values. We can find meaning even in sad or stressful situations – by considering, for instance, that we are doing something valuable.

Some other practical suggestions for finding meaning:

✔ **Create a coherent narrative about your life.** American psychologist Robert Biswas-Diener suggests simple writing exercises (see pp.40–41) in which you describe the best possible self you aspire to be – morally as well as in terms of achievements – and consider concrete strategies for working towards your goals.

✔ **Support others, be generous.** A 2013 American study found that people pursuing happy lives tended to be "takers", while people with meaningful lives tended to be "givers".

✔ **Don't wait for a leader.** A 2016 British study found that, while having bad bosses could make a job feel meaningless, inspirational bosses were barely mentioned: people's sense of meaning came from feeling that their own work contributed to society.

Living with a certain amount of stress can be tolerable, and even desirable, provided you feel it has meaning.

Q WELLSPRINGS OF MEANING

According to a 2016 American paper by researchers Login George and Crystal Park, a meaningful life has three central features:

1 Purpose. Having valued life goals that motivate your actions and guide your choices.

2 Comprehension. Being able to understand your life experiences and see them as part of a coherent whole.

3 Mattering. Feeling that your existence is valuable to others and has significance.

The key is to identify what you care about most in life – what higher purpose or bigger picture you feel you fit into. If you can do that, then the everyday stresses may start to feel less important in comparison.

FEELING IN CONTROL
UNDERSTANDING OUR LIMITS

Much as you may wish to rein in others, the only person you can truly control is yourself. Appreciating the full weight of this life lesson can make it a great deal easier to limit the power that stress has over you.

Few things are as frustrating as trying to control someone who simply won't do as we wish – but by believing we have control over our own actions, thoughts, and feelings, we can empower ourselves to feel calmer and more confident.

Beating the bullies

We can often limit the impact of a tiresome or offensive person by managing our own reaction (see "Taking back control", opposite). However, it's worth noting that studies confirm the stress of being bullied increases our vulnerability to depression and anxiety.

Psychologists define bullying as the use of power and aggression to cause distress, in one of two ways:

- **Direct bullying.** Overt expressions of threat, such as violence, sexual harassment, threats, and insults.
- **Relational aggression.** Causing pain by spreading rumours, gossiping, and deliberately excluding people.

In both situations, you can and should exercise self-care by shoring up your self-esteem (see pp.42–43),

> [Self-control is] among humankind's **most valuable assets**.
>
> **Wilhelm Hofmann**
> American psychologist

but sometimes the best solution may be to find a way to escape them – for example, by switching teams at work. This may take time and can be stressful while it lasts, so reach out to your social supports (see pp.176–179), and fill your life with positive people while you plan how to steer clear of the negative ones.

Is self-control boring?

Often associated with denying ourselves the fun and pleasures of life, self-control can actually make our lives happier. A 2013 study led by American psychologist Wilhelm Hofmann defined self control as "the ability to override or change one's inner responses" and found that people with more self-control tended to have fewer conflicts, a better mood, more life satisfaction, and lower stress. Knowing what we want out of life and moving towards it leads to a happier state of mind, and we feel better if we don't let momentary stress or temptation distract us.

Using CBT techniques can improve your sense of control by challenging stressful thoughts (see pp.52–53), and mindfulness can help you manage your mood (see pp.132–135). There's a limit to what we can control, but it's helpful to remind yourself that you hold more power than you might expect when it comes to your own thoughts, feelings, and actions.

⊝ TAKING BACK CONTROL

Our feelings are shaped as much by our own thoughts as by other people's behaviour. Trying to change someone is more likely to lead to frustration on both sides rather than a reduction in stress. Instead, try reframing how you think about them in order to relocate the emotional control to where it belongs – with you.

INSTEAD OF...	TRY SAYING...
He makes me feel bad about myself.	**I've been letting** his wisecracks get to me.
She's stressing me out with her complaints.	**I get stressed** if I don't set limits on how much I have to listen to her.
They're making me doubt myself.	**My self-doubt** tends to play up around that group of people.

⚲ THE LOCUS OF CONTROL

Do you see yourself as master of your fate, or do you tend to think that "what will be will be" regardless of your actions? If you identify more with the former, you have a high "internal locus of control" – and such people tend to suffer less depression and anxiety. Remind yourself that you have the power to manage your stress: it can be a self-fulfilling prophecy.

HIGH INTERNAL LOCUS OF CONTROL

"I have the power to change my fate."

"I'm in control of my own thoughts and feelings."

LOW INTERNAL LOCUS OF CONTROL

"My life is shaped by chance."

"Others hold the power over me."

BREAKING THE WORRY CYCLE

DEALING WITH UNCERTAINTY

Sometimes the most stressful problem is the one that might happen: if you don't know the outcome, it's harder to plan your coping strategies. Fretting doesn't help, though — worries need to be managed.

If the prospect of a possible problem – one that hasn't happened yet – sends your stress levels climbing, you are probably a worrier. Worry is stressful (worriers often worry that they worry too much), so it's wise to learn some techniques that help you keep worry in check.

Set aside worry time

In the 1980s, American psychology professor Thomas Borkovec developed a four-step therapy for excessive worrying. The principle is that if we worry thoughout the day, we start to associate particular places with worry. When we see those places again, we automatically start worrying. To break this cycle, these are Borkovec's four steps:

1 Identify which of your thoughts and feelings are worry.

2 Set aside a time and place where you will think about the things that are worrying you.

3 If you find yourself worrying outside that time and place, stop, postpone those thoughts until the assigned time, and refocus on what you were doing.

4 Use your "worrying time" to try to find solutions for the problems that are worrying you.

These steps can significantly lower your stress levels: in a 2011 Dutch study, volunteers felt calmer even if they tried just the first step – and if they used all four, their worries decreased considerably.

✔ GOING ROUND AND ROUND

Obsessive worry is described by American psychologist William Doverspike as a negative spiral that grows deeper the more you stress over it, and can become a trance-like state. See if you recognize this pattern:

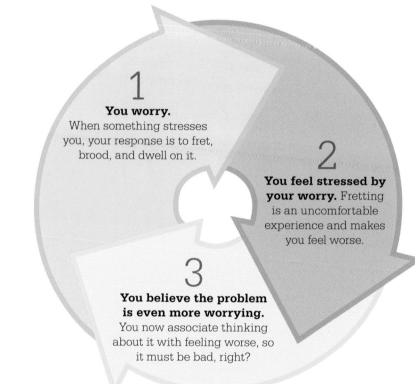

1 You worry. When something stresses you, your response is to fret, brood, and dwell on it.

2 You feel stressed by your worry. Fretting is an uncomfortable experience and makes you feel worse.

3 You believe the problem is even more worrying. You now associate thinking about it with feeling worse, so it must be bad, right?

Breaking out of the spiral takes mental energy, so experiment with some of these "trance-breakers" and see if they help you to steer your stress response onto a more positive track.

- **Change your environment:** for instance, go for a walk and pay attention to your surroundings.

- **Create a different emotional mood:** listen to soothing music or watch an exciting movie.

- **Engage in a hobby:** do something rewarding that you associate with fun and relaxation (pp.150–151).

- **Do something challenging** and interesting that takes all of your attention and creates "flow" (pp.174–175).

- **Use some calming** breathing exercises (p.129), progressive muscle relaxation (p.131), or meditation (p.133).

✎ EMBRACING UNCERTAINTY

Many psychologists recommend creating a worksheet to help you consider how you react to the unknown, which can help take some of the stress out of it:

1 How has needing certainty helped or hindered me?

2 If it's hindered me, how do I tend to cope with that?

3 If I don't know what will happen, do I predict something bad?

4 How likely is it that bad things will happen?

5 If there's only a small chance, can I live with that?

6 Are there uncertainties I can tolerate?

7 How do my friends and family cope with unpredictability?

8 Is there anything I can learn from them?

9 Can I apply those coping skills to different parts of my life?

{ Worry isn't worth what it can cost…After all, most of what we worry about **never happens**. }

Seth Gillihan
American psychology professor

THE GREATEST WEAPON AGAINST STRESS IS OUR ABILITY TO CHOOSE ONE THOUGHT OVER ANOTHER

WILLIAM JAMES, PHILOSOPHER AND PHYSICIAN

DE-STRESS YOUR THINKING

THE POWER OF CBT

Stressful situations happen to us all, but do you ever convince yourself that things are worse than they really are? A form of therapy known as CBT might be what you need to keep things in perspective.

CBT (Cognitive Behavioural Therapy) is a commonly recommended form of talk therapy. A 2012 review of several hundred studies, including patients treated for a variety of mood disorders and other mental illnesses, found very strong evidence that CBT was effective, particularly as a technique to reduce stress levels considerably. If you're prone to having distressing thoughts, you can develop the art of catching them before they make you too unhappy. "Catch it, check it, change it" are the three Cs of CBT.

Catch your negative thoughts.
The 10 common "cognitive distortions" – ways of thinking that make things seem worse than they really are – are listed in the table opposite. If your thinking often contains cognitive distortions, consider trying this:

1 **Identify the thought that's bothering you** – for example, "I've taken on too many projects; I'll miss my deadlines and look bad to all of my clients"

2 **Ask yourself how much you believe the thought.** Assign a percentage – for example, 85%.

3 **Ask yourself if the thought is a cognitive distortion.**

4 **Consider some alternative interpretations** – "I've met tight deadlines before", or "This client can be flexible about dates". You may have your doubts, but try some other interpretations for size.

5 **Look at the evidence as calmly as possible.** Do the facts really support your forecast of doom? Is there any evidence that is more encouraging?

6 **Ask yourself again how much you believe the upsetting thought.** The answer doesn't have to be "Not at all". If you've dropped from 85% to 45%, that's still a marked improvement.

The more you work at catching and re-framing cognitive distortions, the easier it will be. Eventually, it will become your new normal, and you won't have to work so hard to change your thinking.

> Our **emotions start** with our interpretations of events.
>
> **Dr Frank Ghinassi**
> Associate Professor of
> Psychiatry, University
> of Pittsburgh

COGNITIVE TROUBLE-SHOOTING

It's easy to get stressed if we are prone to thinking the worst. Psychology lists 10 common types of distorted thinking, but with cognitive re-framing, it's a tendency we can learn to control.

Cognitive Distortion	How it works	Example	Re-framing with an alternative explanation	Counter-evidence to support re-framing
All-or-nothing	If you aren't perfect, you must be hopeless.	"I failed one of my exams – I'm an idiot."	"That was a tough paper for everyone."	"Gina and Leo failed too, and they usually do well."
Over-generalizing	If it happens once, that is how it will always be.	"Tom didn't call back. I can't keep friends."	"He's just not that great at keeping in touch."	"I have good friends who do keep in touch."
Mental filter	Focusing on a negative detail, screening out the wider context.	"Coach likes my ball control but says I need more stamina. I quit."	"He wouldn't tell me what to improve if he didn't believe in me."	"Ball control is important. I can build up my stamina if I work at it."
Disqualifying the positive	Finding ways to write off good news and positive feedback.	"My boss says I did well – she's just trying to encourage us all."	"Maybe she actually meant it."	"I know she's a truthful person. Why assume it was a false compliment?"
Jumping to conclusions	Mind reading and fortune telling – predicting disaster.	"He hasn't called since our date. He doesn't want to be with me."	"It was only yesterday. Maybe he's just been too busy to call yet."	"'On our last date, he said he'd had a lovely time. I'm an attractive person."
Maximizing / minimizing	Bad news is a disaster ("catastrophized"), good news is no big deal.	"He says my report needs work. He wants to fire me."	"It's just one piece of feedback. If I take it well, I'll look good."	"I've never seen them fire anyone over a small thing like this."
Emotional reasoning	Taking your feelings for facts.	"I feel like a failure, so that's what I must be."	"Maybe I'm just tired and discouraged today."	"I have achieved plenty of things in my life."
"Should" statements	Imposing rules on yourself.	"I mustn't cry over my dog dying. It's pathetic."	"I really loved that old dog. It's good to love."	"Caring doesn't make me weak. I have a big heart."
Labelling and mislabelling	Thinking one action sums a person up.	"I've just let out a friend's secret. I'm a bad friend."	"It was a slip of the tongue. I'll try to make amends."	"I am still a trustworthy person. One mistake doesn't change that."
Personalizing	Blaming yourself if things go wrong.	"My son is moody. I'm a bad parent."	"He's a teenager, he's got a lot on his mind."	"I go to all his matches – he knows I care."

HOW STRESSED?

BETWEEN DISCOMFORT AND DANGER

Some stress in life is inevitable, and when it's below a certain level we can usually cope. Be alert to your own psychological wellbeing, so that you are able to recognize when you might need more help.

The majority of stress is what psychiatrists call sub-clinical – enough to affect your quality of life, but not enough to provoke a diagnosable illness. However, the greater and more prolonged your stress, the more vulnerable your physical and mental wellbeing. Knowing what level of stress you're dealing with is vital for knowing how to manage it.

- **Acute stress** is a short-term crisis, such as giving a public speech. It may be exciting, even useful, in small doses, and does little harm unless it is severe or traumatic (pp.204–207). The negative effects can include emotional distress and physical symptoms such as headaches and stomach aches, but they're usually manageable.
- **Episodic acute stress** is what happens when acute stress is a regular event, such as having frequent crises because you habitually take on too much. Practising assertiveness (pp.92–95), prioritization skills (pp.146–147), and mindfulness (pp.132–135) can help you to reduce its impact.
- **Chronic stress** is a high level of stress over an extended period, such as a boss who consistently overloads and criticizes you. It wears you down and leaves you feeling exhausted. It increases your vulnerability to physical and mental illness, and you may need support from a therapist (pp.208–209) who can help you to improve your coping skills.

? QUALITY OF LIFE

If you feel you're more stressed than you should be, take that feeling seriously. Consider the five questions shown here:

ASK YOURSELF

Am I finding it hard to relax in my free time?
Are my stress levels affecting my general mood?
Is my concentration suffering?
Am I developing some unhealthy habits?
Do I feel like my emotions are hard to manage?

IF THE ANSWER IS "YES" to some or all of the above, stress is definitely affecting your wellbeing. The chapters that follow can help you to identify areas where you may benefit from learning some stress-busting techniques.

How serious is it?

One sign that chronic stress is getting to you – possibly to the point where you should consult a doctor to investigate whether it is seriously affecting your mental health – is "cognitive impairment". If stress makes regular thinking tasks difficult (see far right), this can interfere with your problem-solving and multi-tasking, which worsens stress.

Experiencing acute stress now and then is unlikely to harm you unless it's very extreme, but if it becomes a regular or chronic part of your life, using stress-management techniques may make you a lot happier. Whatever your situation, it's important to develop good self-care and keep your stress levels down to a tolerable level, as we'll discuss in the chapters that follow.

Q WEARING YOU DOWN?

The "stress hormone" cortisol is essential, in moderation, but if we are chronically stressed, a constantly elevated cortisol level can lead to:

■ A suppressed immune system, making us more at risk of infection.

■ Increased appetite and excess glucose production, which may lead to weight gain, high blood sugar, and other health problems.

■ High blood pressure, which can lead to heart disease and stroke.

Chronically high levels of cortisol can lead to damage to brain cells in areas that are critical for memory and concentration. Keeping your stress down can be crucial for your body and mind.

? THINKING CLEARLY?

A 2015 British study identified a series of tests that can suggest there's a problem. If you're worried, test your performance on these:

■ **Reasoning.** Can you solve verbal and numeric reasoning problems at your usual rate?

■ **Reaction time.** Are your reactions slowing down at all?

■ **Numeric memory.** Can you remember a phone number for long enough to dial the number?

■ **Visuospatial ability.** Taking six pairs of cards, randomly arranged face-down, and turning over two at a time, how many tries does it take for you to match them all?

■ **Prospective memory.** If you're given an instruction and then have a delay before you can act on it, can you remember what you were supposed to do?

Everyone has different abilities in these areas, so making mistakes isn't necessarily a concern, but if you notice your skills declining compared with your usual level, or more than you'd expect for your age, it may be a sign that you should see your doctor for advice.

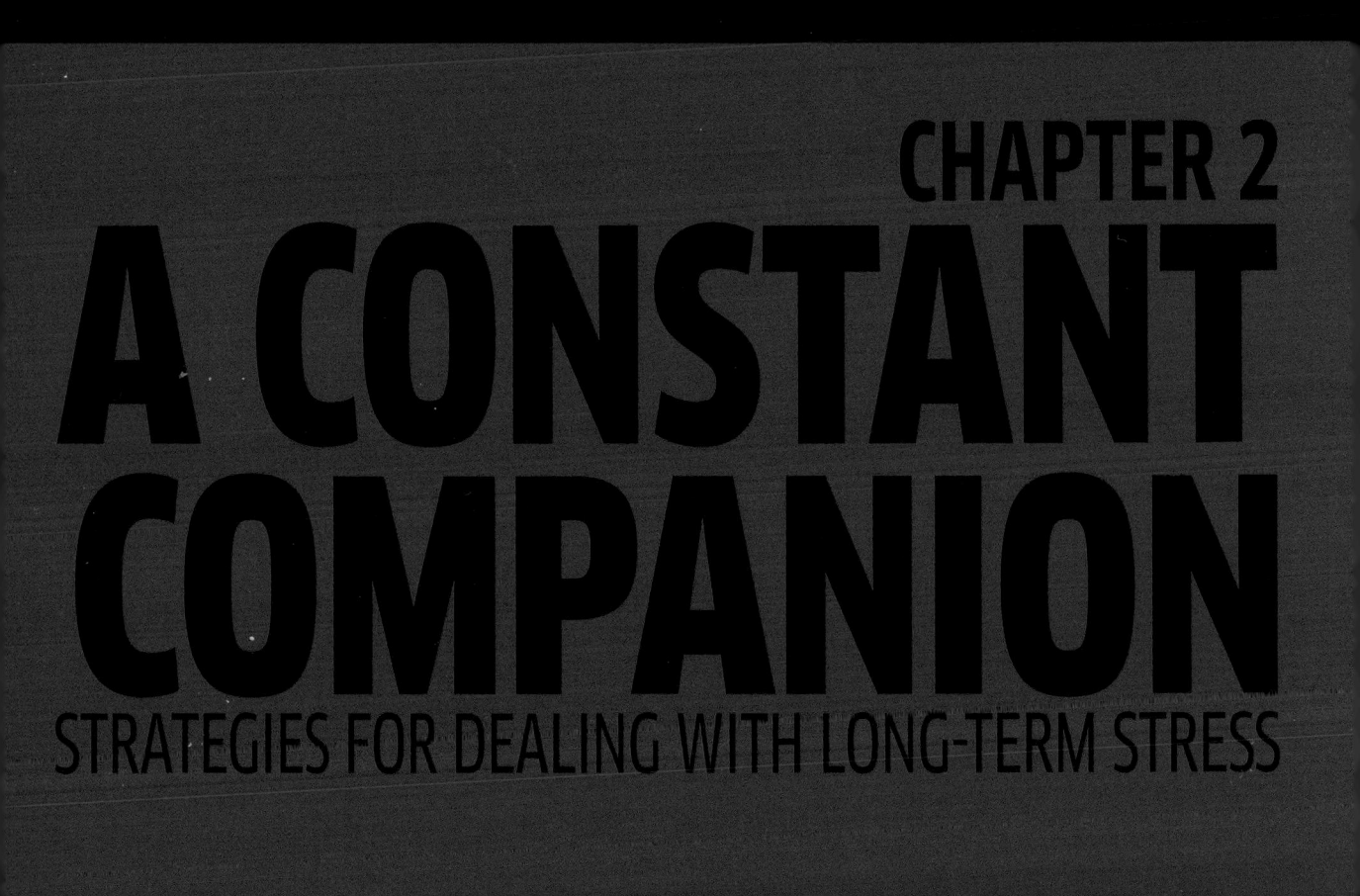

CHAPTER 2

A CONSTANT COMPANION

STRATEGIES FOR DEALING WITH LONG-TERM STRESS

PRESSURES OF TODAY

IS LIFE MORE STRESSFUL THAN EVER?

Modern life is a mixed blessing. We're more technologically advanced than ever before, but the pace of life can be hard to manage comfortably. Let's begin by understanding its particular stressors.

The modern world is one where the pressures of work, productivity, communication technology, and multi-tasking leave many of us feeling like we never get to relax. What effect does contemporary culture have on our stress levels?

> Many people still feel **very squeezed**, just in terms of taking care of their daily needs.
>
> **Katherine Nordal**
> American Psychological Association

Rich and poor

Few people will be surprised to hear that poverty tends to create stress: a 2006 study published in the American journal *Psychosomatic Medicine*, for example, noted that a lower socioeconomic status was associated with higher levels of stress hormones in the body.

However, affluent economies have their own distinct stresses. The key issue is time pressure. A 1999 study of 31 countries by American psychologist Robert Levine and Canadian psychologist Ara Norenzayan found that wealthier, more industrialized nations had a faster pace of life – which led to a higher standard of living, but at the same time left the population feeling a constant sense of urgency as well as being more prone to heart disease. In effect, fast-paced productivity creates wealth, but it also leads people to feel time-poor when they lack the time to relax and enjoy themselves.

Standards of living

An interesting discovery was made in a 2008 American study of quality of life: people living in poorer nations or communities were found, not surprisingly, to experience more problems with life satisfaction, low moods, and painful emotions – but people in wealthier nations were more likely to identify themselves as stressed. Why?

The researchers concluded that the wealthier nations' greater material opportunities led to a "hedonic treadmill". "Hedonic" means "pleasure-seeking", from the ancient Greek word *hedone* (pleasure). More consumer goods and higher material standards meant that people felt they had to work faster and harder to measure up, which made them feel all the more pressured.

❓ CAN MODERN LIFE GIVE US WHAT WE NEED?

An influential model of how we measure quality of life was suggested in 2000 by South African sociologist Ruut Veenhoven in the *Journal of Happiness Studies*. According to Veenhoven, we need four things in order to feel we can comfortably cope with life's stresses:

A LIVEABLE ENVIRONMENT
Unpolluted ecosystem, political freedom, functioning economy, cultural opportunities.

A USEFUL LIFE
A chance to live according to moral qualities such as compassion.

PERSONAL LIFE ABILITY
Good physical and mental health, skills, knowledge, and understanding.

APPRECIATION OF LIFE
Positive emotions and outlook.

Our environment isn't fully under our control, but by managing our own life skills, activities, and outlook, we can reduce our stress considerably.

If this sounds like a familiar problem in your life, consider taking some practical steps to ease up:

✔ **Be moderate** in your use of communications technology; it can be useful, but too much can feel like round-the-clock pressure (pp.60–63).
✔ **Streamline your spending.** If something isn't a true necessity, consider whether it's actually a "hedonic treadmill" purchase – in which case, you could save the money (pp.88–89).
✔ **Seek out opportunities** to live meaningfully rather than just pleasurably (pp.44–45).
✔ **Take time out** to enjoy the simple pleasures in life that don't break the bank, such as a stroll in the park (pp.98–99, 154–155).
✔ **Work on appreciating** what you already have (pp.108–109).
✔ **Be aware of feelings** that suggest you're overwhelmed, so that you take steps to avoid burnout (pp.84–85).

Life today offers many opportunities, but in an increasingly hectic world, it can be difficult to feel calm and competent. Throughout this chapter, we'll discuss the common stressors of modern life and offer simple but tried-and-tested techniques that can help you to reduce stress and increase your enjoyment of meaningful – and inexpensive – recreation and relaxation.

DAILY HASSLES
In 2017, the American Psycholological Association's annual stress survey listed the most commonly reported stressors:

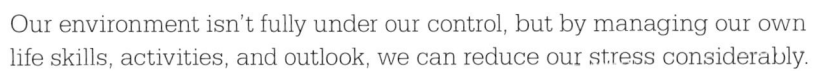

61%

Financial worries were reported to be a major stressor by 61% of the Americans who were questioned.

58%

Work stress was a major pressure for more than one in two people.

50%

The economy was a significant source of stress for half the people surveyed.

80%

For the month prior to the survey, 8 in 10 people reported at least one **physical or emotional symptom of stress** – and both can have consequences for **our health**.

If you find modern life stressful, it's not a sign of weakness: you are in the majority.

TACKLING TECHNOSTRESS

COPING IN THE DIGITAL AGE

As citizens of the Internet age, we are living at an unprecedented level of interconnectedness. Our 24/7 use of communication technology in every area of our lives can call for new methods of coping with stress.

Whether you're a technophobe or a gadget lover, communications technology is a major feature of contemporary life and can create its own stresses. How does a modern citizen manage?

Reduce your multi-tasking

Multi-tasking is a major stressor, and social media makes us more prone to it. A 2009 study at Stanford University found that people who simultaneously used many forms of social media while trying to accomplish other tasks had reduced scores on memory and concentration tests, and were less able to filter out irrelevant information. Ignoring a digital distraction became unbearably stressful and they lost focus.

Social media is distracting. A 2010 American study installed spyware on its students' computers and even though the students were supposed to be working and knew they were being recorded, they had non-work-related software – such as social media – on their computers for an average 42% of the time.

> It's just being **constantly connected** to everything. You are just **unable to switch off**.
>
> **Richard Balding**
> British occupational psychologist, on IT stress

Those distractions can interfere with our performance and the completion of tasks.

Take a break

It is possible to control our use of technology and reduce stressful multi-tasking (see pp.64–65). If juggling media has become an unhealthy habit for you, you may benefit from making a long-term plan to break the habit.

In the short-term, American psychologist and technology expert Larry Rosen also advises "tech breaks": that is, turning off your devices while working, then allowing yourself time-limited tech breaks through the day to check social media – and then turn your devices back off again. In this way, you limit your distraction, allowing you to work more efficiently.

Glued to your smartphone?

A 2014 American study found that people who use their smartphones late at night experience a more disturbed sleep, and find work more stressful the next day. Two possible causes:

- The screen's bright light makes the body suppress melatonin, a hormone that promotes sleep.
- The invasive, always-on nature of the phones makes it more difficult to draw a line between work and rest.

A 2014 Dutch study found that people who were high-frequency users of smartphones found it more difficult to detach from their jobs, which led to emotional exhaustion.

⊘ TECHNO-CLUTTER

Digital clutter can make computer use needlessly stressful. Tech experts offer these tips:

- **Make your computer desktop** simple and easy on the eye – avoid too many icons.
- **Unsubscribe** from unwanted mailing lists and blogs.
- **Delete accounts** you rarely use.
- **Organize your bookmarks** to be easy to navigate.
- **Set up a logical filing system** for your documents, and delete files you don't need.
- **Pick an Internet homepage** that just takes you to a search engine and won't bombard you with news or celebrity gossip.
- **Don't follow** too many online "friends". Limit your social media friendships to people you genuinely care about.

The study noted one exception: professionals who were used to, and comfortable with, their work spilling over into their personal lives felt less stressed when they were able to check their phone regularly: they were reassured that they weren't missing anything crucial.

As a general rule, the best smartphone use allows us to feel in touch, but not invaded. The same is true for all our devices – striking a balance is key, as we'll discuss over the page. **»**

ROUND THE CLOCK

1 hour

According to a 2013 American study, as little as **2 hours' exposure to light** from phones and tablets is enough to suppress the sleep hormone melatonin by up to **23%**. The findings suggest keeping your screen time to **under 1 hour** before bedtime.

Research cited in the *New York Times* in 2010 found that the average computer user checks **40 websites** a day and switches between **37 programs** an hour – which means we change tasks **every 2 minutes**.

Q HOW STRESSFUL?

According to the American Psychological Association's 2017 stress survey, 86% of people say they check their emails, texts, and social media "constantly" or "often". People who checked constantly reported their stress levels at 5.3 out of 10; those who checked less often reported 4.4 out of 10.

❯❯ Need to disconnect?

Being constantly connected might not be good for you. In 2012, a report to the British Psychological Society documented a phenomenon where subjects were so distressed about their social texts that they experienced "phantom vibrations": they felt their phone vibrating even when no message was received.

The researcher, Richard Balding, noted that smartphones might reduce our stress by helping us manage our workload – but that the pressure of feeling the need to be in constant contact with family and friends can actually heighten stress.

Minute-by-minute news coverage can be particularly problematic. A 2013 American study, for instance, found that people who were exposed to constant media reports following the traumatic Boston Marathon bombing experienced more extreme stress than people who had personally witnessed the attack.

As the American Psychological Association advised in 2016, it's wiser to read just enough to stay

✓ TIPS FOR FAMILIES

Parents worry that too much time on gadgets may stunt their children's social development. A 2011 British study found some encouraging facts (see right) and recommends a "Balanced Communication Diet":

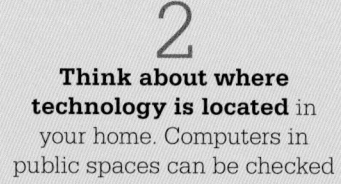

3
Have agreed-upon rules for both parents and children about when is tech-time and when is offline-time.

1
Take notes on how you use technology so you have a clear picture of your habits.

4
Set your children a good example: if you yourself are constantly checking your phone, you can't expect them not to do likewise.

2
Think about where technology is located in your home. Computers in public spaces can be checked more easily without sending the family into separate parts of the house.

5
Find your own balance: every family will have its own comfort zone.

CAN'T GET YOUR KIDS OFF THE SCREEN?

Some reassuring statistics from the 2011 British study:

65%

65% of adults and children preferred **face-to-face contact**.

43%

People aged 10–18 were more likely to be taking steps to **limit their social network site usage**: 43% of young people versus 36% of adults.

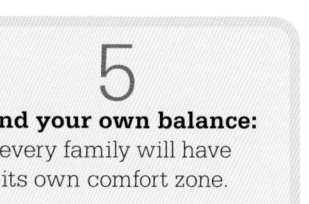

informed; following reports too obsessively is likely to do more harm than good, and it's always important to preserve your own emotional health and stability.

High stakes

The American Psychological Association's 2017 stress survey found that our relationship with social media varies considerably from generation to generation. The younger we are, the more social media defines our identity, and the more stressful we find negative experiences on social media – such as the aggression described right and far right. The older we are, the less we worry about the negative impacts of social media on our wellbeing. If your online life is making you unbearably stressed, try to seek out – or reconnect with – some offline sources of meaning that can supplement your online life (see pp.44–45).

In a 2011 study at Cambridge University, one in three people felt overwhelmed by technology. Young or old, when it comes to stress, technology is a mixed blessing, but moderation and balance are likely to be the best approach.

> You have to make the technology **your servant** and not your master.
>
> **Debra Nelson**
> American work-stress professor

🔍 HOW DARE YOU!

If you like to socialize on websites, you may be familiar with the stress of being berated by unpleasant people. You may also have to admit that you've sometimes been more aggressive than you're proud of. A famous 2004 study by American psychologist John Suler identified this as the "online disinhibition effect", which shows six factors:

1 **Dissociative anonymity.** "What I do online can't be connected to my normal self."

2 **Invisibility.** "No one can see me or pass judgement on me."

3 **Asynchronicity.** "This isn't happening in real time, so I don't have to see the impact."

4 **Solipsistic introjection.** "I can't see these people, so I can presume they are whoever I imagine them to be."

5 **Dissociative imagination.** "This isn't the real world, so I'm not causing real pain to real people."

6 **Minimizing authority.** "Nobody can stop me."

While some online rudeness comes from genuine hostility, remember that a total stranger who makes personal, offensive comments isn't talking to the real you. If you feel distressed by an offensive comment, remind yourself that replying often emboldens people to become more offensive and that their comments say much more about them than you.

⊘ BEWARE OF ONLINE AGGRESSION

Being "trolled" is highly stressful. A 2012 American experiment identified two factors influencing online aggression:

1 **Anonymity** heightens aggression.

2 **Participants exposed to aggressive comments** by other people react more aggressively than those exposed to positive comments.

If you're looking for a friendly place to chat online, check websites for a degree of openness about identity and a good example set by previous posts – they're your best guide to a low-stress environment.

DIGITAL DETOX

In the American Psychological Association's 2017 stress survey,

65% **65%** said a **digital detox** would aid **their mental health**

28% … but **only 28%** of those people **actually took one**.

The evidence suggests we feel less stressed if we unplug occasionally, so if you're thinking you should too, it's worth sticking to your resolution.

BALLS IN THE AIR

THE STRESS OF MULTI-TASKING

When you're overwhelmed, it can be tempting to try to tackle everything at once. Yet the research suggests that this approach is likely to make you feel more stressed and less efficient: one task at a time is best.

Being able to handle several tasks at once would seem to be an advantage. However, the fact is that the human brain is not actually capable of concontrating on multiple tasks at once: you'll manage your stressors better if you handle tasks one at a time.

The perils of juggling

Trying to solve too many problems at once is inherently stressful. As American-Canadian neuroscientist Daniel Levitin points out, it has a number of harmful chemical effects in the brain:

- Increasing production of the stress hormone cortisol (see pp.20–21).
- Burning through the brain's glucose levels at an accelerated rate, leading to lower energy and disorientation.
- Creating a feedback loop similar to addiction. Encountering new information releases the reward neurotransmitter dopamine, which drives us to seek out increasing levels of novelty and makes us less and less able to stay focused.

> Under most conditions, the brain simply **cannot do two complex tasks** at the same time.
>
> **David Meyer**
> American psychology professor

It may be hard to set aside all but one of our tasks if we're worried about getting everything done, but on a biological level, multi-tasking heightens stress and confusion and reduces efficiency.

Dropping the balls

When American neuroscientist Earl Miller scanned subjects' brains as they tried to sort out visual stimuli, the results showed that it is physically impossible to focus on more than one or two things at once.

When we try to multi-task, we are switching our attention rapidly from one task to another – which, as American psychiatrist Edward Hallowell explains, "reduces the quality of the work on any one task, because you're ignoring it for milliseconds at a time". This switching-cost means that multi-tasking can actually slow us down:

- A 2010 Italian study found that subjects juggling multiple tasks were less productive and made more mistakes.
- A 2005 British study found that multi-tasking temporarily reduced its subjects' IQ by as much as 15 points, while their self-reported stress levels rose by 40–100%.
- A 2006 American study found that even if we do absorb information while multi-tasking, it doesn't become a transferrable skill: subjects who were required to learn while simultaneously counting musical tones found it more difficult to adapt their new knowledge to other contexts.

When you have a lot to do, the science suggests that picking one task at a time may help you to finish faster. Yet multi-tasking can be successful if we mix a mental task with a "mindless" physical one, since they use different parts of the brain (see below right). For instance, if you try to compose an email and talk on the phone at the same time, you're unlikely to manage either properly, but if you fold laundry and talk on the phone, your brain won't suffer any stress.

Positive "multi-tasking"

There is in fact a small but positive form of multi-tasking: if you find it hard to focus, have something to fiddle with. Many tasks today are stressful partly because they require us to stay unnaturally still, and recent research suggests that movement may actually be an important part of thinking. A 2011 British essay in *The Lancet*, for instance, argued that doodling helped concentration and alleviated stress by activating neural networks in the brain that promote cognition.

A 2013 American study also reported that the fidget widgets we play with "mindlessly" – such as paperclips or stress balls – help the brain regulate the effects of stress, such as boredom and indecision.

In short, trying to multi-task your way through too many stressful tasks is likely to make you feel more stressed. If you doodle or fidget to help yourself concentrate, or if you combine brain-work with jobs you can do on auto-pilot, you are doing as much multi-tasking as you can reasonably ask of yourself.

29%

For a safe and stress-relieving form of multi-tasking, a 2009 UK study found that subjects allowed to **doodle** performed **29% better on a memory test** than subjects who weren't.

40%

A 2001 American study published in the *Journal of Experimental Psychology* found people were up to **40% slower at problem-solving** when trying to multi-task.

⌕ THE MULTI-TASKING BRAIN

The brain's cerebral cortex handles higher-level thought, like organizing, planning, and self-control, while more routine tasks that can be done "absent-mindedly" – such as combing your hair – are handled by the cerebellum. Save your brain some strain, and let each centre stick to one task at a time.

TO ACHIEVE GREAT THINGS, TWO THINGS ARE NEEDED: A PLAN AND NOT QUITE ENOUGH TIME

LEONARD BERNSTEIN, COMPOSER AND CONDUCTOR

MIRROR, MIRROR

BODY ISSUES

In a culture of mass media that idealizes near-unreachable beauty standards, it's not surprising that many of us feel stressed simply by looking at our body. How do we get more comfortable in our own skin?

It can be hard to feel attractive in a media-saturated world that surrounds us with images of "perfect" bodies we feel we must measure up to. Disliking our own appearance isn't healthy: a 2009 Australian study, for instance, found that poor body image was a predictor for depression in teen boys and girls. Rather than going on a crash diet or extreme exercise regime, a better first step is to start improving our self-image.

Manage your media exposure

Does media affect our body image? The answer seems to be yes. A famous Harvard study in 1998 followed Fijian girls who'd recently gained access to television. Despite their culture traditionally valuing a robust build, by the end of three years, 74% of the girls identified themselves as being too fat. Body anxiety can start early in an image-saturated culture: America's National Eating Disorders Association reports that 80% of ten-year-olds fear being overweight.

It doesn't help that average body weight is increasing, yet

PURSUING PERFECTION

17 million

How real is the pressure to look "perfect"? The American Society of Plastic Surgeons reports just over **17 million cosmetic procedures** were performed in the US in 2016.

professional models are getting thinner. The addiction and eating disorders website Rehabs.com reports that American models weighed 8% less than the average woman in 1975 – and 25% less than the average woman in 2014.

As media images increasingly focus on male bodies, men too are developing body stress. A 2012 British study found that four in five men spoke anxiously about their appearance and many put the blame squarely on the media. A 2004 American study also found that showing men images of an idealized male body made them feel angry and depressed.

Rational acceptance

It can be difficult to avoid media images entirely, but you're likely to be less stressed if you remind yourself that you are not obliged to resemble an air-brushed model.

An American study published in 2005 investigated the body images of both male and female subjects and found that when we're feeling insecure about our bodies, our coping methods can be divided into three broad groups:

- **Appearance fixing.** We dream of looking better, plan to change our looks in some way, or seek reassurance about our looks from others.
- **Avoidance.** We avoid mirrors and try not to think about our appearance.
- **Positive rational acceptance.** We acknowledge our appearance but we know it's not the most important thing about us.

Of these three coping methods, the first two were found to make people feel worse, while positive rational acceptance made people feel more confident about their bodies, and about themselves in general. To see which of these coping methods you tend to use, try the self-assessment test on the right.

Whatever our body image, we need to eat well and stay active: a healthy diet (see pp.158–161) and a moderate amount of exercise (see pp.152–157) are good for both body and mind. When it comes to feeling good about ourselves, the first step is to accept it's really not that important whether we are physically perfect, and that we're valuable no matter how our bodies look.

EATING DISORDERS

Severe problems with body image can lead to eating disorders. If you're concerned that your relationship with your body and food are out of control, it's always best to seek medical help.

1 in 10

A 2011 study estimated that 10 million men and 20 million women in the US – almost **10% of the population** – suffer from an eating disorder at some point in their lives.

? REAL CONFIDENCE

If you feel bad about your body, what are your usual methods of dealing with the discomfort?

A I think about how I could make myself more attractive.

B I avoid looking at myself in the mirror.

C I remind myself that I probably look better than I'm feeling right now.

A I do something to make myself look better.

B I comfort eat.

C I think about good qualities I have which don't depend on my looks.

A I look for reassurance from other people.

B I try to ignore my feelings.

C I tell myself it's not that big a deal.

Results:

A answers indicate "appearance fixing" approaches.

B answers indicate "avoidance" approaches.

C answers indicate "positive rational acceptance" approaches.

According to the 2005 study described under "Rational acceptance" (see left), positive, rational acceptance is the best way of making ourselves feel better.

SECURE IN LOVE?

STRESS AND RELATIONSHIPS

Is your love life a place of calm and support, or one of heartache and conflict? We all want a happy home life, so understanding how stress affects us romantically helps us build a more positive relationship.

When it comes to romance, stress can affect us in two ways: there is stress created by the relationship itself, and stress due to outside causes having an impact on the relationship. The key to a successful romance is managing both so that you and your partner make each other feel safe.

How attached?

One of psychology's most influential concepts regarding relationships is "attachment theory". Formulated in the 1940s by British psychologist John Bowlby – and later developed by his American-Canadian pupil Mary Ainsworth – the theory identifies three main types:

- **Secure** people regard intimacy as natural and are comfortable with it. They expect their partners to care about their needs and to treat them well, and seek to offer the same.
- **Anxious** people want intimacy, but do not see themselves as very desirable and are hyper-vigilant for signs of rejection. However, with a secure partner they tend to relax and become affectionate and loyal.
- **Avoidant/dismissive** people are the "commitment-phobics" who see others as untrustworthy and feel that safety comes only from emotional independence. Subconsciously they fear abandonment, but they tend to manage that fear by hiding their feelings from their partner. As a result, they can give out mixed signals.

❓ WHEN ANXIOUS MEETS AVOIDANT

Do you keep getting your heart broken? Perhaps you have an anxious attachment style but you choose avoidant partners. The anxious/avoidant mix can lead to intense highs and lows. For some anxious people, this can result in them associating relationship stress with passion and finding that secure partners – who would actually make them happy – seem boring and unattractive. If this pattern sounds familiar, it's wise to try dating outside your usual "type".

ARE YOU PRONE TO RELATIONSHIP DRAMAS?

Avoidant partner feels stressed by too much closeness – does something to create a sense of distance

Anxious partner feels rejected and starts to panic – pursues avoidant partner

Avoidant partner pulls away still further

Anxious partner feels dizzying rush of happiness at being close again

Avoidant partner relaxes and draws closer

Anxious partner stifles fears and stops asking for intimacy

Avoidant partner makes it clear that it's "my way or the highway"

Anxious partner becomes seriously distressed

■ **Fearful-avoidant** people (a fairly rare fourth type) have commonly experienced trauma in the past and fear both abandonment and entrapment, resulting in extremely difficult relationships.

Research has found that the most stressful relationships tend to be between anxious and avoidant people (see above). A relationship with a secure partner tends to be the least stressful: a secure partner is able to reassure an anxious partner and isn't threatened by the independence of an avoidant one.

Facing stress together

Even the best relationships aren't stress-free. A 2010 American study sampled 30 couples' cortisol levels (see pp.20–21) over three days, and found that while their positive moods didn't affect each other very much, if one partner's stress level rose, the other's did too.

A set of 2009 American studies found that partners experiencing non-relationship stress also had stronger negative reactions to normal annoyances in their partner, regardless of their attachment style. A couple might usually have good communication and conflict resolution skills, but find it hard to draw on them when under stress.

As a general rule, managing our own stress levels improves our partner's life as well as our own, as we'll discuss further overleaf. **»**

THE TOP TWO

A 2015 study by an American bank highlighted the top two **causes of relationship stress:**

35%

of couples suffer from **money-related worries or conflicts**.

25%

of couples say that their partners' **annoying habits** really bother them.

? STAYING POSITIVE

Why do some couples endure under pressure while others don't? A useful model – developed in 1995 by American psychologists Benjamin Karney and Thomas Bradbury and still in use today – is the Vulnerability-Stress Adaptation Model of Marriage. Karney and Bradbury argue that lasting relationships involve each partner using successful "adaptive processes" (relationship skills) that help mediate the effects of stress.

Initial satisfaction
with the relationship

Enduring vulnerabilities
such as personality traits, past experiences, habits of thought

External stressors
such as work stress, ill health, family problems

Adaptive processes
such as resolving conflicts, trying to understand each other, accepting our imperfections, and tackling other stressors together

Change in relationship satisfaction –
we decide either it's worth the effort or it's too stressful, and the relationship endures or ends

Every relationship involves accepting that nobody's perfect and coming to terms with our partner's vulnerabilities and limitations. The strength of our adaptive processes – our relationship skills – can make the difference between whether we ride out stressful times together or break apart.

⟫ Gender balance?

Do men and women process stress differently in relationships? Two studies suggest they do, if traditional gender roles place more emotional responsibility on women.

A 2006 American study of attachment types asked couples to reflect on their relationship problems, and then measured their stress hormone levels. The avoidant women had the highest levels, while men with secure partners had the lowest. The study concluded that men tended to depend on their partners to help manage their feelings; avoidant women found that role stressful, but secure women managed it well.

A 2010 American study suggested that since men tended to have more power within the family, their feelings set the tone in a marriage. While wives tended to experience their husband's stress – and showed elevated cortisol levels – even if they were satisfied with the marriage, only the unhappily married husbands experienced their wife's distress.

Facing stress together

Researchers suggest the tendency for male moods to affect female partners more than female moods affect the men is due in part to social expectations that women should help men manage their emotions. Men might be well advised to seek out a secure partner, but also to work on their own stress-handling skills, while a woman who already finds intimacy stressful should favour a calm partner. Greater equality in relationships is likely to lead to less stress for everyone.

The happiest couples

How do we make a relationship solid enough to survive the stressful times? According to American psychologist John Gottman – one of the most influential researchers in the field of relationships – there are several key strategies:

✔ Become intimately familiar with your partner's goals, aspirations, and stressors.
✔ Foster fondness and admiration towards your partner.
✔ When your partner makes a "bid" by saying something that invites you to be affectionate, attentive, or playful, turn towards them – that is, validate and respond in kind – rather than ignoring or dismissing them.
✔ Treat each other with respect and let your partner influence you. Gottman notes that this is a skill men generally need to cultivate more; women are often better at it.
✔ When addressing solvable problems, speak with courtesy, de-escalate the tension levels, be prepared to soothe each other, and be ready to compromise.
✔ Respect your partner's dreams, even if you don't share them.
✔ Create a sense of shared purpose and meaning (see pp.44–45).

Gottman calls the people who can manage these strategies "masters" – as opposed to "disasters", who can't. No one is a perfect partner, especially under strain – but if we can keep our relationships secure and supportive, we can have love even in the stressful times.

⊘ THE FOUR HORSEMEN

American psychologist and relationship expert John Gottman identifies four behaviours he describes as the "Four Horsemen of the Apocalypse" – behaviours guaranteed to cause your partner so much stress the relationship may break under the strain. Take care to avoid:

1 Criticism
Polite complaints are effective ("I wish you'd try to be nicer to my mother"), but criticizing your partner as a person is not.

> You're such a jerk, talking to my mother like that!

2 Contempt
Mockery, sarcasm, name-calling, eye-rolling: being the target of these behaviours is highly stressful.

> You forgot the cereal again? You can't remember the simplest thing, can you?

3 Defensiveness
If our partner raises a complaint, it's destructive to behave as if we don't take their feelings seriously.

> I know I didn't call, but look how busy I am. Why can't you be more considerate?

4 Stonewalling
Shutting down and tuning your partner out by saying nothing tells your partner, "You don't exist as long as I'm mad at you".

> Whatever...

Happy marriages are based on a **deep friendship**. By this I mean a mutual **respect** for, and **enjoyment** of, each other's company.

John Gottman
American psychotherapist and psychology professor

NOT TONIGHT, JOSEPHINE

SEX AND INTIMACY

Good sex is de-stressing, but stress can make us feel a lot less sexy. Any long-term relationship can have ups and downs, but if a sexless phase goes on too long, it may be time to work together and fix the problem.

Unfortunately our bodies aren't built to feel stressed and sexy at the same time. When we feel tense or threatened, our sympathetic nervous system fires up its fight-or-flight response (see pp.20–21) – but it's the rest-and-digest response, also known as "feed-and-breed", that makes us want to make love, and it is controlled by the parasympathetic nervous system. As the two systems have opposite effects on the body, we can only activate one at a time. The result can be that when you're stressed, you're not in the mood.

A few sexless nights won't hurt anyone, but if sexlessness is becoming a habit in your relationship and you're unhappy about that, it may be time to consider the underlying causes.

Some common problems
The effects that stress has on our sex lives can be complicated. We may just be feeling too tense right now – or we may be dealing with more long-term issues, including the following:

50%

American sex therapists Barry and Emily McCarthy estimate that around 50% of couples experience **problems with desire** at some point in their marriage. If that includes you, don't panic – it's common, and it's fixable.

- **Feeling undesirable** because one or both partners have gained weight through stress-eating (see pp.158–161). America's National Healthy Marriage Resource Center suggests a softly lit or dark room and paying each other compliments in non-sexual as well as sexual contexts. They add that if you want to improve your diet, it helps to do it as a couple. Don't create the feeling that being seen as attractive is conditional on weight loss, as that will only hurt your partner's self-esteem, but tackle self-improvement together so that it becomes a source of intimacy rather than loneliness.

- **Depression.** Stress is associated with a greater risk of depression, anxiety, and other mood disorders, and this can in turn suppress your sex drive. In cases like this, sexlessness can be an indicator of a deeper problem, so if you think you may be depressed or unwell, consult your doctor.

- **Medication.** Some medications, including many antidepressants, can dull sexual sensation. If this is a problem, ask your GP about alternatives. If a medication change isn't possible, try low-pressure physical intimacies such as massage, caressing, and other activities that feel good whether they result in sex or not.

- **Feeling alienated.** Stress is hard on relationships. If you're constantly tense with each other, you're less likely to feel amorous. In this case, improving the relationship should be the priority (see pp.70–73).

✓ BREAKING THE SEXLESS CYCLE

If stress has caused you to feel less interested in sex for some time, you can get into a vicious circle.

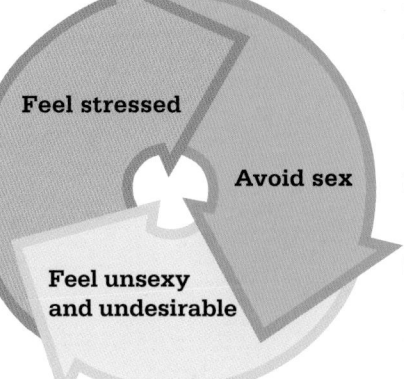

Feel stressed

Avoid sex

Feel unsexy and undesirable

In this situation, American marriage counsellor Michele Weiner-Davis advises against waiting to feel sexy before you have sex: desire can develop after you've begun. It's easy to lose touch with our sexuality, but often we find that our desire returns when we stop waiting for it to find us and start making love.

Taking the pressure off

Performance anxiety is often associated with public speaking (see pp.114–115), but it can also affect our most intimate moments. Feeling that sort of pressure is hardly sexy, so how do we relax about our sexual performance?

Psychologist and sex therapist Linda Savage recommends a useful technique for stressed lovers, called the "pleasure paradigm": thinking of pleasure rather than orgasm as the goal of sex, and achieving this

❓ FEELING UNLOVED?

Even when there is sex, stress can make us withdrawn. The American National Healthy Marriage Resource Center advises being aware of certain pitfalls, and working together to overcome them:

- Does one of you always make the first move?

- Does one of you consent to sex, but seem unenthusiastic?

- Does one of you enjoy sexual favours, but not give many back?

- After sex, does one of you give no particular indication that it was enjoyable?

Partners need to hear they're wanted. If stress distracts you in intimate moments, Canadian psychologist Lori Brotto advises using mindfulness techniques (see pp.132–135) to bring your attention back to connecting with your own sensations and with your partner.

through sensual touch rather than focusing too exclusively on penetrative sex.

Sometimes the best solution is to broaden our definition of sex. There is more to both passion and tenderness than the simple act of lovemaking – and if we decide that any physical pleasure we experience with our partner counts as part of our sex lives, then we both open ourselves up to many more intimacies without adding any more stress.

PRESSURES OF PARENTHOOD
CREATING A CALM HOMELIFE

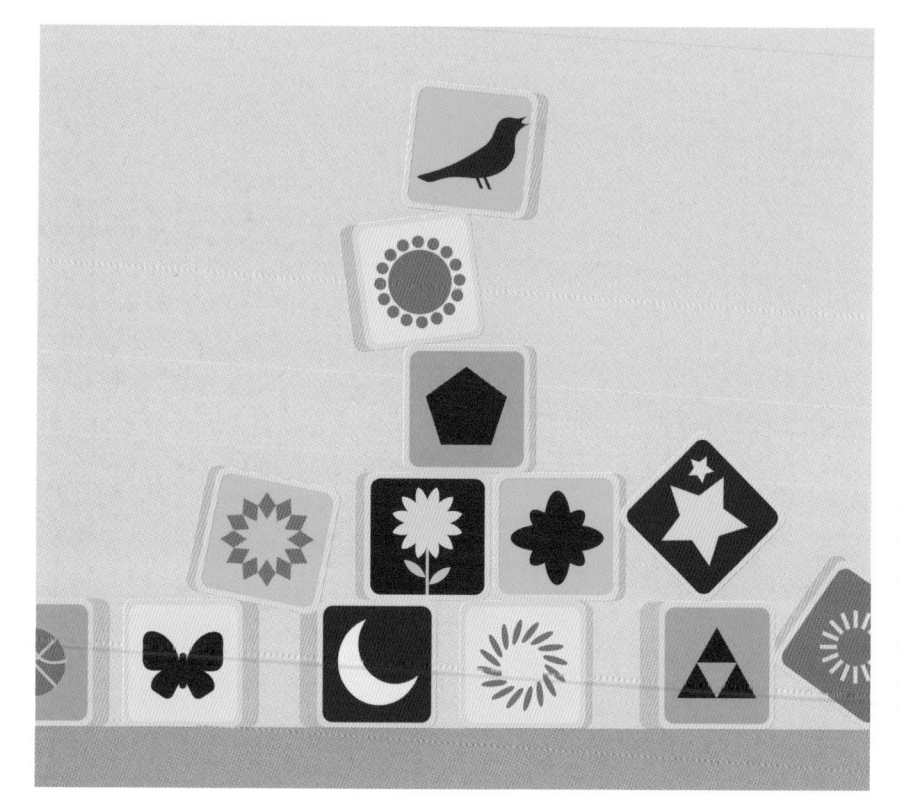

Parenting can be wonderful, but there's no question that it can be stressful as well. We want to help our children feel calm and safe – but that process begins with making sure we're calm ourselves.

Few things give us more joy, pain, and stress than the experience of parenting. As author Elizabeth Stone observed, the decision to have a child is "to decide forever to have your heart go walking around outside your body". Exhausted parents might add that it's also a decision to have your time, sleep, and resources subject to the needs of another person who, being young, doesn't always have the best judgement. Under this much pressure, how does a parent manage stress – both for themselves and their children?

The kids are fine, right?
Children need parents who can provide love and support as well as discipline, which requires parents understand their child's feelings. According to a 2012 American study, we aren't as good at understanding our children as we might think.

The researchers tested families with "typically developing" children – that is, with no health or learning disabilities – aged four to eleven, and found that parents consistently underestimated how much worry and nervousness their children felt, overestimated how optimistic they were, and tended to assume that

> If you care about children, **take really good care of mothers**.
>
> **Rick Hanson**
> American neurologist

their children's feelings were more similar to their own than was actually the case.

The lesson here is that when dealing with our children, there are two things we need to remember:

1 Our children are separate and different from us.

2 Being a child is more stressful than it looks.

It's best not to assume that our children are feeling fine unless they misbehave – or that misbehaviour is caused by naughtiness or anger rather than anxiety. Be alert to your children's fears, and if they're misbehaving, consider whether they are stressed rather than just being willful.

Take a step back

Love is crucial in families, but it sometimes helps to turn down your feelings a notch. Research suggests that parents who feel the deepest empathy for their children may not be the best at nurturing them.

A 2014 American study found that mothers who scored high on an empathy test also showed the greatest physiological response when their children cried. However, mothers with high empathy had to watch their temper. Empathic parents are sometimes more likely to turn to harsh discipline when under stress (see right). On the next page, we'll discuss ways to put some distance between yourself and your stress. ⟫

✓ KEEPING YOUR TEMPER

Do you adore your kids but struggle to be patient when they kick up a fuss? You're not alone: a 2013 Dutch study found that parents who had a strong emotional response to their children crying were also the most likely to overreact and use harsh disciplinary methods at home. Over-empathizing can cause an unfortunate stress reaction:

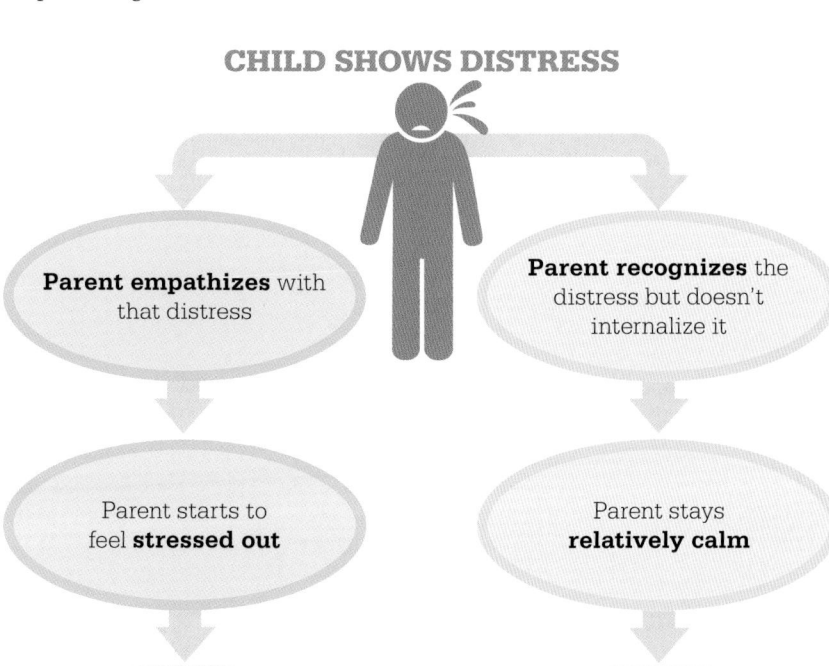

CHILD SHOWS DISTRESS

Parent empathizes with that distress

Parent recognizes the distress but doesn't internalize it

Parent starts to feel **stressed out**

Parent stays **relatively calm**

Parent's **self-control frays** under the pressure

Parent is able to make **better judgements**

Parent **shouts** at the child

Parent addresses the child's behaviour **more constructively**

When we take on our chid's feelings as if they are our own, we lose the ability to nurture the child. It's important to remember that your child is not you, and help them learn to manage difficult feelings appropriately.

» Set an example

Appropriate emotional boundaries are important for parents and for children. Not overreacting to your child's distress, but helping them to manage their emotions is a more supportive, effective approach. Children benefit from a parent who can not only sympathize, but also model a calmer mood for them.

Try not to sweat sleeplessness

We all benefit from a good night's sleep (see pp.162–165), but with young children, sometimes that's not possible. As American psychologist and anthropologist Gwen Dewar points out, "Getting resentful, ruminating, or worrying about your inability to function the next day isn't going to help". Negative feelings can make it harder to sleep even when you have the opportunity, and it's more likely to make you irritable with your children – which may, in turn, worsen their problems with sleep.

A 2010 American study found that the best way to ensure a young child slept well was to make sure that they got "maternal emotional availability" at bedtime – that their mother (or father) could give them their full attention and respond to their feelings with sensitivity. When your child is keeping you up, your best strategy – for their sleep and for your own – is to give them all the patience you have and accept that settling them will take as long as it takes.

Worried about money?

Sometimes we're stressed by our parenting responsibilities, but sometimes we're just stressed people who also happen to be parents. Our background stress

ASSESSING STRESS

A classic model of stress known as the Lazarus model (see p.28) helps us to manage our feelings by making a constructive assessment of our circumstances. Next time your child's behaviour is wearing out your patience, try these steps and see if it helps.

Agent of stress: an event that causes a problem		Appraising the stress: how you view the situation	Coping mechanism: the decision you make	Stress reaction: how you react
At the supermarket checkout, your child whines to be bought an unhealthy snack.	Negative reaction	"He's being disobedient; he knows perfectly well that I said no more sweets today!"	"He's got to learn that I'm not putting up with this kind of behaviour."	"If you don't cut that out, young man, you're in serious trouble!" **Impact:** you escalate the conflict and upset your child.
	Positive reaction	"He's tired and bored; this is a stressful environment for him."	"I'd better let him know I understand, but remind him what I expect."	"Darling, I know this isn't fun for you, but you need to be patient. I'll fix you a snack at home." **Impact:** you manage the conflict and support your child.

level does affect our children and how we relate to them. According to a 2015 review by the University of Minnesota, numerous studies confirm that parents experiencing economic hardship are more likely to take a child's misbehaviour personally – and assume that, for instance, a failure to put away toys is a sign the child is deliberately trying to be annoying rather than just forgetful or distracted.

The same review reports that parents can protect their children from the stress of poverty to a significant degree if they show plenty of affection and make sure they know what's going on in the children's lives. The challenges are greater, but if you can manage to remain patient and warm despite worries about paying the bills, the evidence suggests your children can feel as safe and supported as those in more affluent families.

Parenting isn't easy, and even the most loving and responsible people find it a challenge. Keeping that in mind, you can take real pride in doing a good job. No family is perfect, but with warmth and good coping skills, parents and children manage stress more effectively as a family.

Q THE TOP TWO ESSENTIALS

According to American sociologist Christine Carter, the most important predictors of a child's wellbeing are:

- Getting enough love and affection.
- Having parents or caregivers who can manage their own stress levels.

Children pick up on parents' emotions, so don't feel guilty if you put some time and energy into self-care: it'll help your kids as well. The happiest families are those where every member is happy, including you.

✓ THE COPING CHILD

A happy child generally makes for a happy parent, so ensuring your children feel safe is likely to help you as well as them. In the US, the Center for Effective Parenting advised in 2006 that the tactics a parent can use to create a safe-feeling and low-stress home are:

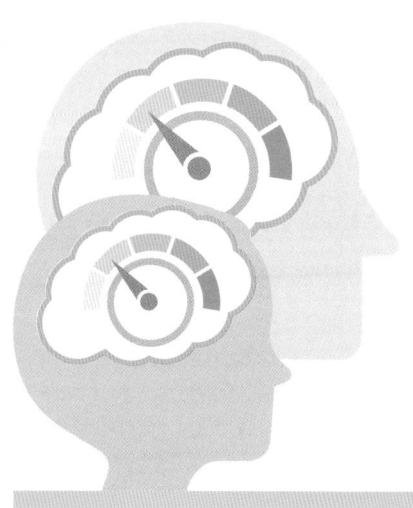

✔ **Provide a good balance** between giving warmth and setting reasonable rules.

✔ **Be available,** supportive, and reassuring.

✔ **Help your child understand** their own signs of stress, such as sleeplessness, headaches, upset stomach, moodiness, or irritability.

✔ **Listen when they talk,** and ask open-ended questions such as, "What do you think of...?" or "How does that make you feel?"

✔ **Don't overprotect:** children will need to learn how to manage stress effectively.

✔ **Build up their self-esteem** (pp.42–43).

✔ **Teach them** to handle criticism (pp.34–35).

✔ **Help them learn** how to limit stress with effective time management (pp.146–147).

✔ **Teach them problem-solving skills** and cognitive re-framing (pp.26–29, 52–53).

✔ **Make sure they have enough sleep**, good nutrition, regular exercise, and challenging and engaging activities (pp.174–175).

✔ **Teach assertiveness** (pp.92–95).

✔ **Encourage a sense of humour** (pp.182–183).

✔ **Model calm, optimistic, and confident moods.**

IN THE WORKPLACE

PRESSURE TO PERFORM

One of the top sources of stress in everyday life is our work: earning a living can be anything but relaxing. We need to find ways to come to terms with the pressure and improve our ability to cope.

A challenging job can be interesting and exciting, but some job situations are challenging and unhealthy. What stresses us varies between individuals, but the most common workplace stressors are:

- Demanding, dull, or upsetting work
- Low control over how you work
- Unclear expectations, creating no-win situations
- A high-conflict, bullying, or unfair environment
- Low recognition for your efforts, and few opportunities for promotion or development
- Changes at work being badly managed

In short, we don't thrive doing work that feels unrewarding or disempowering: over time that sort of environment can wear us down.

Making you sick?

Can a stressful job negatively impact your health? Sustained high levels of the stress hormone cortisol are unhealthy, but according to a 1997 Australian study, work stress doesn't necessarily raise our blood pressure. The researchers found that workers in stressful jobs might be prone to high blood pressure, but only if they used "maladaptive" coping strategies. In other words, the workers who drank, binged on unhealthy food, smoked, used drugs, or isolated themselves socially in response to stress showed an increased rate of high blood pressure. The workers who exercised, used relaxation techniques, used problem-focused coping such as re-organizing their work time, or made good use of social support, remained physically well. The problem wasn't workplace stress as such, but unhealthy coping mechanisms: if you turn to healthy coping strategies, your body needn't suffer.

Coping tactics

Some workplaces are simply impossible – if your boss is a bully, for instance, quietly looking for a new job may be the only solution – but when the main source of stress is the work, rather than the people, several tactics are recommended by doctors and psychologists:

1 Begin every day by taking just 10 minutes to plan and prioritize a realistic set of targets (pp.146–147).

2 Keep track of your stress through the day. Use a Stress Diary to make a note of where stressful events happened, who you were with, and how you reacted (pp.40–41). Identify situations to avoid in future, and cultivate healthy coping mechanisms.

3 Have "no-work" times in your schedule. Plan them in advance, then turn off your phone, don't check your email, and put work out of your mind (pp.60–63).

4 Use time off to the full. Take annual leave, and make your holidays and weekends periods of recharging and recovery (pp.150–151).

5 Use relaxation techniques such as exercise (pp.152–155), yoga (p.157), and meditation (p.133).

6 Identify allies at work. Ensuring employees can be effective is part of a supervisor's job, so talk to yours about plans for making your schedule workable and your environment tolerable. If your supervisor doesn't have a sensible attitude, look for colleagues with whom you can share the load and get mutual support (pp.176–179).

7 Get support from any health and safety or HR departments to make sure your workplace is safe and comfortable – not unbearably loud or liable to give you repetitive strain injury, for instance – so that your physical wellbeing isn't an extra worry.

8 Don't try to control the uncontrollable. Company structures and colleagues' personalities, for example, may be outside your control, so don't exhaust yourself obsessing about them (pp.46–47).

9 Avoid perfectionism. If the work is done and adequate, don't push yourself to do more (pp.34–35).

10 Find the funny side. Laughing at a situation helps reduce its hold on us (pp.182–183).

11 Appreciate the positive. Try to focus on pride in your own work, your colleagues' good points, and anything else that keeps you seeing the brighter side of things (pp.180–181).

Appropriate boundaries are as important at work as they are in your personal life: knowing that you are much more than your work and giving an appropriate amount of your time and energy to work is central to establishing a healthy work–life balance.

Q THE THREE "E"s

Harvard professor of cognition and education Howard Gardner identifies three intertwining aspects that make up "good work" – work that feels more rewarding than stressful:

Excellence. You are satisfied that you're working to a high standard.

Engagement. You enjoy your work.

Ethics. You are doing the right thing, both in your field of work and by your team.

Tackling tasks

When a task is stressful, the natural tendency is to procrastinate. In a work situation, this is obviously problematic: putting off the task results in heightened stress as you rush to meet a deadline while facing a growing workload – or the work doesn't get done and you get into trouble with your colleagues. How do we stop procrastinating and face the project and the stress head-on?

Don't wait to feel motivated

American psychologist Joseph Ferrari points out that it's easy to delay starting work because we're not in the "right mood" – but by doing that we are making a fundamental mistake. We're succumbing to the false belief that we will somehow feel more in the mood later, even though nothing has changed – or if it has, the only difference is that the job has become more urgent, resulting in more stress, causing us to feel even less like tackling the work.

Instead of waiting for a task to feel manageable, we're better off making a start even if we don't feel motivated. As American psychiatrist David D. Burns, CBT expert and author of the best-selling *Feeling Good: The New Mood Therapy*, observes, once we've started the task, we usually discover some motivation – and we have definitely lessened the stress of procrastinating.

> **Action must come first**, and the motivation comes later on.
>
> **David D. Burns**
> American psychiatrist and CBT expert

Tackle the worst stressors first

An old proverb is helpful here: if you begin your day by eating a live frog, you can enjoy the comfort of knowing that nothing else that happens to you today will be that bad. If you have a "frog" to cope with, it's going to stress you out knowing that it'll have to be dealt with at some point, so if your schedule allows for it, do the thing you're most dreading first and get it out of the way. After that, your other stressors will feel less daunting.

Reward yourself

American psychologist Robert Eisenberger proposes a theory he calls "learned industriousness": put simply, if we come to associate working hard with being rewarded, hard work in and of itself begins to feel more rewarding and less stressful. If you're lucky enough to have an employer who praises your efforts, you may already be experiencing this benefit. Studies confirm that praise is a sufficient reward – even if you have to reward yourself in small ways. A 2007

✓ WORK SMART

An acronym pioneered by American consultant Peter Drucker during the 1980s is still recommended by psychologists today, and can help you set workplace goals that feel manageable rather than daunting:

S Specific	Choose goals that can be clearly articulated. (The "S" can also stand for "simple" or "sensible".)
M Measurable	Have a way of tracking your progress. (Sometimes identifed as "meaningful" or "motivating".)
A Achievable	Aim for realistic targets. (Sometimes identified as "agreed" or "attainable".)
R Relevant	The outcome must be useful. (Also "reasonable", "realistic", "resourced", or "results-based".)
T Time bound	Set a date by which you intend to have your task completed.

American study found that the most important elements of a reward are that it should be quick and reliable. If you've decided to reward yourself for a job well done, keep that promise to yourself.

Create "mastery" experiences

According to a 2004 study by Canadian psychologist Fuschia Sirois, people are more prone to procrastinate if they have a low opinion of their own efficacy – in other words, they don't trust their own competence and abilities (see pp.42–43).

One of the best ways to improve your confidence in your own efficacy is to consider your life outside work and build up a memory bank of accomplishments, great or small. This allows you to look back and recall times when you proved to yourself that you are, in fact, able to get things done when you set your mind to it. With that knowledge, tackling work projects may feel less intimidating.

If you are finding work difficult, you're far from alone. A 2013 survey by the American Psychological Association found that only 36% of employees felt they were given enough resources to help manage workplace stress. With good coping tactics, though, and some time set aside as work-free, you can do a lot to manage the stress yourself.

ROOM FOR IMPROVEMENT?

Workplace stress is, unfortunately, the norm. If you find yourself under pressure, you can limit the impact by managing the aspects you control, so take a look at your own work habits and work on your coping strategies.

54%

A 2016 American survey found that 54% of professionals said they had increased their commitment to a **better work–life balance** in the previous year.

58%

In 2017, the American Psychological Association's annual stress report found that 58% of the people surveyed described work as a very or somewhat **significant source of stress** in their lives.

 ## STRIKING A HEALTHY BALANCE

Workplace experts recommend these tips for a healthy balance between personal and professional commitments:

Set aside distraction-free time to focus on what really matters (pp.146–147).

Limit communications technology. If it's outside working hours and you don't absolutely have to send that email, let it wait (pp.60–63).

Look into reducing your commute. Telecommuting, or flexible time that lets you skip the rush hour, can reduce stress considerably (pp.96–97).

Plan your time off well in advance, and keep it work-free. If you have to keep in touch, only check in at specific, pre-agreed times.

JOB BURNOUT
KNOWING WHEN TO STOP

At a certain point, work strain passes the point of ordinary stress and becomes outright toxic. Self-care doesn't just make work more pleasant; sometimes it's necessary if we're going to keep working at all.

It's not unusual to feel tired at the end of a working day, but what if you're feeling exhausted and repelled by your job all the time? You may be looking at burnout – and if so, you need to take your wellbeing seriously.

Isn't this just normal stress?

Burnout is not same thing as job stress: it is the endpoint of unmanaged stress. Experiencing too much stress for too long leaves us feeling not just anxious and overloaded, but disengaged, apathetic, cynical, despairing, and even disgusted with our lives.

The symptoms of job burnout are very similar to the symptoms of clinical depression (see pp.202–203). Indeed, a 2013 French study published in the *Journal of Health Psychology* argued that the "between-syndrome overlap" of burnout and depression was so high that it was unscientific to call them two separate conditions.

If you suspect that you may be succumbing to clinical depression, it's always wise to consult a doctor. On the other hand, if you aren't there yet but you feel you are on your way to burnout, what are your options?

> **Burnout** can affect almost any professional, from top boss to rank-and-file employee.
>
> **Phil Sheridan**
> UK recruitment specialist

Spot the dangers

How at risk are you? According to advice given by psychologists and workplace experts, the biggest predictors are:

- **Lacking control** in your job.
- **Confusing expectations** that are hard to meet.
- **An unhealthy work culture,** such as a bullying boss or backstabbing colleagues.
- **A workplace that doesn't suit** your values, skills, interests, and personality.
- **An uncomfortable pace,** either very boring or very hectic.
- **Excessive working hours,** giving you too little time to recuperate and creating a work–life imbalance.
- **Your sense of identity** being overly bound up with your job.
- **Working in an emotionally demanding profession** such as healthcare, teaching, or ministry.
- **Lacking people** who support you, in the workplace or out.

THE BURNOUT ZONE

According to Dutch expert Arnold Bakker, we are most at risk of burnout when we are pushed too hard and helped too little. Some jobs are more inspiring than others, but demands that exceed resources can wear down our motivation, as the chart below shows. Be aware of how well you're being supported and if you feel yourself moving into the red burnout zone, prioritize self-care.

Resources: Situations and experiences created by an employer that help workers meet demands. Good support, helpful feedback, and the freedom to manage your own time are examples.

Demands: Pressures that call on us to use our resourcefulness and energy – physical, mental, and emotional – all of which can be stressful if we're overtaxed and inadequately supported.

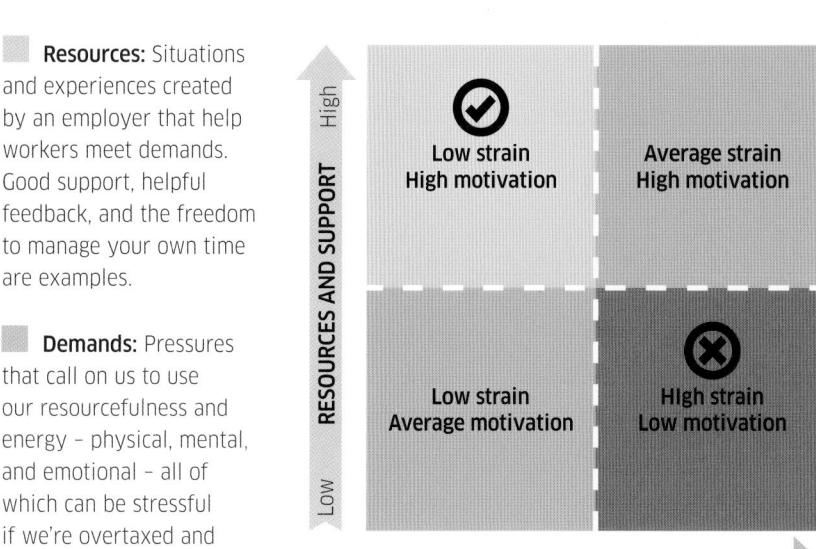

WHO IS STRUGGLING?

Be aware of the risks. According to a 2013 survey of HR directors in Britain's leading companies,

1 in 3

Around 1 in 3 professionals were struggling with **burnout**.

2 in 3

2 in 3 survey respondents said that the **main reason** was having too large a **workload**.

1 in 2

More than half cited overtime or **long working hours** as a secondary reason.

1 in 4

More than 1 in 4 said that they and their colleagues were struggling because it was hard to manage a good work–life balance.

Preventing burnout

If you feel you are at risk, it's best to face facts and make working on your stress management an urgent priority: a 2014 Spanish study found that those most likely to burn out were those who tried to avoid thinking about their situation.

With that in mind, be pro-active about making your days as tolerable as possible – to that end, consider these helpful tips:

✔ **Spend time with supportive colleagues** you know and trust (pp.176–179).

✔ **Have a time each day** when you unplug from contact via your electronic devices (pp.60–63).

✔ **Keep your body moving** – don't sit for more than an hour at a time (pp.152–157)

✔ **Make space in your life** for laughter and play (pp.182–187).

✔ **Look for positive moments** in your day, even something small, like chatting with your colleagues (pp.80–83).

✔ **Make time outside work** for family and friends (pp.148–149).

✔ **Connect with a community** or cause that reflects values that matter to you (pp.44–45).

If stress wears us down, burnout can be the ultimate consequence. Prioritize taking care of yourself: it's the best long-term strategy.

THERE IS MORE TO LIFE THAN SIMPLY INCREASING ITS SPEED

MAHATMA GANDHI, LEADER OF INDIA'S INDEPENDENCE MOVEMENT

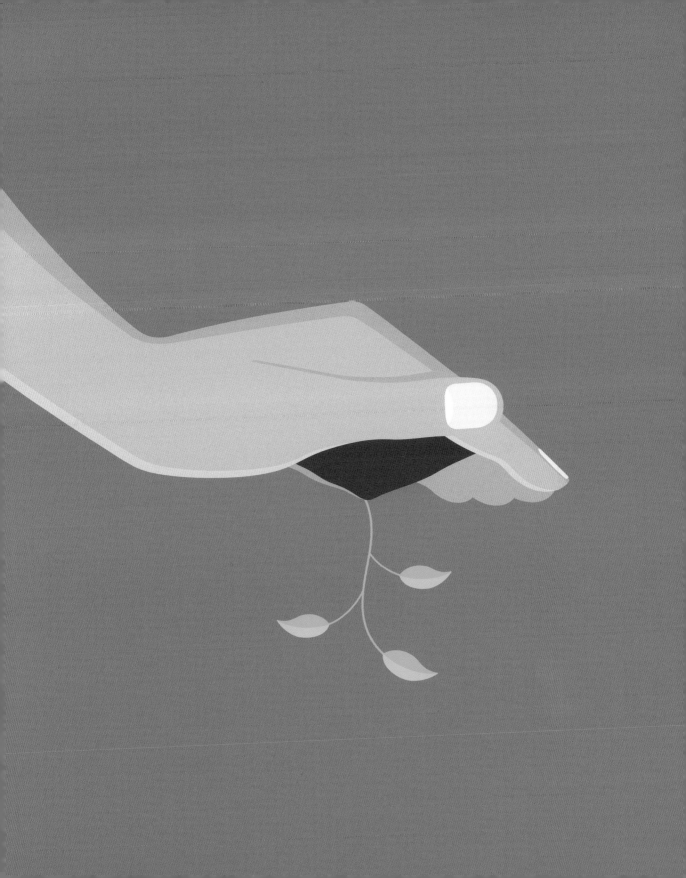

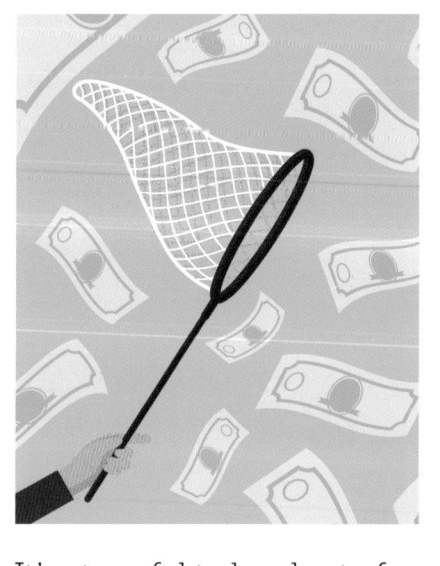

THE PRESSURE TO SPEND
MANAGING YOUR MONEY

It's stressful to be short of money, but it can be hard to keep track of purchases, especially in an environment designed to make us spend. Some psychological savvy can make us more cash-efficient and calm.

To make your finances less stressful, it helps to have a good grip on your day-to-day spending. The retail industry invests large sums on researching effective ways to part us from our money – American consumer psychologist Kit Yarrow points out some examples:

■ **Placing everyday items** at the back of the store, so you have to pass a barrage of promotions.

■ **Presenting slightly untidy displays** so shoppers are more comfortable picking up items – and once we have an item in our hands, we're more likely to buy.

■ **Playing music** to create emotional associations – loud music makes us more likely to grab an item and go, and slow, quiet music more likely to linger and consider more purchases.

If you're planning to go shopping, make a list and resolve to stick to it. If you're shopping online, beware of "free shipping" deals that pressure you to buy more items, and remind yourself that clicking a mouse is still spending real money.

Does "retail therapy" work?

Buying may give us a temporary boost, but what kind of expenditure makes us happy in the long term? A 2008 Canadian study confirms that spending money on others feels better than spending it on ourselves. A 2011 Canadian study adds that emotional closeness is key: a loved one is a better choice for your generosity than a "duty" purchase for a relative you never confide in.

Buying experiences rather than things not only reduces your clutter at home but also lowers your stress levels. As American psychologist Matthew Killingsworth put it in 2010, "A wandering mind is an unhappy mind" – when we have little to think about, our worries tend to resurface. Experience purchases can be a buffer against stressful rumination. American psychologist Thomas Gilovich finds that, while waiting for a material purchase is frustrating and the novelty tends to wear off, waiting for a holiday, theatre trip, or other experience purchase gives us a sense of pleasant anticipation, and the memories remain warm.

Reward yourself wisely

Keeping a spending diary may help you keep track of which purchases heightened your stress and which ones made you feel good. It's less stressful to motivate yourself with rewards than punishments, so when wrestling with temptation, consider keeping a log of what you didn't buy, too. Adding up the amount you've saved on resisting impulse buys can feel highly rewarding.

Q THE DENOMINATION EFFECT

People are generally more reluctant to spend a single big bank note than its equivalent in smaller currency, but often spend more once they've broken it.

Tip: to avoid what a 2009 American study called the Denomination Effect (or the "what-the-hell effect"), keep small notes handy for making smaller purchases.

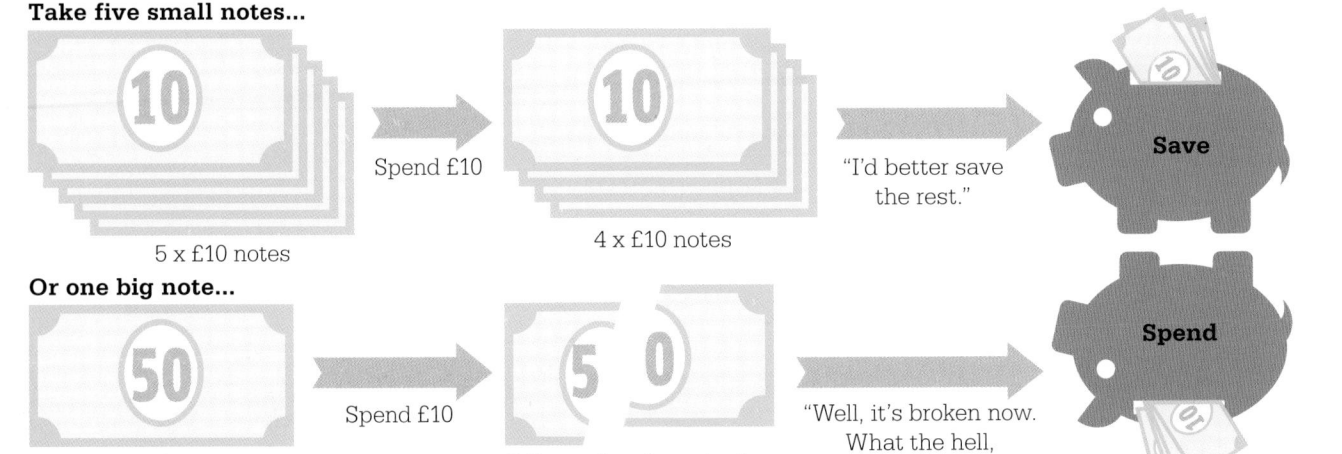

Take five small notes...

5 x £10 notes → Spend £10 → 4 x £10 notes → "I'd better save the rest." → **Save**

Or one big note...

1 x £50 note → Spend £10 → £50 note has been broken with a small purchase → "Well, it's broken now. What the hell, I'll spend more." → **Spend**

Q THE HEDONIC TREADMILL

Spending more doesn't necessarily make us happier. According to an influential theory developed in 1971 by American psychologists Philip Brickman and Donald Campbell, increased income can become a "hedonic treadmill" – a cycle of pleasure-seeking that keeps us overworked and dissatisfied.

If your lifestyle is currently modest but tolerable, it's likely you'll get more pleasure from living simply and having more leisure time than from earning more by working extra hours. If you do get a pay raise, you may be happier if you resolve to keep your current lifestyle and save for a more secure future.

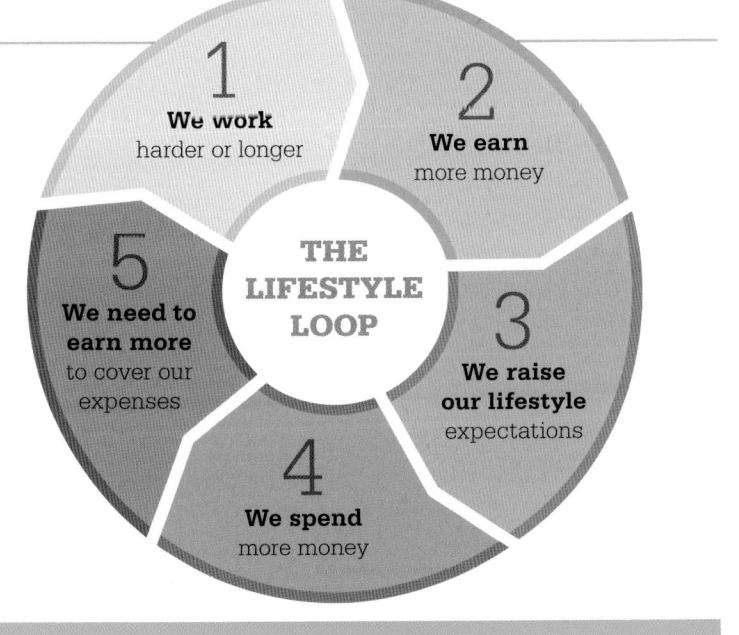

THE LIFESTYLE LOOP

1 **We work** harder or longer

2 **We earn** more money

3 **We raise our lifestyle** expectations

4 **We spend** more money

5 **We need to earn more** to cover our expenses

MONEY WORRIES

SURVIVING DEBT AND INSECURITY

We live in an era where many people struggle with debt, and many more worry about paying the bills. Sound financial advice will help to manage stress levels when money is tight.

In today's economy, a degree of debt is common: according to data from the 2016 US Census Bureau and Federal Reserve Bank of New York, the average American household has more than $16,000 of credit card debt alone. Being in debt can be hugely stressful, but it can be tackled with practicality.

Hurting financially?

Financial stress can be literally painful. According to an American study published in 2016:

- **Households** where both adults are unemployed spend 20% more on over-the-counter painkillers.
- **People** asked to describe either a period of economic instability or security, and then how much pain they felt while describing it, reported almost twice as much pain when describing financial instability.
- **Students** displayed a higher tolerance to physical pain when reading a paragraph encouraging them to believe they'd enter a stable job market compared to students who read a paragraph describing an unstable one.

A COMMON CONCERN

62%

In the 2017 American Psychological Association stress survey, 62% of Americans anticipated that money would be a **significant source of stress** in the next few years.

Q FEELING GUILTY?

Synthesizing economic data in the US in 2016, the website NerdWallet shows that in recent years, the cost of living has risen faster than the median household income. If you've taken steps to reduce your spending, but still find yourself in debt, this doesn't prove you're incompetent – you may be dealing with challenging circumstances. As the American Psychological Association reported in 2017, "Higher stress is disproportionately reported by Americans with lower incomes". Don't let guilt add to your stress.

■ **The amount of pain** we report correlates to both our own financial insecurity and economic instability on a state level.

A 2004 American study also found that patients with arthritis reported more health problems during periods of financial stress. Clearly, money worries are common, and for some they are a chronic stress, affecting both physical and mental health.

How to manage?

If you're struggling with debt, your first step will need to be problem-focused coping (see pp.26–29):

✔ **Create a plan.** You are not alone. There are charities and agencies that offer free or means-tested debt counselling and reputable inexpensive firms that assist in reorganizing debt payments. Consider taking advantage of the help that's available in your local community.

⊘ PAYING OFF MULTIPLE DEBTS

When we owe money to several creditors, it's important to do the maths, particularly concerning rates of interest. A 2011 American study presented people with a simulated debt situation in which there were multiple creditors with different interest rates and found that the stress of owing money interfered with their judgement.

The optimum strategy the researchers identified for people with multiple debts is as follows:

1 **Settle the minimum payment** for each debt, to avoid surcharges and penalties.

2 **Use all available money** left over to pay down the debt with the highest interest rate.

3 **Once that debt has been paid** in full, use available money to pay down the debt with the second-highest interest rate.

4 **Keep paying off debts** one at a time, but always pay off the higher interest rate first.

However, none of the subjects in the study followed this strategy: they spread their money between creditors, thus paying higher interest rates overall, and ended up owing more. Don't let the discomfort of debt discourage you from doing the maths: pay the minimum charges first, then concentrate on discharging debts one at a time.

✔ **Budget your expenses.** Track where the money goes and see if there are any non-essentials you could cut, or shop around for less expensive necessities. If you're unsure how to track your spending, search online for free budgeting programs or apps.

✔ **Favour cash over credit cards** – paying by cash makes it difficult to overspend – but beware of the "Denomination Effect" (see p.89).

Robert Leahy of the American Institute for Cognitive Therapy also recommends we separate our self-esteem from our finances, and ease the strain by enjoying as many meaningful experiences as we can. Debt can be managed, and stress lowered, if we keep it in perspective.

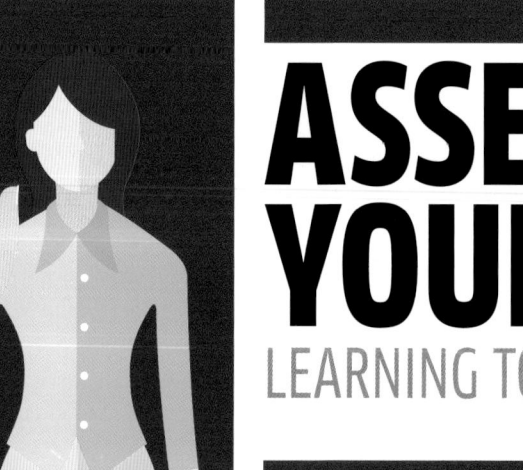

ASSERT YOURSELF
LEARNING TO DRAW THE LINE

Few things are more stressful than feeling you can't stand up for yourself in the face of others' demands. Improving your assertiveness will help you to feel more in control of your life.

If stress means feeling unable to cope with life's demands, then clearly we need to keep life's demands at a manageable level. But what if you find it hard to tell other people you've already got enough to deal with and you can't take on any more? To avoid such situations, it is important we learn to assert ourselves.

The fear of aggression

Some people have trouble asserting themselves because they're worried that if they say "No" or "Stop that", they'll come across as aggressive. However, aggression and assertiveness have an important difference:

■ **Aggression is focused on winning.** The "loser" ends up having their rights, feelings, and needs trampled.

■ **Assertiveness is focused on fairness.** An assertive person tries to appreciate that other people have rights too, and only disregards their wishes if it is impossible or unreasonable to do so.

MORE PERSUASIVE

If refusing a request, avoid implying that you'd do it if you could. A 2012 American study found that people are **8 times more likely** to accept an **"I don't"** statement than an "I can't" one.

If you feel guilty for saying "No", remind yourself that pushing for a fair outcome is not aggressive. It's appropriate.

Self-knowledge

You may seem less aggressive to others than you fear, especially if you tend to feel uncomfortable with asserting your needs. A 2014 study published in the *Personality and Social Psychology Bulletin* found that many people who felt they were coming across as overly pushy were in fact rated as "appropriately assertive" by their fellow participants.

This isn't necessarily a sign that you should ramp up your assertiveness: among the over-assertive participants, the same study found that 64 per cent saw themselves as appropriately or even under-assertive. It is probably wise to ask a few trusted friends or colleagues how you are coming across. But if you fear you might look pushy, consider the possibility that you may simply look confident.

✓ THE PERFECT BALANCE

If someone asks you to do something you don't want to do – such as cancel your plans and spend the evening helping with DIY – how do you draw a line without coming across as too weak or too hostile? Consider who seems to be "winning" the discussion; you want both parties to end up feeling reasonably satisfied. To keep stress levels low, an assertive response is best:

ASSERTIVE
I win – You win
Example: "Sorry, I'd like to help, but it's not possible this evening."
Likely outcome: You establish a reasonable boundary.

AGGRESSIVE
I win – You lose
Example: "You're joking – not after the day I've had!"
Likely outcome: You offend others and may lose social support in future.

PASSIVE
I lose – You win
Example: "Well, okay – if you really want me to…"
Likely outcome: You feel overwhelmed, stressed, and possibly resentful.

PASSIVE AGGRESSIVE
I lose – You lose
Example: "I'm so tired, but if I must … No, I've said I'll do it, so I'll do it."
Likely outcome: They feel annoyed, and you feel unappreciated.

Practise, practise, practise

If you feel your assertiveness could be better, how do you improve it?

- **Start small.** Asserting yourself over low-stakes issues will make the process less daunting.
- **Rehearse.** Act out boundary-setting in front of a mirror, or with a trusted friend, so you get comfortable with the words (see "Saying it right", above right).

- **Remember** you have a right to your assert own needs. Assertiveness is a skill, and skills develop and improve with practice. Over time, you should find you're more comfortable with saying "No", which should free you from both the stress of the uncomfortable, unwanted situations and the stress of worrying about how to assert yourself when they arise.

✓ SAYING IT RIGHT

What is the key to an assertive response? A weak phrase sounds as if you just need persuading; a strong phrase should be both polite and non-negotiable. When drawing a boundary, stick to strong phrases.

WEAK
- ✖ I'm not sure I agree…
- ✖ Do I really have to…
- ✖ I'd rather not…

STRONG
- ✔ I understand your perspective, but I still think that…
- ✔ I think that would be difficult – let's set a time to discuss other options.
- ✔ I appreciate the offer, but it's really not my kind of thing.

✓ 3 STEPS TO "NO"

To challenge a behaviour you dislike, use a three-step "I-statement" to focus on your own perspective rather than make an accusation:

1 **Describe** the other person's behaviour.

2 **Describe** your feelings.

3 **Make a request** (politely but firmly).

For example, "When you make fun of my accent, I feel embarrassed. Please stop teasing me about it."

SPEAKING UP

ASKING FOR WHAT YOU WANT

Stress can be caused by having to deal with too many demands, but it can also be caused by having unmet needs. Learning how to articulate what you want is a key skill for preserving your wellbeing.

Do you feel confident stating your needs, even in the face of stonewalling or criticism, or does that prospect send your stress levels climbing? Some self-training might help you become more confident and effective.

Challenging others

Standing up for what we want is difficult for some of us. American psychologist Nando Pelusi observes that as a social species, we tend to factor power and dominance into most of our interactions and most of us err on the side of submission. Asking for what we want can feel like we're challenging someone's status, which feels risky. Pelusi calls this "Neanderthink" – a primitive instinct that generally doesn't apply in the modern world. His advice:

- **Accept** that doing what you believe is right or asking for what you want may feel awkward, and practise tolerating that discomfort.
- **Be clear** about your preferences.
- **Be civil** and reasonable: asking doesn't have to be pushy.
- **Accept** that you are entitled to ask, and others to refuse.
- **Allow yourself** enough time to think when called upon to answer any questions.

Tricks of the trade

An Egyptian study published in the *Journal of Nursing Science* in 2015 studied the effects of assertiveness training on psychiatric nurses – a profession that requires the ability to balance the needs of others with one's own needs and the ability to remain calm when facing criticism.

Useful techniques involved:

- Calmly repeating the same simple refusal no matter what was said.
- When presented with an unclear or uncomfortable situation, asking for more information.
- Insisting on putting off angry conversations until all parties had calmed down.
- If criticized constructively, confidently agreeing that they had faults and made mistakes.
- In the face of hostility, using "clouding" or "fogging" – that is, finding a small part of the criticism they could agree with, and affirming it without becoming defensive or making any promises.

When the study's nurses used this approach at work, they experienced a significant increase in their self-esteem and a reduction in their stress levels.

While asserting your needs can sometimes be challenging, with practice you may feel more confident and better able to protect yourself from avoidable stress.

SCARED TO START?

Sometimes it's more stressful to stay silent than speak up, but asserting what you think or want can be daunting. Treat it as a skill you can learn and try some of these simple, low-stakes examples to get you used to it.

Tell a friend that you respect a talent or virtue they possess.	"Those marathons you run for charity are really impressive."
At a bar or restaurant, ask for a small customization of your order.	"Ice, no lemon, please."
If you have a positive thought about a stranger (as long as it's not too intimate), tell them so.	"Hey, nice hat! Where did you get it?"
At a bookshop or library, describe your own tastes confidently and ask for a suggestion.	"I enjoy historical thrillers. Is there anything you can recommend?"
Be sure to comment if a colleague did a good job.	"I thought the way you handled that difficult customer was really smart."
If you particularly admire someone's taste or skill, ask for pointers.	"I'd love to listen to more of that music you played yesterday – where's a good place to start?"

By describing things you like, you build your ability to speak about what you admire and want in a low-stress way – which is a good place to start asserting your own feelings.

CAN I ASK A FAVOUR?

In a 2016 study, American psychologist Vanessa Bohns told volunteers to ask strangers if they could borrow their cellphone. How many people, she queried, did they think they'd need to ask in order to get three who'd say yes? The result shows we needn't be too timid:

3 in 10

Volunteers estimated they'd have to ask 10 people to get 3 loans – in other words, **a 70% rejection rate**.

3 in 6

The actual number they had to ask was 6 people – a **50% acceptance rate**.

STOP CROWDING ME!

COPING WITH BUSY SPACES

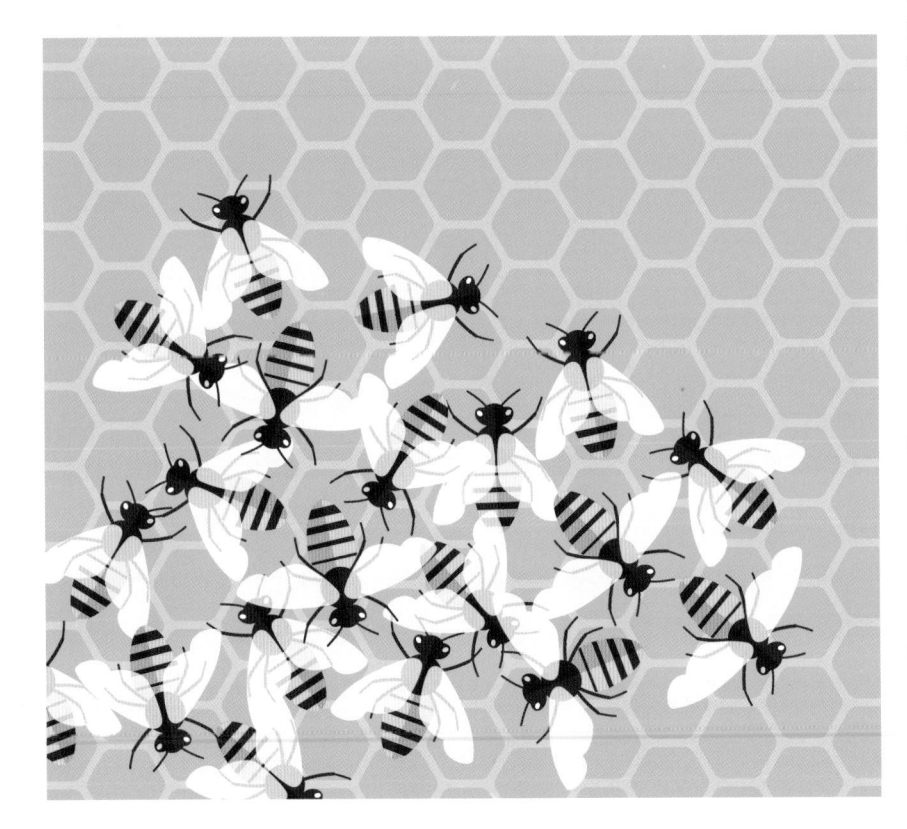

Whether you live on a noisy street or commute on a packed bus, it's stressful to have your personal space invaded. We can't entirely control our environment, but we can take steps to reduce its impact.

Crowded train carriages, cramped neighbourhoods, open-plan offices, busy streets: we're often thrown together with people wo didn't choose to be close to – and that close proximity may strain our nerves.

Calming down

To feel comfortable, American environmental psychologist Sally Augustin advises that we need to regulate how much access we give people. She gives several tips on creating calm spaces in our lives:

- **Get into nature** – even city gardens, zoos, and parks help restore our mental energy.
- **Insulate your work space.** Noise can break our concentration and heighten tension. If you can, rearrange your furniture, plants, or even the objects on your desk to deflect and reduce sound waves.
- **Pad your home space.** Flat surfaces amplify sound but soft objects act as a muffler. Cushions, curtains, and rugs can all make a place more peaceful.

Sorry, it's taken

According to a 2012 American study, people resort to a wide range of strategies to be able to sit alone on public transport:

> **Privacy** is a fundamental human need.
>
> **Sally Augustin**
> American psychologist

TOO MUCH CLOSENESS

Why is it so stressful to be crowded? According to American psychology professor Robert Feldman, there are three interpretations: knowing which one is applicable can help you find a solution:

What's the problem?	Finding a solution
Getting overloaded In close proximity, other people's voices, the heat of their skin, and their smell are much more intrusive. When our senses have to process so much information at a rate we can't control, we feel stressed.	**For sensory overload,** try blocking out what you can. Close your eyes, listen to music on headphones, or carry a sachet of something with a soothing scent.
Needing protection We feel threatened by people coming too close because if they chose to attack us, we'd be vulnerable.	**If you feel tense or panicky,** try calming your breathing (see pp.128–129). A genuinely creepy stranger is best avoided, but if they don't seem like a potential threat, focus on relaxing.
Managing relationships We prefer to stand further away from people we don't know well beacause if we're unable to maintain our personal space, it creates more intimacy than we're comfortable with.	**If you feel there's too much intimacy,** try American psychotherapist Deb Elkin's "shield" technique (see right). The creative play can itself reduce stress.

Passive:

- Avoiding eye contact.
- Listening to music on our headphones and pretending not to hear someone ask if the adjacent seat is taken.
- Pretending to be asleep.

Confrontational:

- Stretching out to take up more space.
- Piling the adjacent seat with belongings.
- Pretending the seat is already taken.

It may not be entirely ethical, but the study found everyone does this sometimes, regardless of age, gender, race, or class. If you're worn out and you need some peace, it's best to stick to the gentler, passive methods and be prepared to give way if someone does sit next to you. Using the confrontational methods could backfire if somebody decides to challenge you.

We can't always keep others at arm's length, but insulate yourself where you can, and use peaceful moments to counter-balance.

✓ CREATE YOUR SHIELD

According to American psychotherapist Deb Elkin, we can reduce the stress of over-crowding by creating an imaginary shield around our bodies, devising a different design for different situations. Next time someone's in your space, start building yours:

- Is it made of glowing light, thick chainmail, solid marble?
- Is it heavy and tough, or thin and flexible?
- Is it precious metal, or solid iron?
- Does it have beautiful decorations?
- Does it have sharp spikes?

Enjoy your creativity
and have fun designing your shield: it will give you a greater sense of control.

IN GREEN PLACES
THE TIME-HONOURED NATURE CURE

For those of us who live in crowded cities and towns, or work in a noisy location, our daily environment can be stressful. A walk in the woods can offer a calm respite from the crowds and noise.

In the 1970s, a hospital in Pennsylvania, USA, made a now-famous discovery among its post-surgical patients: patients in some rooms had brighter moods, experienced less pain, and healed more quickly than patients in other rooms. What accounted for the difference? The patients who had rooms with windows that looked out onto trees felt better. Wherever we live, a little exposure to nature can have a positive impact on our wellbeing.

Close to nature
While a nature walk can provide gentle exercise, which is good for our mental and physical health (see pp.152–155), research shows that just contemplating nature can be beneficial. Here are some striking examples of its resorative effects:

■ **Cardiac health,** which stress can worsen, is improved by viewing nature. A 2015 Canadian study found that city-dwellers who lived on tree-lined streets enjoyed a health boost equivalent to a $20,000 gain in income.

■ **Children experiencing bullying** or difficult family circumstances were found, in a 2003 American study, to suffer reduced wellbeing because of the stress – unless they lived in green environments, in which case they continued to thrive.

■ **Women suffering from breast cancer,** according to a 2003 American study, experienced a reduction in stress and an improved ability to meet mental challenges after spending two hour-long sessions every week in natural environments.

Q NATURE SOUNDS

In 2013, Swedish psychologist Matilda Annerstedt subjected volunteers to a deliberately stressful interview, and then allowed them to recover in one of three conditions: a plain room, a room with a silent, "virtual" forest projected around them, or a virtual forest with natural sounds added. Those listening to the sounds showed their stress hormone and heart rates returning to normal substantially faster. If a walk in the woods isn't an option, closing your eyes and listening to a "nature sounds" recording could be a good compromise.

Soothing surroundings
Developed in the 1980s, a popular Japanese form of stress therapy is guided nature walks, known as *shinrin-yoku,* or "forest bathing". In small experiments reported in 2010, subjects taking a gentle stroll in a forested environment experienced several physiological benefits, including lower cortisol levels. If you're suffering from

stress, head for your nearest forest, park, or garden: research suggests it will help.

Also in the 1980s, American environmental psychologists Rachel and Stephen Kaplan developed Attention Restoration Theory. They argued that urban environments place a constant pressure on our attention: we have to remain on the alert, constantly switching our focus from the crossing lights, to the oncoming traffic, to the glare of a neon sign. Natural surroundings can be considered at leisure – the Kaplans called it "soft fascination" – which gives us the opportunity to replenish our energy.

Effortless engagement

Recent research continues to confirm nature's long-term benefits for our mental health. A 2013 study in Edinburgh attached EEGs to read the brain waves of healthy volunteers: while the urban walkers' brains showed frustration and stress, those walking through parks showed states of effortless engagement, similar to meditative states (see pp.132–135).

That effect was reported again in a 2015 American study that took volunteers with no mental illnesses on a walk through either a scenic grassland or a busy street. Only the nature-walkers showed a decrease in rumination – dwelling on worries or frustrations – which is known to increase the risk of depression.

Whether for maintaining our mental health or recovering from overstimulation, walking in green spaces does, neurologically speaking, calm the mind.

WALK WITH A THEME?

A 2015 American study published in the *Journal of Holistic Nursing* found that stressed adults showed a marked increase in wellbeing after taking meditative walks through ornamental gardens, using each walk to dwell on a certain healing concept at specific points along the way. If you're planning a stroll in the park, consider reflecting on one of these themes:

AWARENESS

POSSIBILITY

REFLECTION

FORGIVENESS

JOY

TRUST

GRATITUDE

CONNECTION

JOURNEY

FREEDOM

TRANSITION

MUSIC AND SILENCE

THE EAR AS HEALER

The research is conclusive: relaxing music has a de-stressing effect. A 2013 Canadian meta-analysis of 400 studies, for instance, confirmed that music not only lowers stress levels but also boosts the immune system. Just listening to music before surgery lowered patients' anxiety better than prescription medications. Music can be a powerful tool to reduce stress, so how can we make it work for us?

✓ PICKING THE STYLE

If you're wondering which genre is the most relaxing, research best supports the calming properties of classical music. A 2004 American study found that listening to classical music calmed volunteers more than jazz or pop, and an American study in 2008 found that classical won out over heavy metal. The best choice, however, is the one you make yourself; psychologists agree that simply having control over what you hear reduces stress.

If you need to soothe or distract yourself, try the effects of music. Listening to a pleasant track – or to a moment of genuine quiet – can be an ideal buffer against stress.

When I hear music, **I fear no danger**. I am invulnerable, I see no foe.

Henry David Thoreau
American writer, 1857

PICKING THE PACE

According to a 2015 German-American study, there is an ideal tempo for relaxation – or rather, several ideal tempos. To feel safe and relaxed, the brain prefers to process a limited amount of complexity per second. The most soothing speed for music depends on the complexity of the rhythm. The study found that the most relaxing tempos were these:

- **For simple rhythms:**
  160.8 beats per minute

- **For moderately complex rhythms:**
  126.0 beats per minute

- **For complex rhythms:**
  113.6 beats per minute

You're likely to perceive this instinctively – as the study's subjects did – but if you're trying to choose some tracks to help you de-stress, follow this useful rule of thumb: "The more complex the rhythm, the slower the tempo".

60%

A 2010 Indian study found that **athletes exposed to soothing music** before a high-stakes competition had a **60% drop** in the stress hormone **cortisol**.

THE POWER OF SILENCE

Music is calming, but what about no sound at all? The results are mixed. Some studies have found certain types of music are more calming, but in 2005, Italian physician and amateur musician Luciano Bernardi tested a variety of musical styles and found that his subjects' heart rate, blood pressure, and breathing were calmer in the pauses between the music than during the music itself – and the contrast between music and quiet made the quiet more powerful.

TAKING PART

If listening to music is relaxing, what about creating music? Studies confirm that music-making has a significantly calming effect. When you're making music for comfort, relaxation, and pleasure, skill is not important. Allow yourself to be musically creative without expectations or pressure. Rather than trying to play a challenging instrument or a complex piece of music, American neurologist Barry Bittman advises that you jam for your own amusement on an accessible instrument such as a digital keyboard – that way, you get to relax without worrying about your performance.

SINGING TOGETHER

If picking up an instrument isn't appealing but you enjoy singing, consider joining a choir: a 2016 British study found that active choir members had lower cortisol levels and healthier immune systems. A 2005 Canadian study also found that people benefitted from their choir regardless of their experience or training, particularly if they refused to feel self-conscious. So find a supportive group, set aside any worries, and let yourself have a good time.

PREPARING FOR STRESS

When you are approaching a stressful event – such as a big speech, an exam, or a competition – music can be a good way to help you prepare. A 2013 international study tested the stress levels of 60 volunteers under three conditions: resting in silence, resting while listening to the sound of rippling water, and resting while listening to classical music – in this case, Allegri's "Miserere", a famously meditative choral work. The volunteers then completed the Trier Social Stress Test, which stresses subjects by making them perform challenging tasks for unresponsive judges. The test was stressful for all the volunteers, but those who had previously listened to music experienced a more rapid reduction in their stress after the test compared to the other groups.

STRESS AND OLDER PEOPLE
GROWING OLD GRACEFULLY

We may hope to mellow as we age, but since life is likely to keep providing stressors, will we really be more relaxed? Research suggests that your perspective may change, but your coping abilities should stay solid.

As we age, we face more physical challenges, but we also know that with age comes wisdom. The emotional skills we develop throughout our lives are usually maintained. In fact, the evidence suggests that our resilience increases as we age.

Keeping our wits

Aging affects the brain: on average, it decreases in weight by about 5% per decade after the age of 40. So does that mean our ability to solve problems also decreases as we get older?

Published in the *Canadian Journal of Aging* in 2011, a study that tested coping methods in a group of volunteers ranging from age 20 to 90 offers reassuring news. The older subjects did show a certain amount of decline in cognitive performance – their working memories and mental processing speeds were somewhat slower. However, unless they had clinical dementia, they could still use problem-focused ways of coping. Age didn't limit their coping skills: they were just as capable of being active, effective problem-solvers.

11.5%

In a 2016 study of retirement, 33% of subjects expected to be **lonely** in later life, but eight years later only **11.5%** of them actually were; the study posited that swapping our stereotypes about loneliness for a more **positive** outlook lowers the risk of loneliness in old age.

A 2009 Brazilian study found that its elderly subjects tended to use more problem-focused coping methods than emotion-focused ones – they were more likely to try to fix a problem than resign themselves to it – though both methods were effective in managing stress.

Less stressed?

A 1996 study for the Gerontological Society of America found that the elderly report fewer stressors. They generally encounter fewer upheavals in their lives, and the stressors they face are more likely to be chronic, such as health conditions, which are best met with an emotion-focused, "what can't be cured must be endured" attitude rather than complaining.

Older people also have more practice in managing their lives to avoid problems altogether. Research suggests we may become more resilient as we age, but when there's a problem that needs solving, older people can use their own judgement just as effectively as younger people.

SELF-CARE IN OLD AGE

Doctors and psychologists agree these are effective techniques for reducing stress as we age::

- **Maintain social contacts.** A 2014 Indian review published in the *Journal of Clinical and Diagnostic Research* confirmed that loneliness in old age is a potentially dangerous stressor. American psychologist John Cacioppo's research found that good social support reduced the risk of early death by half.

- **Find new purposes in life.** Once we retire and our children leave home, what next? Each of us has a different answer, but political involvement, community engagement, mentoring, and creative endeavours provide a sense of meaning, which can significantly reduce the burden of stress (pp.44–45).

- **Organize for independence.** You may need more help getting around: plan ahead to ensure maximum access to transport so you enjoy as much freedom of movement as possible.

- **Take care of your health.** Gentle exercise, a balanced diet, and a good doctor can keep you well and active for much longer, lowering your stress levels.

- **If you are caring for your partner,** take care of your own needs, too, and create a solid support network (pp.104–105).

PLANNING FOR RETIREMENT

One of the major psychological theories of retirement was pioneered by American sociologist Robert Atchley: that retirement is a process, not an event – and each phase of life comes with its own stressors. That process is less stressful if we know what to expect, so it's wise to prepare by considering the stages described below:

Stage	Challenges	Stress reduction tactics
1. Pre-retirement	■ Making arrangements for your future security ■ Emotionally disengaging from your previous routine	✔ Get good financial advice. ✔ Have post-retirement plans to look forward to. ✔ Arrange to stay in touch with work friends.
2. Retirement	Atchley identifies three common points of view: ■ "Honeymooners" treat retirement like a holiday and have fun ■ "Immediate routine" retirees get straight into their new normal ■ "Rest and relaxation" individuals take a break	✔ Don't overspend, especially as you're probably getting used to a lower income. ✔ Be aware that this phase may not last.
3. Disenchantment	■ Boredom ■ Loss of previous identity	✔ Plan for the future by developing new interests and establishing yourself as part of a community.
4. Reorientation	■ Making new plans for a future life	✔ Research any major decisions before you do anything irreversible such as moving to a new town.
5. Retirement routine	■ Settling into a new structure of life	✔ Expect some daily hassles to deal with.
6. Arranging for care	■ Health starts to fail	✔ Organize good medical care and support.

ALWAYS THERE FOR YOU

HOW TO BE A STRONGER CAREGIVER

Caring for another person – be they an elderly relation, a sick spouse, or a disabled child – is highly stressful. It's a life that calls for organization and resilience, but don't forget to care about yourself as well.

Caring for someone who, because of chronic illness or disability, is unable to fully care for themselves is a common, and often unpaid, responsibility. In 2015, there were an estimated 7 million caregivers in the UK and 43.5 million in the US. If you are a caregiver, you need extra skills in managing your own stress (see opposite).

The stress of caring

The physical and emotional demands of caregiving are stressful. A set of American studies in 2009 found that mothers of autistic adolescents and young adults showed levels of cortisol, the stress hormone, similar to those of combat soldiers. Caregiving is a difficult job.

Many caregivers feel frustrated at times, which is normal and doesn't mean that you're a bad caregiver. Recognize that what you do is work as well as love. America's National Family Caregivers Association reported in 2001 that after people fully identified themselves as caregivers (rather than just family members helping out), 90% became more pro-active about seeking out needed resources and skills.

The charity Carers UK reports that **83% of caregivers find their role stressful**, so if you do too, don't feel guilty – you're in the majority.

WHAT CAN I DO?

Psychologists and mental health charities agree that the following methods are helpful for keeping your stress in check:

✔ **Be an educated caregiver.** Learn about your loved one's medical condition and what resources are available to you.

✔ **Share your feelings.** Friends, family, and support groups can all be helpful, especially if they are well informed and non-judgmental.

✔ **Be realistic** about what you can do, and set appropriate boundaries. You'll cope better if you don't ask yourself to do the impossible.

✔ **Get organized.** Use schedules or planners to prioritize and remember commitments; keep important information in one accessible place.

✔ **Try to stay healthy.** Physical activity, good nutrition, and adequate sleep are all essential: caregivers must care for themselves.

✔ **Take breaks when you can.** Some agencies offer much-needed caregiver respite: investigate what is available to you.

✔ **Use relaxation techniques** such as meditation (pp.132–135) and yoga (pp.156–157). These are helpful for both mind and body, increasing your sense of control over your emotions and reducing frustration.

? SPOT THE SIGNS

Are you nearing the point where you should ask for some support or respite? Experts in the area of caregiver burnout recommend looking out for the following signs:

1
Exhaustion.
"I'm too tired to deal with this."

2
Sleeplessness.
"I can't sleep; what if she wanders and gets hurt?"

3
Irritability.
"Just go away and leave me in peace!"

4
Denial.
"She'll be better next year, I'm sure."

5
Anger.
"You could do more if you just made an effort!"

6
Anxiety.
"What does the future hold? Maybe I won't be able to cope."

7
Depression.
"It feels like life is over for both of us."

8
Social withdrawal.
"I can't face getting together with friends."

9
Poor focus and memory.
"Oh no, the appointment was yesterday, wasn't it?"

10
Health problems.
"I seem to catch every bug that's going round."

If you are a caregiver and these sound familiar and commonplace, consider reaching out for help, whether from your doctor or a community support agency.

LETTING THINGS GO
THE POWER OF FORGIVENESS

Many religions counsel us to forgive. "Forgiveness Psychology" studies the benefits of that advice: under the right circumstances, and approached thoughtfully, letting go can substantially reduce stress.

Why should we forgive someone who has wronged us? According to the American Psychological Association, if we approach it correctly, forgiveness contributes to mental and physical health. When given freely, forgiveness is empowering, which can significantly reduce stress.

The Forgiveness Project

A major development in the field of forgiveness psychology is the "Stanford Forgiveness Project", which conducted a series of experiments at the turn of this century. The study found that for forgiveness to be beneficial, one must be able to answer yes to the question, "Can you at least imagine that you could learn to feel differently about the concern that you bring to the study?" If you can answer yes about your concern, try these steps:

1 Be clear about how the situation made you feel, and explain what you found unacceptable. Convey this to one or two people you trust.

2 Commit to forgiving the person who has wronged you. Know that your forgiveness will be for your benefit, not for the benefit of others.

> First, you must **feel anger** before you can **begin to forgive**.
>
> **Judith Orloff**
> American psychologist

3 Understand that forgiving someone doesn't mean you have to condone their behaviour or befriend them.

4 Recognize that your distress is coming primarily from the thoughts and feelings you're experiencing now and not from the original grievance, which is now past.

5 When feeling distressed, try some simple stress management techniques, such as a breathing exercise (pp.128–129), PMR (pp.130–131), or a mindfulness meditation (pp.132–135).

6 Accept that the actions of others are not within our control. Having unenforceable rules about how things "should be" will increase your stress, but you can still hope and strive for good things.

7 Identify your positive life goals: what do you want? The time and energy you'd otherwise spend

✅ WHAT ABOUT JUSTICE?

Forgiveness can't be forced, and being pressured to forgive when you aren't ready will only heighten your stress. A 2015 American paper aimed at therapists working to help their clients with forgiveness identified some important rules:

1

Forgiveness takes emotional effort. Just saying "I forgive" is unlikely to make the forgiver feel better.

2

Forgiveness is not forgetting. We may forgive someone while still feeling the effects of the harm they have caused: the aim is to become more at peace with that harm.

3

Forgiveness doesn't mean forgoing consequences. You can forgive someone while still holding them accountable – for example, by reporting wrongdoing or by pressing charges.

4

Forgiveness takes time and shouldn't be attempted before you feel ready.

5

Anger and resentment are a healthy response to being wronged. Forgiveness aims to move past them, but they should be respected as a normal and natural starting point.

dwelling on your bad experiences can be used to reach your goals.

8 Remember the power of living well to help you overcome hurt or loss. Focus on the love, kindness, and beauty you see in the world.

9 Change your story. Rather than viewing yourself as a victim, see yourself as a victor, successfully overcoming adversity and learning from experience.

This approach has proved effective even for people with deeply personal injuries and resentments. Published in 2000, a study of both Catholic and Protestant women who had lost loved ones during Northern Ireland's sectarian violence found that six months after first learning this technique, their stress levels had dropped by 50%.

World conflicts past and present demonstrate only too well that exacting revenge serves only to

escalate tension. Little wonder that the sayings attributed to the ancient Chinese philosopher Confucius include this advice: "Before you embark on a journey of revenge, dig two graves."

Forgiveness isn't easy and shouldn't be attempted if it feels simply impossible. However, if your anger and resentment are causing you distress, a systematic attempt at forgiveness may leave you stronger and happier.

GIVING THANKS

HOW GRATITUDE CAN LOWER STRESS

Gratitude may be a virtue, but it's also an effective form of self-care. If the challenges of life are weighing you down, research suggests that counting your blessings is a good way to maintain your wellbeing.

It may feel counter-intuitive to say that we should feel grateful in times of stress: after all, having more problems than you can comfortably manage doesn't feel like a blessing. However, psychologists have determined that cultivating a sense of appreciation – even if only for small things – helps to reduce stress.

Feeling better

Positive psychology, which studies the processes by which people thrive, has found strong evidence that gratitude lowers our stress. For instance, a study titled "Counting blessings versus burdens" was published in 2003 by American positive psychologist Robert Emmons, a leading gratitude researcher. The researchers asked subjects to keep a record of either neutral life events, daily hassles, or experiences that provoked gratitude. Those who recorded their blessings showed heightened wellbeing compared to the other two groups.

> It is precisely **under crisis conditions** when we have the most to gain by **a grateful perspective on life**.
>
> **Robert Emmons**
> American positive psychologist and gratitude expert

A 2008 British study followed people through a transitional period in life and monitored their emotional states. The subjects who showed the highest levels of gratitude perceived greater social support and showed lower levels of stress and depression. These positive effects were independent of the subjects' personality traits as measured on the Big Five scale (see pp.30–31): gratitude lowers everyone's stress levels.

Beating stress

Gratitude has several other beneficial effects that can also help to lower stress levels:

- **Stress can disrupt sleep** (pp.162–165), but a 2009 British study found that grateful people sleep better.
- **Painful memories** are stressful, but a 2008 American study found that people who recalled an unpleasant event and then wrote about something positive they'd learned from it felt better and were more able to move on (pp.40–41).
- **Relationship problems** can be stressful, but a 2011 American study found that people who expressed gratitude for their partner to a third party were also more comfortable raising concerns and communicating with their partner (pp.70–73).

Taken together, the research suggests that a regular gratitude practice can be an excellent way of keeping your stress levels in check.

✓ EVERYTHING IN MODERATION

Of course, gratitude isn't a complete cure-all. American gratitude psychologist Amie Gordon adds a few warnings:

- ✖ Don't push yourself to be grateful all the time (see right).

- ✖ Don't waste your gratitude on someone who is actually treating you badly.

- ✖ Don't use gratitude to dismiss problems that need to be tackled (pp.140–141).

- ✖ Don't be so grateful for your good fortune that you take no credit for your successes and ignore your self-worth (pp.42–43).

- ✖ Don't confuse gratitude with indebtedness – you can appreciate someone without owing them.

In short, do appreciate the good things in your life, but don't forget to solve problems, set reasonable boundaries, and appreciate your own hard work: these are positive acts of self-care.

Don't forget to solve problems

▮ KEEPING A GRATITUDE JOURNAL

Psychologists and gratitude researchers recommend that we keep a gratitude journal to maintain a sense of wellbeing in the face of life's stresses. Some suggestions for creating your journal:

1 **Plan your time.** A daily entry is too much; in fact, American gratitude researcher Sonja Lyubomirsky found that people who wrote one entry per week for six weeks felt happier, but people who wrote three entries per week didn't. Once or twice a week is enough.

2 **Make a conscious decision** to become more grateful – the more committed you are, the more beneficial your diary will be.

3 **Quality, not quantity.** Noting just one thing and writing in detail about why you're grateful is more effective than writing a few words about many things.

4 **Be grateful for people** more than things.

5 **Watch out for surprising blessings:** these leave more of an impression than expected ones.

Be grateful for **people** more than things

CHAPTER 3
STRESS IN THE MOMENT
TROUBLE-SHOOTING TACTICS FOR SHORT-TERM STRESS

TURNING POINTS

STRESS IN TIMES OF CHANGE

It makes sense that we feel stressed when life changes for the worse. Surprisingly, though, for some of us, changes for the better can also be stressful: a lot depends on what we feel we deserve.

Any change that disrupts the flow of our life and requires us to make adjustments – in our practical circumstances or in our attitude – is challenging. If we believe we cannot meet the challenge, even positive change can be stressful.

Self-esteem and stress

In order to avoid excessive stress, we need to feel that our lives are, for the most part, what they ought to be. If we have good self-esteem, we generally believe that our lives should have a healthy proportion of positive events, but if our self-esteem is poor, it's hard to believe that we deserve good fortune – so good fortune can become a source of stress.

In a 2004 study on the effect of life events on health, American psychologist Timothy Strauman asked his students three questions:

1 What kind of person do you think you are?

2 What kind of person would you like to be?

3 What kind of person do you think you ought to be?

Strauman then measured the subjects' levels of infection-fighting white blood cells, which usually decrease under chronic stress. Some students' answers showed "self-discrepancy" – their answers to the three questions showed serious differences. For instance, for question 3, "I should be hard-working", but for question 1, "I'm lazy." These students had a lower white blood cell count: the stress of self-discrepancy had undermined their wellbeing.

When your answer to question 3 is "I don't deserve success", actually succeeding means that your answer to 1 – "I'm successful" – creates a self-discrepancy, and that can be just as stressful as failure. Students who were both self-confident and successful had good immunity, but successful students with lower self-esteem had a lower white cell count. To enjoy your successes, you need to believe that you're the kind of person who ought to succeed.

What can I do?
If your self-esteem is fragile, it's wise to work on improving it (see pp.42–43), but in the short term, some useful coping methods are:

- **Seek out** and foster more supportive relationships.
- **Put energy** into people and activities that reflect your values.
- **Engage in activities** that help you to express your feelings.
- **Exercise good self-care,** ensuring you get enough sleep, nutritious food, and recreation.
- **Recall times you've coped** in the past and identify your best coping strategies.

It may seem strange to advise that you should brace yourself for good times, but they come with their own stressors. Once you know whether you may be at risk, you're better able to cope with stress, good or bad.

Q THE THREE Cs

According to American psychologist and founder of the Hardiness Institute Salvatore Maddi, change calls for us to deploy three positive attitudes:

Challenge. Accept that life is naturally stressful, and view change as a learning opportunity.

Commitment. Even if things are stressful, don't sink into alienation: stay involved.

Control. Reject passivity, and believe you have the power to turn whatever happens to your advantage.

A HEALTHY ATTITUDE
If we don't feel we deserve good things, success or good fortune can be stressful enough to make us ill. An influential study in 1989 by American psychologists Jonathan Brown and Kevin McGill followed 261 students over four months. Their answers to a 33-point questionnaire showed that positive life events had an opposite effect, depending on self-esteem: the students who felt good about themselves showed improved health, while the students who had a poor self-image got sick more often.

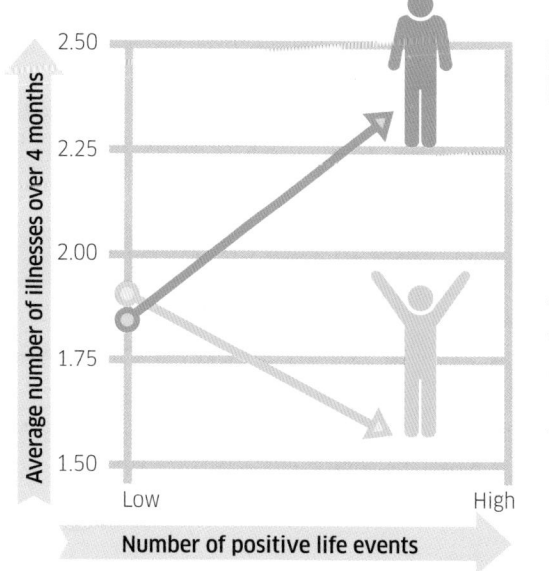

Average number of illnesses over 4 months

Low self-esteem
High self-esteem

Number of positive life events

The findings suggest that if you do have doubts about your self-worth, you should take extra care of yourself if something goes well for you.

THE BIG DAY LOOMS

HANDLING PERFORMANCE ANXIETY

If you're familiar with that dreadful sinking feeling when it's time to make a speech, you're far from alone. Performance anxiety is a very common stressor, but it needn't stop us achieving our goals.

Few people feel completely relaxed before a public appearance, but sometimes the anxiety can be so overwhelming that it undermines our performance. Fortunately, there's a useful method we can use to settle our nerves and focus the mind.

Finding our centre

In the 1970s, American sports psychologist Robert Nideffer developed "centering", a technique that was adapted for performing artists by fellow sports psychologist Don Greene. It is based on the idea that the brain operates as two separate hemispheres: the left brain is associated with logic, language, planning, and judgement, and the right with sounds, sensations, images, and emotions.

When we practise for a speech or a performance of any kind, we're using the planning, "left brain" mode of thinking, but to give the most inspired performance, we need to use the creative "right brain". Unfortunately our more imaginative "right brain" can be hampered by the critical "left brain", which can provoke anxiety. So how do we find the right balance?

25%

According to a 2016 survey by Chapman University, just over 25% of Americans **dread public speaking**.

Pre-performance promoters

Before your speech, follow these steps to prepare yourself:

1 Use positive self-talk: ask yourself what you want to achieve and then put that goal in encouraging terms: for instance, rather than "I hope they'll like my speech", say "I'm going to speak with clarity, authority, and sincerity".

2 In front of someone you trust, practise your speech, avoiding "filler" words like "um" or "ah", which are distracting.

3 Come up with a mental image (such as the audience clapping) or a phrase ("Be brave") that reminds you you're prepared and you're going to be fine.

4 Visualize your presentation from beginning to end – this helps prepare you for the real thing.

5 As you stand before an expectant crowd, pick a focal point to fix your gaze on. It should be slightly below eye-level and comfortable to look at. This reduces distractions.

6 Before you begin speaking, take a deep, cleansing breath. People often hold their breath when nervous, which heightens anxiety.

7 Use your positive mental image or encouraging phrase.

8 Live what you visualized in your preparation: you've already done it and you can do it again.

BE YOUR OWN SUPPORTER

Performance anxiety is not helped by negative self-talk – telling ourselves things that only make us feel worse. Check how you talk to yourself. If you're being too negative, try to re-frame these thoughts in a more positive light.

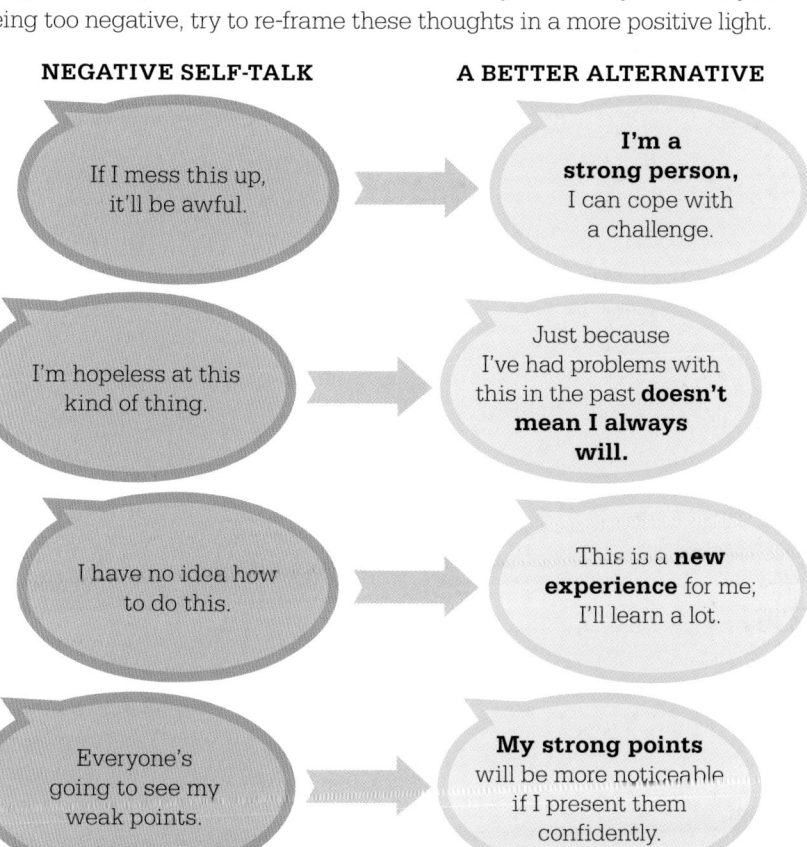

NEGATIVE SELF-TALK

If I mess this up, it'll be awful.

I'm hopeless at this kind of thing.

I have no idea how to do this.

Everyone's going to see my weak points.

A BETTER ALTERNATIVE

I'm a strong person, I can cope with a challenge.

Just because I've had problems with this in the past **doesn't mean I always will.**

This is a **new experience** for me; I'll learn a lot.

My strong points will be more noticeable if I present them confidently.

How afraid we are of performing isn't necessarily related to how well we actually do it. From Mahatma Gandhi to Hugh Grant, the great and the gifted in all walks of life have known the rush of panic when the time came to perform. Performance anxiety is not a sign that we're about to fail. With practice and some calming techniques, you can gain mastery over your anxiety and present yourself with confidence.

Q WRITE IT OUT

In 2011, American psychologists got students to write down their thoughts and feelings about an upcoming test. The result: all the students' scores improved, especially the ones most prone to exam stress. Downloading performance anxiety onto paper can be a good way to get a better handle on it.

AT ODDS WITH OTHERS

MANAGING THE STRESS OF CONFLICT

Nobody gets through life without having occasional arguments or personality clashes with others, and most conflicts are stressful. In the face of disagreement or hostility, how do we keep calm and confident?

I n an ideal world, we'd all live our lives without quarrels or conflicts of interest, but in reality, that's all but impossible. We stand a better chance of managing stress if we feel self-confident even in the times when we are at odds with others.

Authenticity

Research suggests one of the best tools for managing stress during conflict is authenticity. Defined in 2006 by American psychologists Michael Kernis and Brian Goldman, authenticity in the psychological sense consists of four dimensions:

- **Awareness.** Knowing and trusting our own thoughts, feelings, motives, personality, and needs.
- **Unbiased processing.** Taking feedback and accepting outcomes without being defensive.
- **Behaviour.** Behaving in ways that are consistent with our own values and preferences.
- **Relational orientation.** Having honest relationships in which we choose to let both our faults and our virtues be seen.

If we can preserve this kind of authentic relationship with ourselves, the pressure of other people's behaviours and opinions becomes less stressful.

Integrity

How do you tend to approach a disagreement? In 1983, a team of American researchers led by Alan Sillars defined three main tactics:

- **Distributive acts.** Fighting to win, using hostility, pressure, and insults.
- **Avoidance acts.** Indirect communication or passive acceptance to reduce the level of disagreement.
- **Integrative acts.** Saying what you think and working on problem-solving.

In 2010, American researchers studied these three methods to see which caused the greatest stress and negatively impacted health. The results: all subjects felt equally agitated and experienced intrusive

ANYTHING HOLDING YOU BACK?

Handling a conflict well requires skills that don't come naturally to many of us. A 2014 American study identified a variety of barriers to good communication in stressful situations, and the best solutions to each.

Communication problem	Solution	Example
A family, cultural, or organizational taboo against making trouble	Openly acknowledge the taboo.	"I feel a little awkward bringing this up, but…"
Poor conflict-management skills	Work on respectful disagreement and staying calm.	"We're all getting heated; let's take a break and cool off."
Difficulty with understanding others	Practise social skills and empathy.	"I know this isn't easy for you."
Unresolved emotional issues from past conflicts	Take responsibility for your own actions.	"I get too worked up, I know I shouldn't have done that."
Poor problem-solving skills	Try to approach problems more collaboratively.	"We both want what's best for everyone; let's find a solution."
Poor self-esteem	Allow yourself to feel upset, but take a step back and try to be objective.	"This isn't easy to hear, but I'm trying."
Limited self-knowledge	Ask trusted people for their input.	"People say I can be too aggressive – do you think that's true?"

thoughts after an argument – but those thoughts had no ill effect on the health of "integrative" arguers.

Communicating honestly and trying to resolve conflicts may not make arguments more comfortable, but they can be less distressing if you can reflect on your behaviour with few regrets. Avoiding clashes entirely is unlikely, even if we're co-operative by nature. Maintaining a sense of personal authenticity, and approaching conflicts as problems to be solved rather than battles to be avoided or won, may minimize the stress of conflict.

Q SELF-DETERMINATION THEORY

The concept of authenticity comes from a school of thought known as Self-Determination Theory, developed since the 1980s by American psychologists Edward Deci and Richard Ryan. The theory proposes that our three most powerful needs are:

Autonomy. The need to maintain control over the course of our lives.

Competence. The need to feel capable and effective.

Relatedness. The need for positive relationships with other people.

When any of these three needs are threatened, we experience stress. Conflict with another person – especially if we are battling for control, our competence is questioned, and the relationship has (at least temporarily) turned hostile – is therefore stressful on a very fundamental level. A secure sense of personal authenticity is crucial to maintaining wellbeing. It's the best way to know that, even if we can't control what other people think, we are comfortable with ourselves.

I CAN'T STAND IT!

HOW TO DEAL WITH FRUSTRATION

It's always stressful to deal with obstacles we can't overcome or people who persist in hindering us. With practice, we can build our tolerance for frustration, and approach problems with a calmer attitude.

Essentially, frustration is the discomfort we feel when what is happening is different from what we believe *should* be happening. A certain amount of frustration in life is inevitable, but by increasing our tolerance levels, we can lower the emotional impact of frustration.

Tolerating frustration

The stress caused by the obstacles we face is closely aligned with our overall ability to tolerate emotional discomfort. British psychologist and frustration expert Neil Harrington advises the following techniques to improve our coping skills:

- **Risk-taking.** Expose yourself to safe and moderate discomforts, such as taking a scary ride at a fairground or watching a horror movie.
- **Staying put under pressure.** Practise not leaving a situation at the first sign of discomfort, such as persisting with a boring book or an irritating talk show.
- **Exercising your discomfort muscles.** Stand in the slower-moving queue to build up your patience, or wear a silly hat to reduce your fear of shame.

These simple exercises teach us that we can survive discomfort. By learning this lesson, our ability to tolerate frustration increases. Rather than magnifying our stress by telling ourselves we shouldn't have to feel this way, we can experience our discomfort as a temporary annoyance, rather than a disaster.

> Frustration intolerance [is] an inability to accept the **divergence** between our **expectations** and **reality**.
>
> **Meghan Keough**
> American psychologist

Tolerating loved ones

As American physician Alex Lickerman observes, the people who frustrate us most are often those who are closest to us – partners, children, or parents. The combination of frequent contact with, and high expectations of, the people we love can result in a conflict between what we feel they should be doing and what they actually do.

Lickerman advises that the best approach is distraction, and the best distraction is gratitude (see pp.108 109). Imagine that the person who is currently annoying you is suddenly no longer in your life. What would you miss about them? When you consider how you'd feel without them, the stress caused by the temporarily maddening person is likely to dissipate or at least reduce.

No one enjoys frustration, of course, but since we cannot entirely avoid it, the less stressful route is to appreciate the good things in life and remember that a degree of discomfort is not the end of the world.

? HOW EASILY FRUSTRATED ARE YOU?

Frustration can be a complex emotion: a lot depends on exactly how we feel we're being thwarted. In 2005, British psychologist Neil Harrington proposed a "Frustration Discomfort Scale" to measure just how stressful we find different kinds of frustration. See how many of these statements you agree with: they may offer an insight into your own stress levels and how best to cope.

1
- I can't stand grinding away at difficult tasks.
- I need the easiest way of solving things.
- I can't stand having to do things I don't feel like doing.

2
- I can't stand waiting for what I want.
- I can't stand being criticized, especially when I know I'm not at fault.
- I can't stand being taken for granted.

3
- If I get upset, I need to get rid of those feelings fast – I can't bear them.
- I can't stand to feel emotionally out of control.
- If things don't change, there's no way I can be happy.

4
- I can't lower my standards, even if it would be convenient.
- I can't stand being unable to fulfill my potential.
- I can't stand leaving work unfinished or imperfect.

TYPES OF FRUSTRATION

1 = Discomfort Intolerance: stress at coping with daily hassles.

2 = Entitlement: stress at either being denied gratification or having to put up with injustice.

3 = Emotional Intolerance: difficulty in coping with emotional distress.

4 = Achievement: stress at feeling that you're prevented from reaching your goals.

COPING STRATEGIES

✔ Developing a sense of persistence (pp.192–193) can help you keep going in the face of discomfort.

✔ A more philosophical approach to life's unfairness (pp.124–125) can help make these frustrations feel more tolerable.

✔ Mindfulness practice (pp.132–135) can improve your coping skills.

✔ Reducing your perfectionism (pp.34–35) can help you stay productive but lower your frustration.

WHEN LOVE ENDS

BREAK-UP AND DIVORCE

Almost everyone has experienced heartbreak and knows how miserable it can be. By taking good care of yourself when the relationship ends, you may find that the hurt fades more rapidly.

Divorce, separation, and break-ups are among the sad facts of life: sometimes love doesn't work out, and we have to go through the painful process of adjustment as a relationship ends. Take care of yourself, and while you will undoubtedly experience stress, you will almost certainly cope.

Can I survive this?

There is no question that the end of a relationship hurts. How worried should you be about your stress levels as you come to terms with the loss? In 2015, an American review of the research noted an apparent contradiction: some studies suggest that people tend to be quite robust about break-ups, while others suggest that divorce and separation increase our odds of drinking problems, stress related illness, and depression.

The review's conclusion was that for most people, break-ups are upsetting, but that most people bounce back. However, 15–20% of people find the experience distressing enough to seriously impact their wellbeing.

> Most people are **psychologically resilient** and fare quite well following divorce.
>
> **David Sbarra, Karen Hasselmo, and Kyle Bourassa**
> American psychologists

How to remain robust

To ensure you remain in the robust 80–85% who cope well with break-ups, note the researchers' advice:

- **Try not to obsess** about why the relationship has ended. It won't help and it will raise your stress levels.
- **Don't keep trying to re-unite** with your ex. Knowing that things are over is difficult, but if you refuse to accept it, you only prolong the pain and damage your wellbeing (pp.124–125).
- **Re-frame your situation.** Telling yourself that your future looks bad without your partner, or that you'll never find anyone else, will only make you feel worse; focus instead on reasons to feel more hopeful (pp.26–29).
- **Think about who you are** apart from the relationship. The clearer your sense of personal meaning and self-worth (pp.42–43), the less daunting it is to face the future without your ex.
- **Get enough sleep.** To manage your feelings, you need your rest (pp.162–165).
- **Be alert to your mental health.** If you have a history of depression, the stress of separation can exacerbate it, so be sure you're getting good support and treatment (pp.202–203, 208–209).

With patience and positivity, you will be able to keep yourself going until the initial stress of the break-up passes and life returns to a new normal. Break-ups are painful, but the pain does not last for ever.

EVERYONE NEEDS CARE

TAKING CARE OF THE CHILDREN

Separation and divorce can be hard on children, so keep a close eye on their emotional wellbeing:

- **Particularly important** is to show as little hostility towards your ex as you can; research confirms that children whose parents disparage or attack each other suffer serious stress as a result. As much as possible, keep things calm in front of the kids.
- **Don't give yourself** the extra stress of guilt. A 2016 Spanish study noted that children whose parents separate after a high-conflict relationship tend to do better after it ends. The best thing you can do for your family is to be the most loving and supportive parent you can be.

SELF-CARE

Whether or not you have dependents, prepare yourself for what's ahead:

- **Self-compassion** is a good technique to get you through the bad moments (pp.38–39). Don't let the sadness of a broken relationship deter you from looking after yourself, both physically and emotionally.

You have a new life to live, so treat stress management as part of your responsibilities and give yourself and your children the care you need.

MANAGE YOUR RESOURCES

A 2011 Israeli study identified three ways in which a recently separated individual can shore up their resources against stress:

- **Socioeconomic resources.** Separating finances can be hard work, but do all you can to get back on your own feet. The more financially stable you can make yourself, the more secure you are likely to feel.

- **Cognitive resources.** Find a narrative about your situation that makes sense to you and gives you the feeling that it is manageable (pp.44–45).

- **Emotional resources.** The more social support you have, the more confident you will feel (pp.178–179).

45%

If your marriage ends, don't let it feel like failure: it happens to a great many people. The US Census Bureau estimated in 2011 that 40–45% of **first marriages** end in divorce.

LIFE AFTER LOSS

HOW TO DEAL WITH BEREAVEMENT

Even the most resilient people feel deep pain at the loss of a loved one. We can't avoid the grief that comes with bereavement, but we can weather the storm by showing ourselves patience and compassion.

P sychologists define bereavement as the period of sadness that follows the death of someone we love. Mourning a loved one is a normal emotional experience, but the deeply painful sorrow can feel overwhelming. This is a period of great stress, so if you've lost someone you care about, it's important to be patient with yourself because healing does take time.

Common reactions

Though painful, grief is a healthy process. Grief counsellors advise that you can realistically expect to experience some of the following:

- **Numbness,** shock, or disbelief, especially if a death is sudden.
- **Anxiety** over how you will cope without the loved one.
- **Distress and tearfulness:** emotions often come in waves or bursts that initially can feel overwhelming. Dreams or imagining that you see or hear your loved one are also common and normal.
- **Anger** at the unfairness of it all, or at the deceased for leaving you.
- **Difficulty carrying on** with day-to-day activities because of the grief, which makes us feel that nothing matters or that we cannot survive the pain.

{ **Grief** is the price we pay for **love**.

Queen Elizabeth II
speaking at a remembrance service for victims of the 9/11 attacks }

Be patient

There is no right or wrong way to grieve, so don't criticize yourself for anything you feel, even if it seems irrational or undignified.

Some researchers advise that if you are still intensely sad two years after the death, you could be depressed and might benefit from some extra support (see pp.202–203, 208–209). For most people, though, with time the pain lessens and life does feel worthwhile again.

Embrace the positive

We can sometimes feel guilty for enjoying life when our loved one has died, but as American psychiatry professor M. Katherine Shear observes, "Positive emotions are natural during this time and

6-12 months

Most studies suggest that the intensely stressful **first phase of grief** usually begins to settle down after **6–12 months**.

opportunities to experience them should be gently encouraged".

Mourning is a learning process: we gradually create a new life in which the lost person's absence can be accommodated. In between the waves of grief (see below), you do your loved one no dishonour – and are likely to reduce your own stress – if you embrace a sense of meaning and gratitude, and enjoy the good moments as much as you can.

Q THE MOURNING PROCESS

American psychiatrist M. Katherine Shear identifies an instinctive process by which grief evolves from the acute initial shock to the lower-stress phase during which the loss becomes bittersweet rather than devastating. You will take yourself gradually from one stage to the next.

ACUTE GRIEF

EVOLVES INTO...

> **Processing** the new world that you find yourself in and your place within it.
> **Alternating** between confronting the pain and avoiding it.
> **Finding ways** to express your grief in line with your cultural traditions and your own personality.

Q RIDING THE TSUNAMI

Canadian psychiatrist Diane McIntosh (a consultant on this book) uses an analogy with grieving patients that she calls the "grief tsunami". Bereavement hits us as a shattering blow, and after the first impact, the pain tends to come in waves – moments of relative calm punctuated by swells of stress and sorrow. Those waves may keep coming for the rest of our lives – anniversaries and holidays are often particularly difficult – but with time, the swells come less often and they don't hit as hard, so they're less painful. When grief is rising, remember that

you can ride out this wave and be assured that when it subsides, you will be safe on the other side.

Initial loss

Early grieving stages

Time passes and the waves begin to settle

INTEGRATED GRIEF

> **Accepting the death** and its consequences.
> **Allowing feelings** to gradually settle into a less stressful model, built around memories of the deceased.
> **Finding** that life eventually seems purposeful again.

FACING UP TO THE FACTS

ACCEPTANCE AND COMMITMENT

Stress is always going to be a part of our lives. ACT (Acceptance and Commitment Therapy) can be a good way of embracing that reality and – by embracing it – reducing its power to hurt us.

Your level of stress may be increased by the false belief that life-stress is down to a personal flaw, as if there's something wrong with you rather than the situation. If, instead, you accept that stress is part of life and focus on living the life you want, despite fears and setbacks, you'll feel far stronger.

Acceptance and commitment
Founded in 1986 by American behavioural therapist Steven Hayes, ACT has two central goals:

- **Acceptance** of unwanted personal experiences that we can't avoid. Stress may be uncomfortable; trying to control the uncontrollable is more so.
- **Commitment** to, and action towards, a life that reflects our values despite the discomforts.

As American co-founder Kirk Strosahl puts it, people thrive by being "in touch with their personal values so that they are geared towards living life to its fullest". By focusing on a life of meaning and satisfaction, rather than on our stress levels, we may find that our stress decreases of its own accord.

42%

LESS STRESS
In a 2011 Swedish study of highly pressured people, ACT helped **42% reduce their stress levels** by a clinically significant amount.

✅ THINKING IN IMAGES

ACT founder Steven Hayes often uses metaphors to help illuminate ways of dealing with stress:

- **Bus passengers.** Stresses can be like disruptive passengers. Don't stop to argue with them: keep driving in the direction you want your life to follow.

- **The beach ball.** Trying to ignore stressful issues is about as effective as pushing a beach ball underwater: the issues, like the ball, will just pop back up.

- **Leaves on a stream.** Imagine yourself sitting by a stream. Your stressful feelings are floating along the surface like leaves. Let them eventually drift out of sight.

- **Quicksand.** Struggling to stop feelings of distress can make you sink deeper: accept you're feeling that way for now.

- **Thought train.** Look at your feelings. Imagine a train is passing, with each carriage having a negative thought or feeling written on the side. Don't climb aboard: watch it pass.

When working to process stress, try using some of these images: they may help you feel more empowered to accept and manage your feelings.

🔍 STRESSING CLEANLY

ACT distinguishes between two kinds of discomfort, and recommends that we stick to the "clean" kind.

- **Clean discomfort.** We have to deal with a problem and may feel stressed. Such situations are challenging, but normal and healthy. As life always contains problems to solve, this kind of discomfort is inevitable and needs to be accepted.

- **Dirty discomfort.** We dislike our clean discomfort and struggle against our reaction to it. By fighting our feelings, we rapidly amplify them. If we stop trying to avoid our clean discomfort, we can avoid the stress of dirty discomfort.

CORE PRINCIPLES

How do we develop acceptance and commitment? ACT recommends six core tactics we can use to help ourselves – which in turn will lower our stress levels.

Core tactic	What it means	What it looks like
Cognitive defusion	Notice your thoughts, but don't treat them as objective truths (p.53).	Not, "I'm a loser", but, "I'm having insecure thoughts".
Acceptance	Make room for your feelings, but don't fixate on them.	"I'm really nervous right now. That's okay, I'll carry on."
Contact with the present moment	Develop mindful awareness skills (pp.132–135).	"I can observe my own feelings without over-analyzing them."
The observing self	You are an ongoing consciousness, not just your momentary feelings.	"I'm always me, stressed or not."
Values	What means most to you in the world? Live for that (pp.44–45).	"I believe in generosity. I can be generous even when I'm feeling bad."
Committed action	Set meaningful goals, and take action to achieve them (pp.192–193).	"Stressed or not, I'm still going to turn up for my children's school play."

WHO DO YOU WANT MAKING DECISIONS FOR YOU IN YOUR LIFE – YOUR ANXIETY, DEPRESSION, ANGER, OR YOU?

KIRK STROSAHL, PSYCHOLOGIST AND CO-FOUNDER OF ACCEPTANCE AND COMMITMENT THERAPY

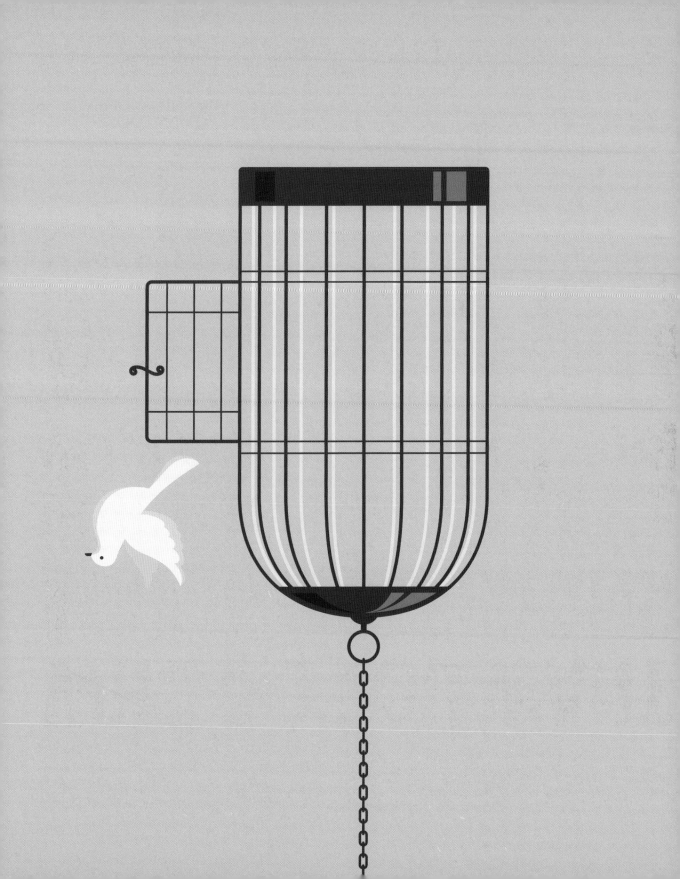

IN-BREATH, OUT-BREATH

BREATH CONTROL REMEDIES

When you feel stressed, your body is likely to respond by breathing in a more shallow, rapid manner. Taking control of your breathing pattern is a good way to lower your stress levels and feel more in control.

Breathing rapidly is a natural response to feeling threatened: in "fight-or-flight" mode, the body assumes it needs more oxygen and we start panting. However, when we don't actually need to escape, rapid breathing can make us feel worse, and can even trigger a full-blown panic attack (see pp.204–207). Some simple breathing exercises (such as the one opposite) can help you to control your breathing when you feel under pressure.

Be kind to your body

According to psychologists and respirologists, shallow breathing can actually cause you to feel more stressed. However, it's an easy habit to fall into. Deep breathing requires relaxed abdominal muscles, which lets the lungs expand fully. Holding in those muscles – if we're trying to make our belly look flat, for example – affects our breathing patterns, which can heighten stress. It's best to allow yourself to be completely free of concern about how you look when you try the breathing

According to a 2002 Belgian-Canadian study, our **voluntary breathing pattern** – the way that we control our breath – can account for as much as **40% of our emotional response**.

exercise below, and to focus only on the movement of air in and out of your lungs.

A word of warning

If you are feeling extremely tense physically and on the verge of panic, trying to breathe too deeply could be the wrong tactic. Anxiety attacks can cause hyperventilation, which means the body expels too much carbon dioxide, creating dizziness and faintness. Taking deeper breaths further reduces carbon dioxide levels, making us feel even worse.

A technique developed in a 2010 study by American psychologist Alicia Meuret used capnometers to measure subjects' breathing rates and help them learn how to adjust their breathing rates based on feedback from the devices. Her findings: when trying to avoid panic, it helps to take shallow breaths initially, and gradually slow the rate down.

In short, if you're stressed, try to breathe slowly and deeply – but if you're panicking, take slow, shallow breaths. With these techniques, you'll calm both body and mind.

Q KEEPING CALM

A 2006 American study asked a group of volunteers to spend 15 minutes either worrying, thinking of nothing in particular, or doing a mindful breathing exercise. The volunteers were then shown images from the International Affective Picture System – pictures chosen to be pleasant, neutral, or unpleasant. The results: those who had been practising peaceful breathing reported a much lower level of distress when shown upsetting images.

BREATHING EXERCISE

Breath control can be used as a general meditation, but it can also tackle stress. If you need to calm yourself, try the exercise below, which doctors and psychologists often recommend. Make a regular practice of this during stressful times, and you should find it easier to relax.

1
Sit or lie somewhere comfortable. If you have time, begin with a Progressive Muscle Relaxation (see pp.130–131) in order to get your body completely settled.

2
Take a normal breath, and see how deep it goes.

3
Take a deliberately deep breath. Let your abdomen expand and breathe slowly.

4
If you feel it would help, keep alternating shallow and deep breaths for a while, so you teach your body how a deep breath feels.

5
When you're comfortable with deep breathing, spend 10–20 minutes doing just that. As you inhale, tell yourself that you are breathing in calmness and peace; as you exhale, tell yourself that you are breathing out stress and tension.

LEARNING TO LOOSEN UP
PROGRESSIVE MUSCLE RELAXATION

Stress tenses our bodies, which can lead to a variety of painful physical symptoms. Fortunately, there's a well-supported technique that can easily fit into your day and can help you feel more at ease.

One of the major physical effects of stress is muscle tension. In the face of a short-term threat, it's a healthy response, allowing us to fight or flee (see pp.20–21). In the long term, though, chronic muscle tension can lead to headaches, back pain, cramps, and aches all over the body, as well as contributing to insomnia (see pp.162–165) – which further adds to our stress. If your muscles are tightening up in the face of stress, you may benefit from a technique known as PMR – Progressive Muscle Relaxation.

Daily care routine

Developed in 1929 by American physician Dr Edmund Jacobson, PMR is still used today to treat tension and sleeplessness. Contemporary research provides substantial evidence for PMR. For instance: a 2011 Malaysian study found PMR helpful for calming young soccer players; a 2006 study in Hong Kong found it improved quality of life and lowered blood pressure in patients with heart disease; and a 1992 American study found patients with epilepsy suffered 29% fewer seizures when they used the technique regularly.

> An anxious mind cannot exist in a **relaxed** body.
>
> **Edmund Jacobson**
> American physician and founder of PMR

PMR is a quick and easy way to relax physically and emotionally. A typical practice takes less than 10 minutes, although you can spend longer if you have the time. Do as much as you feel able to manage – even a brief session can help you to relax during stressful times. Although it's helpful at any time of day, PMR can also improve your sleep.

🔍 SEEING A THREAT?

Is this stick figure walking towards or away from you? It's designed so that you could read it either way, but anxious people tend to be quicker to assume it's walking towards them – because a figure approaching us is more likely to be a threat. A 2014 Canadian study asked people to do PMR before viewing the figure, and found that their "facing-the-viewer bias" was significantly lowered: PMR had made them less afraid.

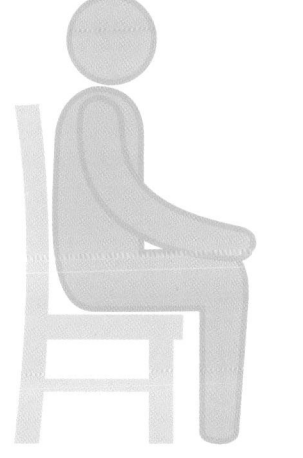

If you saw this figure walking, would you think it was moving towards or away from you?

✅ THE PMR TECHNIQUE

If we're habitually tense, it can be hard to fully relax. PMR involves clenching groups of muscles tightly, and then relaxing them – which creates a greater sense of release. If you have an injury, first ask your doctor whether this is a safe practice for you. PMR should be done sitting down so you can relax, or lying down, if you don't mind nodding off afterwards.

Muscle Mantra

> Clench and inhale.
> Hold for 5–10 seconds.
> Relax and exhale.
> Rest for 10–20 seconds.
> Repeat for each part of the body.

By tightening and then relaxing each part of your body – followed by a brief pause before you move to the next part of your body – you reduce muscle tension, leaving you feeling calmer and more comfortable.

Begin with your feet, and work your way up your body:

1 **Starting with one foot,** clench your muscles by curling your toes tight. Then relax.

2 **Move to your lower leg:** pull your toes upwards towards you, which tenses the calf, then relax.

3 **Clench your thigh muscles** as well as your foot and calf, then relax.

4 **Repeat all three exercises** for your other leg.

5 **Clench one hand** by making a fist, then relax.

6 **Tighten your arm** in the "bicep flexing" pose, with your hand clenched as well, then relax.

7 **Repeat both exercises** for your other arm.

8 **Tighten your buttocks,** then relax.

9 **Suck in your stomach,** then relax.

10 **Take a deep breath** to tighten your chest, then relax.

11 **Squeeze your shoulders** up to your ears, then relax.

12 **Stretch your mouth** open wide, then relax.

13 **Squeeze your eyes** tight shut, then relax.

14 **Raise your eyebrows** high, then relax.

TAKE A MOMENT
MINDFULNESS AND MEDITATION

The concept of mindfulness has been a part of traditional religions such as Buddhism for centuries. In recent decades, it has been increasingly studied by Western science as well – with notably positive results.

In 1979, American professor of medicine Jon Kabat-Zinn founded the Mindfulness-Based Stress Reduction Clinic at the University of Massachussetts Medical School. Mindfulness has since become a major field of study, finding benefits in areas as diverse as anxiety reduction, psychological resilience, and the management of physical pain. Incorporating some mindfulness techniques into your life is a powerful way to keep stress levels under control.

The benefits of mindfulness
What is mindfulness? Put simply, it's a form of non-judgemental awareness of your feelings and experience. A 2004 Canadian-American study defined the key benefits as:

- **Sustained attention** that keeps you focused in the present moment, which helps develop calmness and concentration.
- **Stimulus selection.** During meditation, your mind invariably wanders: the discipline lies in observing this has happened

> To be mindful is to wake up, to **recognize** what is happening in the **present moment**.
>
> **Christopher Germer**
> American psychologist and psychotherapist

and choosing to redirect your attention back to the meditation. This gives you excellent practice in learning how to switch your mind from one subject to another, which can be very helpful when you need to break out of a worry cycle (pp.48–49).

- **Observing your own thoughts.** Mindful awareness makes you better at noticing your thoughts – which means that even when you're not meditating you're better able to identify and challenge the ones that bother you (pp.52–53).
- **Viewing your emotions with curiosity** rather than fighting them. This robs stress of some of its power over you, as you no longer compound it by becoming stressed about being stressed.

Taken together, these effects add up to an increased ability to manage your attention and an improved insight into your feelings – all of which helps stress management. A 2015 British meta-analysis of the research also noted that mindfulness is particularly good at decreasing our reactivity to stress – that is, you can experience stress without blowing it out of proportion.

On the following pages, we'll discuss the most helpful attitudes to bring to meditation. In a few cases, though, it can produce a state called "relaxation-induced anxiety". If meditation makes you feel anxious, try some shorter sessions; if it still feels uncomfortable, try a more physical form of relaxation, such as PMR (see pp.130–131) or some gentle exercise (pp.152–155). »

BASIC MINDFULNESS EXERCISE

If you want to try mindfulness, the central exercise on which most others are based is a simple breathing meditation. Find a time in your daily routine where you can practise uninterrupted, in peace and quiet.

1 Sit somewhere comfortable. Don't lie down, as you want to stay alert. Rest in a position that's upright, but not tense, and close your eyes.

2 Let your attention settle. There will be sounds around you, sensations in your body, and thoughts floating through your head. Allow them to happen: don't try to ignore them, don't start a train of thought about them. Just let them come and go.

3 Focus your attention on your breath. Feel the inhalation, the exhalation, and the sensations and rhythm your breathing creates.

4 If your attention wanders – which it will – don't worry about it. Quietly bring your focus back to your breath. Carry on for 5–10 minutes, or longer if you like, then gently relax your attention and open your eyes.

Even a short mindfulness practice, done regularly, can help you become calmer and more aware of your feelings and your environment. There is no goal except the mindfulness itself, so don't pressure yourself to do it "correctly": simply enjoy it, and let whatever happens happen. Done regularly, meditation can greatly improve your stress management skills.

✅ THE MINDFUL ATTITUDE

The Center for Mindfulness in Medicine, Health Care, and Society at the University of Massachussetts highlights seven important aspects to a good mindfulness practice:

1
Non-judging
Approach your experience with mindfulness as an impartial witness.

2
Patience
Your attention will wander, and your emotions will fluctuate. Don't expect to get it "right" all the time.

3
A beginner's mind
Expecting every meditation to go the same way can distract you from how this particular one is actually going. Approach each moment of mindfulness as if it's your first.

4
Trust
You know your own feelings better than any teacher or guru: listen to your intuition and be yourself.

5
Non-striving
Thinking "I'm stressed, now I'm going to get de-stressed" creates the pressure of something you "should" be achieving. It's more effective just to let whatever happens happen.

6
Acceptance
See things as they are, even if "as they are" isn't something you're completely happy about. If there's something about yourself that you don't care for, don't wait to change it before starting to like yourself.

7
Letting go
Don't cling to certain mental states and reject others: they're all part of human experience. Let them come, and let them go.

By embracing these open and accepting attitudes, you make your practice of mindfulness as non-stressful as possible, and are most likely to benefit from it.

Q FEELING POORLY?

Among its other harmful effects, stress tends to lower our immune system. Good news: mindfulness can help. A 2003 American study tested subjects who had recently been vaccinated against 'flu – a time when their immune systems were facing a challenge – and found that those who practised mindful meditation during the previous eight weeks showed a markedly stronger immune response. If stress is wearing you down, some mindfulness practice may help you fight off infections.

» The right attitude

According to the Center for Mindfulness in Medicine, Health Care, and Society – a leading centre of mindfulness therapy, founded by Jon Kabat-Zinn at the University of Massachussetts Medical School – to get the most benefit out of mindfulness practice, you need to approach it with an attitude that is sceptical but open. Assuming that it won't work is likely to be a self-fulfilling prophecy, but assuming that it will magically cure all your ills is likely to set you up for disappointment. Simply take an interest in what will happen, and

✓ STOP STRESSING

Trying to fit mindfulness into a busy life? American psychologist Elisha Goldstein recommends a simple acronym for short practices you can do at odd moments such as taking a shower, walking, eating a meal, or travelling:

S	**Stop**	Stop what you're doing. Close your eyes if it's safe to do so.
T	**Take**	Take a few breaths, focusing your awareness on the sensation of air going in and out.
O	**Observe**	Observe how you are feeling physically, emotionally, and mentally.
P	**Perceive**	Perceive the sounds around you, listening to them without judgement.

Goldstein reports that even five minutes a day of mindfulness can make us less stressed and more satisfied with our lives.

accept that mindfulness is a skill you teach yourself and have to practise consistently.

The Center adds that meditation, while powerful in itself, tends to need some personal vision to make it fully meaningful. Ask yourself who you might be if you let go of the stress that's holding you back.

Mindfulness won't turn you into a different person, but it can be a foundation for positive progress towards your best self – and if stress is making it hard for you to be the person you'd like to be, it can be an excellent technique to incorporate into your daily routine.

A regular mindfulness practice can create a still centre point in a stressful life, in which you experience your emotions rather than fighting them, and let yourself simply be who you are. Stress is a feeling we all struggle with sometimes – but sometimes it's good to create a psychological space where you stop struggling and take a much-needed rest.

> Mindfulness is **awareness** that arises through paying attention, on purpose, in the **present moment**, and non-judgmentally.
>
> **Jon Kabat-Zinn**
> American founder of mindfulness-based therapy

LET'S CELEBRATE

MAKING FESTIVITIES WORK

Has the thought of Christmas or other holidays ever made you feel stressed or depressed? Celebrations can be difficult for some of us, so don't burden yourself with impossible expectations: prepare for self-care.

There's a lot of pressure to be cheerful during family get-togethers, but they can also be an extremely tense time. If you're dreading the festivities, it can help to plan how you'll manage them well in advance.

According to a 2008 American Psychological Association poll, **8 in 10 Americans anticipate stress** during the winter holiday season.

Coping with celebrations

If you aren't looking forward to the pressure of celebrating, a few tips from the experts:

✔ **Plan ahead.** American psychologist Janet Frank advises that, if your family exchanges gifts at Christmas, it's wise to shop "piece by piece throughout the year". That way you can spread the financial burden, spare yourself from having to buy everything in a rush, and avoid the holiday crowds.

✔ **Maintain your habits.** American blogger and author of *The Happiness Project* Gretchen Rubin points out that if we disrupt our usual routine, it's hardly surprising we feel stressed. Go to bed and rise at your regular hours, maintain your usual exercise regime, and – allowing for a few treats – eat the way you generally do. Whatever else the season requires you to deal with, your body will have the protection of consistency.

✔ **Establish your own boundaries** (see pp.92–95). Christmas sometimes means saying no, whether it's explaining the limits of your budget to children or telling distant relations that you won't visit them this year.

Know what you can and cannot manage, and be prepared to make it clear to others.

> Grown siblings start to behave as if they're **eight years old**.
>
> **Pamela Regan**
> American psychology professor

5% SAD

A 2010 American study estimated that **1 in 20** Americans suffers **Seasonal Affective Disorder** in a given year. SAD is more prevalent the further we are from the equator: statistics may vary depending on where you live, but some extra self-care in winter benefits everyone.

Beating the winter blues

In the northern hemisphere, major holidays such as Christmas and Hanukkah fall during the winter season. For some people, more hours of darkness can lead to Seasonal Affective Disorder (SAD), a form of depression that is usually resolved as the hours of sunlight increase in the spring.

SAD is treated like ordinary depression (see pp.202–203), but also with "light therapy". This exposes patients to artificial light that stimulates the brain to secrete serotonin – an anti-depressant neurotransmitter – and melatonin, a hormone that regulates our sleep cycle. The British Seasonal Affective Disorder Association estimates that light therapy can be effective in 85% of cases, and can reduce symptoms within two weeks of starting treatment, although the full effect may take somewhat longer.

If you feel that the winter months are getting you down, it's always wise to consult your doctor.

✅ FAMILY FUN?

Many get-togethers involve time with the family. Convention would have us believe this is good news, but if your family isn't picture-perfect (and whose is?) the reality can be stressful. Some tips for a tolerable holiday:

PUT IT IN PERSPECTIVE

To quote American sociology professor Terri Orbuch, "The best thing you can do is manage your expectations, to set realistic ones so that you don't get frustrated". Whatever the traditional image of a festivity, the people you'll be spending it with are imperfect human beings, so be prepared for an imperfect event (see pp.34–35).

BEWARE OF OLD PATTERNS

Family time can reactivate old family roles; as American psychology professor Pamela Regan observes, we tap into long-buried habits and behaviour. Hold on to your patience and remember that you're an adult.

ASSESS YOUR LIMITS

Ken Duckworth, medical director of America's National Alliance on Mental Illness, suggests asking yourself, "Why am I doing things that make me miserable?" If you really hate the idea of spending time with particular people, remember that you can opt out.

PICK YOUR BATTLES

You may have to spend time with difficult relations, but as American psychology professor Pamela Wiegartz puts it, "If you need to sort through personal and ideologic differences, find another time when you can discuss these things privately". At least for one day, take a deep breath and let it go.

I NEED A DRINK

STRESS AND ALCOHOL

Many people drink alcohol, and most manage it fine. Stress, though, can complicate our relationship with drinking. If you're under pressure, it's wise to be aware of the risks of using alcohol to cope.

We all know that drinking excessively isn't healthy, but in trying times, it can be tempting to pour a glass and forget our troubles for a while. What's key is to keep our alcohol use within reasonable bounds so that it doesn't ultimately make stress even worse.

The benefits of moderation

A 2011 Dutch study tested people's cortisol levels throughout the day and found that heavy drinkers (which meant having more than three drinks per day) had higher cortisol levels at night, woke with higher levels in the morning, and showed more physiological reaction to stress throughout the day – whether or not they had problems with alcoholism.

Moderate drinkers actually experienced less stress than teetotalers, but drinking large amounts disrupted the body's stress response. If you regularly have more than three drinks a day, you may reduce your stress by cutting back.

ALCOHOL ABUSE

1 in 12

America's National Council on Alcohol and Drug Dependence estimates that **1 in 12** adults experiences **problems with alcohol abuse or dependence**. If you're worried about your drinking, you're far from alone, so don't be afraid to seek medical help.

Stress and cravings

Stress can trigger excess drinking. A 2016 American study subjected lab rats to acute stress for an hour, and then gave them access to sugar water laced with alcohol. The control rats, which hadn't been subjected to stress, drank significantly less than the stressed ones – and those stressed rats kept drinking more for several weeks afterwards.

What the researchers found was that the rats' brains had been altered: stress had flipped a switch that blunted their dopamine response – the neurotransmitter associated with the pleasure of reward – so they had a compulsion to drink more but experienced less pleasure. In other words, the more stressed you are, the more alcohol you'll need to feel relaxed, and the harder it can be to stop.

Save alcohol for the less pressured times, and use more effective relaxation methods to relieve your stress, such as mindfulness, PMR, and breathing exercises (see pp.128–135).

If you are already concerned that you are drinking too much (see above right), reducing your stress levels can help, but make sure you seek medical advice as well: an understanding doctor can provide a great deal of support.

Issues with other substances?

Multiple studies confirm that stress makes us more vulnerable to all kinds of addiction, and more likely to relapse if we're trying to stay clean. If that's a problem for you, it's all the more important you take care of your stress levels.

? DEVELOPING A PROBLEM?

Not everyone who drinks to excess is an alcoholic, but alcohol is potentially addictive. If you wonder whether you may be becoming dependent, consider these questions:

- **Do you find** it difficult to stop drinking once you've started?

- **When other people** comment on your drinking, do you feel angry or defensive?

- **Do you black out** or become "another person" when you drink?

- **Do you feel guilty** about how much you drink?

- **Do you hide or lie** about how much you drink?

- **Would a "dry spell"** be difficult for you?

- **Do you ever worry** about your drinking?

You may also like to search online for the AUDIT or CAGE questionnaires, two well-regarded tests for problem drinking. There's no shame in tackling dependency constructively.

A 2013 Iranian study noted something particularly helpful: the subjects who were addicts used significantly less problem-focused coping (see pp.26–29) and had less stress tolerance (see pp.118–119) than the non-addicts. As well as seeking medical support – which you should do as soon as possible – improving your coping skills supports your recovery.

✓ WANT TO CUT BACK?

Stress can increase the desire for more alcohol, but reducing your intake can be difficult, which can further heighten stress. This vicious cycle reduces the likelihood of successfully cutting back. British psychologist and addiction expert Mark Griffiths offers some tips to make the process easier to manage:

- ✔ **Find friends and family** who want to cut back, and do it together (pp.176–179).

- ✔ **Socialize in smaller groups,** and try not to drink in rounds: such arrangements tend to end up with everyone matching the pace of the quickest drinker.

- ✔ **When you're out at a bar** or restaurant, buy smaller measures, diluted drinks, or soft drinks.

- ✔ **Avoid temptation.** Know what your triggers for drinking are – such as passing a favourite bar – and plan ahead on the best way to avoid them.

- ✔ **Remind yourself of the benefits.** Treat cutting back as a positive, aspirational goal (pp.170–171): with less drinking, you're likely to get more sleep, consume fewer calories, and feel healthier.

- ✔ **Reward yourself.** Keep a spending diary (p.88) and set aside the money you would usually spend on alcohol to buy something nice.

AVOIDING AVOIDANCE

HOW TO STOP STRESS RULING YOU

When something stresses us, our instinctive desire is to avoid it, but avoidance can exacerbate our stress in the long term. Confronting issues, rather than avoiding them, is a far more effective way to overcome the stress.

Avoiding the things that bother us can become a vicious circle that leaves us feeling more stressed than ever. Tackling the problem is more likely to put it in perspective.

Dodging the issue

New Zealand psychologist Alice Boyes highlights various ways we use avoidance as a method of dealing with stress:

- **Refusing** to think about something. "My tax return is overdue. I'm off to see a movie."
- **Avoiding** things that might trigger painful memories. "I got told off at school for asking silly questions. I'm not going to ask my boss what he means."
- **Not testing** whether your fears are true. "That lump might be cancer. I'm not going to the doctor, it's too scary."
- **Avoiding social situations.** "I'll only make a fool of myself, so I'll skip going to the party."
- **Avoiding challenges.** "I'll feel bad if I don't do well in the competition. Better not enter."

> **Avoidance** is tricky because it works, kind of … but it **costs us** dearly over the **long term**.
>
> **Ellen Hendriksen**
> American psychologist

In all these situations, the end result may be that your circumstances actually get worse – but even if they don't, you remain fearful.

By refusing to confront the issue you're stressed about, you subject yourself to what behaviourists call "negative reinforcement" (see below): you've made it more likely that you'll keep avoiding the issue, and you won't learn how to deal with the stressor.

Negative reinforcement

The concept of reinforcement was pioneered by American behaviourist B. F. Skinner. Avoidance involves negative reinforcement:

1 Something is making me feel stressed.

2 I respond to the stressor by acting in a certain way.

3 The stressful issue is resolved as a result.

4 The next time something is stressing me, I'll probably respond the same way.

Negative reinforcement can be useful. for instance, if our car sounds an annoying alarm that only switches off when we fasten our seatbelt, the alarm is a negative reinforcer, making it more likely that we'll buckle up and stay safe.

Sometimes, however, a problem still needs to be fixed. Avoiding it may reduce the stress, but only temporarily – experiencing less stress can reinforce the value of avoidance, and so we're more likely

THE CYCLE OF AVOIDANCE

Avoiding stressors means that we don't learn to cope with them. It's far better to tackle our problems head-on, building up our ability to tolerate stress and find solutions.

AVOIDANCE

> Something stresses you.
> You avoid it.
> Your stress temporarily drops.
> You avoid it more.
> You don't learn to cope with it.
> It builds in your mind as something you can't cope with.

PROBLEM-SOLVING

> Something stresses you.
> You tolerate the discomfort.
> You tackle the problem.
> You discover that you can survive the discomfort.
> You learn ways to deal with it.
> It becomes less stressful.

to resort to avoidance the next time. Over time, it becomes even more difficult to confront and overcome the problem.

There are many coping methods we can use to deal with stressful situations, because in the long run,

GRADUAL EXPOSURE

CBT "exposure therapy" is a form of Cognitive Behavioural Therapy (see pp.52–53) that helps to gradually reduce avoidance. For instance, suppose you once had a panic attack in a shop and dread going in there for fear of having another one: you can expose yourself in small steps to gradually build up your stress tolerance:

1 With a trusted friend, walk up to the shop and stand outside until you can relax.

2 Stand in front of the shop on your own.

3 With a friend, walk a few metres into the shop, stay there until your anxiety settles, then leave.

4 Walk a few metres into the shop by yourself.

5 Go into the shop and buy one small thing.

6 Carry on making longer and longer trips until the shop is a place you can tolerate calmly.

it's better to confront issues than to avoid them. As we discuss on pp.26–29 and throughout this book, it is possible to learn these coping techniques, which will get easier and more automatic the more we use them.

STAYING WELL
STRESS AND ILL HEALTH

Being ill is stressful in itself – but stress can also increase the chances that we'll get sick. In both cases, good self-care is the best way to protect both your psychological and physical wellbeing.

Getting sick can make us more vulnerable to stress, and vice versa. Reminding yourself of how the mind and body interact can help you anticipate when your health might be at risk and improve your self-care.

Post-illness blues
There is a biological reason why we can feel miserable when we're sick: our bodies release proteins known as cytokines, which help regulate the immune system – but they can also contribute to a low mood.

A 2001 American study found that 45% of patients whose treatment included artificial cytokines developed depressive symptoms unless they were already on antidepressants. During and shortly after sickness, keep an eye on your mental health: unchecked stress can lead to depression (see pp.202–203), and cytokines increase the risk.

The let-down effect
Have you ever had a period of stress come to an end, only to be struck

LEISURE SICKNESS

Dutch psychologist Ad Vingerhoets estimates that 3% of people suffer from **"leisure sickness"** – sudden ill health following a period of pressure. His advice: **improve your stress-spotting skills**, identify when you're pushing yourself too hard, and then **slow down** rather than crash down.

down with illness just as you had a chance to relax? You were probably suffering from what American psychologist Marc Schoen calls the "let-down effect". The problem: during acute stress, stress hormones activate the immune system, but in the process they can also re-activate viruses that were lying dormant, leading to a flare-up as your immune system settles down after the stress is resolved.

Arthritis and other chronic pain conditions may also feel worse in the "let-down" after a period of high pressure. Brain chemicals such as cortisol and norepinephrine can suppress pain perception during the stress response, causing some to overstrain the body without realizing they're exceeding their usual limits. The effects might not be felt until the stress chemicals return to normal.

Schoen's advice: as you come to the end of a crisis, don't switch to relaxation mode too suddenly. Instead, have a cooling-off period (see opposite), to allow your brain's stress response to adjust more

✅ NEED A SICK DAY?

If you're too sick to work, you're too sick to work, so don't add to the stress of being unwell by feeling guilty if you have to take a day off. These are some useful phrases when calling in sick, to remind both yourself and your employer that you're doing the right thing:

I need a day's rest to **get me back on my feet.**

I don't want everyone else to catch what I've got.

I'll lose less work time if I can take a day or two to really shake this off.

I can't manage work today, **I'm too sick to think straight.**

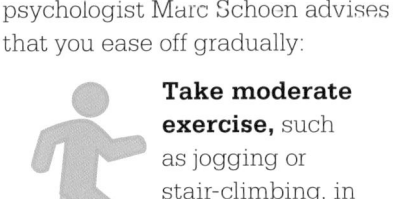

gradually, keeping your immune system active enough to fight off any infections.

Whether a period of stress is making you ill, or an illness is making you more susceptible to stress, the solution is to let yourself down gently: avoid the extremes and ease back into your regular life.

Supportive friends

If you suffer from a chronic illness or disability, you may find that some people pressure you to rise above it with platitudes such as "Everything happens for a reason." Most sick or disabled people find such comments add to their stress rather than alleviating it, as the message they really communicate is that the speaker doesn't want to hear any complaints. It may be comforting to know that doctors don't want patients to underplay their symptoms. A 2007 Indian study concluded that those who

minimize the seriousness of a condition commonly delay, avoid, or fail to comply with treatment.

Social support can help a great deal (see pp.176–179), so choose companions who can cheer you up while allowing you to be honest on the days when you feel down.

Pay heed to symptoms

Stress can sometimes make us feel ill even if there's nothing physically "wrong": from headaches to skin rashes, emotional strain can produce real, physical symptoms (see pp.196–197). If you often experience physical symptoms with no obvious causes, ask your GP if stress might be the reason. This doesn't mean the symptoms aren't real and are "all in your head". It's important not to underestimate the power of stress to provoke uncomfortable, even painful effects. Your stress levels are part of your overall health, so taking care of one helps take care of both.

✅ COOLING OFF AFTER STRESS

Want to avoid a sudden illness after a period of stress? American psychologist Marc Schoen advises that you ease off gradually:

Take moderate exercise, such as jogging or stair-climbing, in 5–6-minute bursts several times a day.

Do mental challenges such as puzzles or chess games for 30–60 minutes at a time.

If you keep up this level of challenge for three days – which Schoen describes as a critical window – you have a better chance of staying well.

CHAPTER 4

DE-STRESSING YOUR LIFE

CREATING A CALMER EXISTENCE

TOO MUCH ON YOUR PLATE

HOW TO PRIORITIZE

For many of us, managing competing demands is one of the constant pressures of modern life. With so many expectations to worry about, how can we use our best judgment when making decisions?

Stress can fluster us – and when we're flustered, we don't always make the best decisions. This can affect how we organize and manage all the tasks we're facing. The first step to prioritizing is to attempt to look at our tasks less emotionally and more objectively.

Making the sensible choice

We can better handle competing goals by the way we interpret the tasks involved. A 2016 British–Australian study gave participants two projects to complete: one that was already in "good" shape and one that was in "bad" shape, or less likely to be completed successfully. The experimenters offered a small cash reward of 6 pence for finishing both tasks and half that amount for finishing just one. Because the "bad" project was designed to have only a 20% chance of success – as opposed to 80% for the "good" one – prioritizing the "bad" project meant that the participants would probably be unable to finish either and get no money at all.

However, the researchers also presented the situation in one of two ways: some of the participants were told they would make money by completing the projects, and others were told they'd lose money by failing to complete them.

The result? Subjects who were told they would make money if successful played it safe and earned more. Subjects who'd been given the "avoid a loss" scenario tended to prioritize the low-chance-of-success goal, and often ended up failing both tasks.

Q GETTING SOME DISTANCE

As a 2008 Israeli–American study points out, we often plan less effectively under the pressure of immediate stress – an effect that can be improved by creating the idea of some emotional "distance" between ourselves and the situation. The study identified four options:

- **Imagine temporal distance.**
  What would someone 10 years from now think was the priority?

- **Imagine physical distance.**
  What would be the priority if this was happening on the other side of the world?

- **Imagine social distance.**
  What would you consider the priority if this was happening to a stranger?

- **Imagine as a hypothetical.**
  What would be the priority if this wasn't a real situation, but an imaginary one?

All of these methods helped people clarify their thinking under pressure. If a problem seems overwhelming to you, try putting some imaginative space between it and you.

Aim for gains

Humans are loss-averse creatures: the stress of avoiding a negative outcome can cause us to take more risks. When trying to decide which task to tackle, try to think in terms of potential gains rather than feared losses: it's a more logical and less stressful approach.

Q PUSH OR PULL?

Psychologists define two different categories of goals:

Approach goals
Aiming at a positive outcome:
"I'm going to ace my exams."

Avoidance goals
Aiming to avoid a negative outcome:
"I'm going to stay out of debt."

A 2014 British study found that we tend to feel more stressed and anxious when we're focused on avoidance goals. If you can find ways to re-frame your goals in terms of a positive outcome rather than avoiding a negative one, you may find it easier to keep your spirits up while juggling tasks.

BUDGET YOUR EFFORTS

Since we don't have the time or energy to give 100% of our effort to every task, we should plan accordingly. By having a well-structured to-do list, we can reduce the stress of feeling we're spread too thin. American psychologist Jeff Szymanski has created a simple ranking system:

Ranking	What they involve	How much effort?
A tasks ★★★★	Tasks it's really important to do well.	Pick 3 things to give 100% – that is, do your absolute best.
B tasks ★★★	Tasks where an adequate job would be acceptable.	About 80% per task – try fairly hard, but be satisfied with "good enough".
C tasks ★★	Basic tasks that require only minimal effort.	Apply just enough effort to get by.
Other tasks ★	Time-consuming but unimportant.	Don't waste effort – set aside for an unoccupied moment.

Whether we're juggling work, study, or personal projects, Szymanski suggests we ask, "What do I want my life to stand for?" By prioritizing what's most important, you can improve your efficiency and reduce your stress at the same time.

BALANCING ACT
HOW TO JUGGLE WORK AND HOME

Trying to strike a balance between home and work commitments is one of the most challenging stressors we face. The balance is rarely perfect, but maintaining a strong support network definitely helps.

Very few families these days can afford to have only one earner: usually both partners work – and single parents are shouldering an extra load of responsibility. It can be difficult to find a good balance between work and home, but the key is solidarity, mutual support, and being flexible and creative about time together.

Coping with overload

When there's too much to do at both work and home, a 2010 Canadian study published in the *Journal of Marriage and Family* identified a range of common strategies:

- **Scaling back:** cutting down on a perceived demand on our time, be it work, housework, or sleep.
- **Seeking support,** by turning to friends and family or paying for extra services such as cleaning.
- **Restructuring work roles,** adjusting a work schedule, for example, or limiting how much we take on.
- **Restructuring family roles,** by getting children and partners to help with chores, planning family time, and covering each other's jobs when necessary.

Women were found particularly likely to scale back on their relaxation time. Restructuring work roles was helpful when people were willing to do it, but men tended to be less willing than women. The most effective method was found to be restructuring roles within the family rather than work roles.

Fitting it in

As the Canadian study above found, men have a harder time restructuring their work situation than women. Gender roles can be limiting: a notable 1984 Canadian

The 2016 US Bureau of Labor statistics show most parents work. Children who are loved and well cared for learn how to create a healthy work–life balance.

48%
In almost half of the married couples, **both spouses worked**.

70.5%
More than **2 out of 3 women** – and 9 out of 10 men – **with children under 18** worked.

study, for instance, found that the most successful single parents tended to be those who took on an "androgynous" role in the family – that is, not letting stereotypes limit either their authority or their nurturing side.

For men finding it hard to strike a work–life balance, American management professor and working-parents advocate Scott Behson has advice that working mothers will find helpful too:

- **Use work breaks** – lunchtime, for example – to do small family tasks such as calling home or paying bills.
- **Arrange "time-shifting"** – if your workplace is reasonable about being flexible, leave work early or come in late in order to meet family obligations, and make up the time at evenings or weekends.
- **Identify "time holes"** at work, such as breaks, where you can fit in extra work to finish sooner.

Having to juggle family and work commitments will always be demanding, but how stressful it is can depend on how well supported you are, and how confident you feel about managing your time. Take advantage of any opportunities to get breaks from work so that you can maintain your communication and connections with your partner, give them as much support as possible, and appreciate one another for the efforts you all make. By doing so, you may very well find that you can find a healthy work–life balance as a family.

HOW TO COPE?

Sometimes the stress of juggling home and work responsibilities can be so challenging that we're not quite sure how to handle it. A 2005 study by American psychologist Gloria W. Bird created a helpful breakdown of coping methods – see whether any of these might be the solution you're looking for.

Coping method	Applied to work	Applied to home
Problem-focused coping as an individual	✔ Break a big task into smaller tasks. ✔ Prepare well. ✔ Work faster. ✔ Seek information and advice. ✔ Accept your own limitations.	✔ Speak up about your needs. ✔ Put aside time to be family-only – no phone calls, texts, guests, or other distractions. ✔ Set more realistic standards.
Emotion-focused coping as an individual	✔ Use positive self-talk. ✔ Withdraw from unsolvable problems. ✔ Use relaxation techniques. ✔ Maintain a calm, self-controlled public face.	✔ Keep your temper. ✔ Accept that different family members have different personalities and ideas. ✔ Exercise. ✔ Rest and relax.
Coping as a couple	✔ Take over chores and childcare when one of you has a work crisis. ✔ Act as a sounding board. ✔ Give advice. ✔ Draw out a partner who appears distressed.	✔ Make time to talk. ✔ Establish a united front. ✔ Avoid particularly difficult members of your extended family.
Coping as a team (with colleagues and with family)	✔ Create good relationships with colleagues. ✔ Offer space or distractions for stressed colleagues. ✔ Raise concerns with colleagues when necessary. ✔ Offer a sympathetic ear.	✔ Be a supportive family member. ✔ Be willing to accept support. ✔ Promote a family culture of "we can rely on each other".

WHY FREE TIME COUNTS

THE VALUE OF LEISURE

Stress is exhausting, and sometimes all we want to do in our spare time is chill out. However, research suggests that challenging hobbies may be a better way to replenish ourselves.

Do you love to paint, go rock-climbing, or play chess? These and other absorbing hobbies may help you to build a better buffer against stress.

Behavioural Activation

In the 1970s, a team led by American psychologist Peter Lewinsohn developed a theory known as "Behavioural Activation" (BA). Originally aimed at treating depression, BA may also help us to stay positive in the face of stress.

Whatever the source, stress can make life feel less rewarding. If that feeling permeates other aspects of our lives, we may withdraw from activities we usually enjoy – and reducing these rewarding experiences can, in turn, further heighten stress.

BA takes an outside-in approach to this problem: by engaging in activities we enjoy, we experience emotional rewards that lead to more positive thoughts and feelings.

⚲ PLEASURE AND MASTERY

"Vegging out" occasionally is not a bad idea, but sometimes the most refreshing way to counterbalance stress is to enjoy a challenge. Psychologists identify "pleasure" and "mastery" experiences as key to wellbeing. In this context, pleasure means an activity you enjoy, while mastery means an activity that also makes you feel competent and enhances your self-esteem. Both help to create resilience, which can help you withstand difficult times.

Q DON'T LET STRESS STOP YOU

When life is difficult, we may feel we don't have the time or energy to do the things that usually relax us or cheer us up. As American Behavioural Activation founder Peter Lewinsohn noted, this can create a vicious circle: by letting stress disrupt our usual pleasurable activities, we create a new behaviour pattern that is less rewarding – which leaves us with fewer pleasurable experiences to counter-balance. By making the time to do the things you love, especially during a stressful period, you'll have fun and you'll reduce the stress.

We experience stress, which undermines our motivation and energy

We stop doing the things we enjoy

We experience less sense of pleasure and mastery in life

TRAPPED IN A BEHAVIOUR CYCLE

We do less to manage our lives

We feel unhappier and more helpless

We become less confident and more self-critical

Under stress, it's in your best interest to keep doing what you enjoy or what makes you feel good about yourself.

Optimal experiences

An enjoyable and interesting challenge may leave you feeling even more energized than resting when you feel tired. Using your BA skills can create what Hungarian psychologist Mihály Csíkszentmihályi called "optimal experiences" – that is, moments of flow (see pp.174–175) in which you feel so engaged, powerful, and confident that the stresses of life feel less intense. Make space for challenges in your spare time: they can help you build your resilience against stress.

TRACK YOUR SATISFACTION

If leisure leaves you feeling unfulfilled, try this: for two months, keep a simple diary of your free time, and note which activities give you the most pleasure and mastery (see opposite). Then make a point of scheduling more of those activities: that's an excellent way to build your stress resilience.

Day	Activity	Pleasure (points out of 10)	Mastery (points out of 10)
Friday	Cooked dinner	4	7
	Browsed online	5	3
Saturday	Went jogging	3	9
	Practised my guitar	7	8
	Watched a movie	8	2

FIGHTING FIT

THE ROLE OF EXERCISE

One of the most powerful ways to fight stress is also one of the simplest: exercise. Besides the obvious physical benefits, exercise can also help us to feel calmer, more resilient, and better able to cope with life's challenges.

Stress activates the body and the mind – raising the heart rate, for instance, and sharpening our focus. Exercise does this too, which is why it helps us to cope: putting the body under pressure gives it practice in coping with stress and recovering from it.

Balancing our stress chemicals

When we feel threatened, levels of the stress hormone cortisol and the neurotransmitter noradrenaline rise as the body prepares either to confront or to flee from a threat (see pp.20–21). Exercise, too, requires cortisol and noradrenaline – and using these brain chemicals when we exercise can lower our response to day-to-day stress.

By reducing the amount of cortisol we produce through regular exercise, we can also reduce the risk of chronic stress-related illnesses, such as heart disease and depression. This is a key reason why regular exercise protects our long-term physical and mental wellbeing.

Improving mental health

Exercise also tends to make us happier, by stimulating the steady release of two major brain chemicals: serotonin, which creates a positive mood and antidepressant effect, and norepinephrine, which reduces pain and anxiety. There is a well-established link between regular exercise and the reduction of depression symptoms. In fact, many healthcare providers routinely recommend exercise for the treatment of mild to moderate depression. For milder forms, a 2013

✅ HOW MUCH SHOULD I EXERCISE?

For healthy adults, doctors generally recommend the amount of exercise shown below. You can also create a regime that mixes vigorous and moderate exercise every week; one minute of vigorous exercise is approximately equivalent to two minutes of moderate exercise. If you have any health concerns, ask your doctor to help with drawing up a safe exercise plan.

WEEKLY MINIMUM #1   OR   WEEKLY MINIMUM #2

150 minutes
Moderate aerobic activity
such as fast walking, swimming,
cycling, or gardening
2 times per week
Strength exercises
such as yoga, sit-ups,
or weight lifting

75 minutes
Vigorous aerobic activity
such as running, martial arts,
football, or other energetic sports
2 times per week
Strength exercises
(see left)

◉ BUILDING A RESILIENT BRAIN

Exercise can build our emotional resilience. In a 2013 Princeton study, lab mice were given an exercise wheel for six weeks and were then briefly exposed to a stressor (cold water). The researchers found that exercise has a positive impact on the brain in two important ways:

- **It promotes the growth of new brain cells** in brain regions necessary for emotional regulation and moderating the response to stress. This is a medium- to long-term effect.

- **It also releases GABA,** a neurotransmitter that plays a central role in reducing anxiety in the short-term.

In other words, exercise gives us a quick boost of calming chemicals in the present and builds our long-term ability to manage stress in the future.

British review of 39 separate studies confirmed that exercise can be as effective at reducing symptoms as medication or psychotherapy. Since depression is strongly associated with chronic stress, a regular exercise regime may help maintain mental health when times are tough.

Protection from distress
Exercise can reduce the impact of stressful experiences. A 2013 American study tested the response of healthy young adults when they were shown upsetting pictures

after either resting or exercising: those who had just been resting experienced elevated stress levels, but those who had exercised remained calm. When we encounter emotionally stressful situations, exercise can moderate our reaction.

Boosting efficiency
Facing more tasks than we feel we can handle is a common source of stress. A 2012 New Zealand study found that exercise improves "executive function" – the ability to think critically, think ahead, organize

our thoughts, and manage our behaviour. This ability is crucial to problem-focused coping, which is improved with regular exercise.

What sort of exercise works best? Anything that gets you moving, raises your heart rate, and potentially raises a sweat can help (see "How much" above). The important thing is to choose an exercise regime you enjoy so you're more likely to stick with it. Ideally, it becomes a rewarding daily activity that helps to build your physical and mental stamina and emotional resilience.

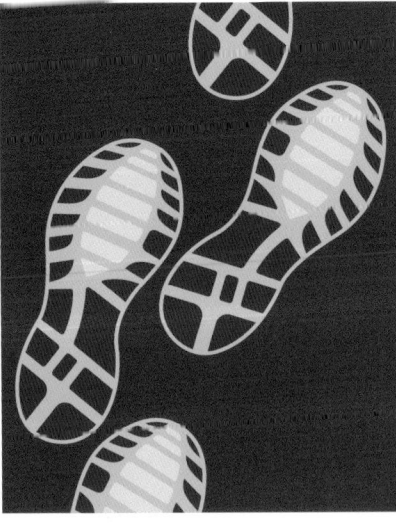

THE WALKING CURE

HOW TO DE-STRESS WITH A STROLL

Exercise has been proven by multiple studies to be helpful for reducing stress – and walking is an especially calming activity. If you need to relax, make time in your life for a ramble.

While many of us find it hard to make time to go to the gym, walking is a form of exercise available almost anywhere, be it getting off the bus a few stops early or strolling around the block on your lunch break. It's also an excellent stress-reliever.

> Walking seems to have a special relation to **creativity** ... outdoors or on a treadmill.
>
> **Marily Oppezzo and Daniel L. Schwartz**
> Psychologists at Stanford University

Benefits of walking

According to doctors and psychologists, some good reasons to take a walk include:

✔ **Walking quickly** is aerobic exercise that helps to maintain physical and mental health (pp.152–153).
✔ **Walking releases brain chemicals** that help to lower the level of stress hormones, such as cortisol (pp.20–21).
✔ **Walking promotes healthy new brain cell growth,** which improves mood.
✔ **Walking can be a social activity,** which promotes supportive bonds (pp.176–179).
✔ **Walking is free.**

In short, walking is an accessible and easy way to reduce stress.

IMPROVED MEMORY

20%

According to an American study published in 2008, no matter where you walk or what the weather's like, **walking improves memory and attention by up to 20%**.

Focusing your mind

A particularly good opportunity to practise mindfulness (see pp.132–135) is while you're walking. In a German study published in 2012, volunteers aged 18–65 who suffered from high levels of stress were asked to try a mindfulness-based walking programme. Within four weeks, the majority of participants reported feeling significantly calmer.

If you're keen to try some mindful walking, the key dos and don'ts are as follows:

- **Focus your attention** on your physical sensations while walking; observe them without comment or judgment.
- **Don't try to think about anything** except the feeling of walking.
- **If you're troubled** by an uncomfortable thought, focus your attention on your breathing until the moment passes.

Freeing your mind

As well as providing an opportuntiy to practise mindfulness, there's also an opposite benefit to walking: it can be a good time to practise "mindlessness". As American psychologists Rebecca McMillan, Scott Barry Kaufman, and Jerome Singer argued in 2013, "zoning out" can be beneficial. "Positive constructive daydreaming", as they term it, allows the mind to relax its usual controls and make connections that might not have been made consciously.

The result might lead us to find solutions to stressful problems or produce creative ideas that provide insight, relieve stress, and impart a sense of satisfaction. Indeed, a 2014 American study found that subjects who walked before a creativity test showed more innovative thinking than those who'd been sitting. Being engaged in a low-demand physical activity such as walking is ideal for creating a state of constructive daydreaming.

Tune out the din

As American positive psychologist Robert Biswas-Diener also points out, the daydreaming that walking

encourages can also protect you from a stressful environment. Walking in a natural environment has been shown to be especially helpful (see pp.98–99), but wherever you choose to go for a stroll, letting your attention wander can help to protect you from the stressful effects of living and working in crowded or noisy surroundings.

Whether you go for a walk in the woods or just down the street, meditating or daydreaming, walking can be a positive form of low-strain exercise that relaxes your mind as well as your body.

✅ THE PERFECT POSTURE

Whether you're out for a leisurely stroll or a power-walk, holding your body correctly can make walking more comfortable and efficient. Follow these tips and good posture will soon become second nature:

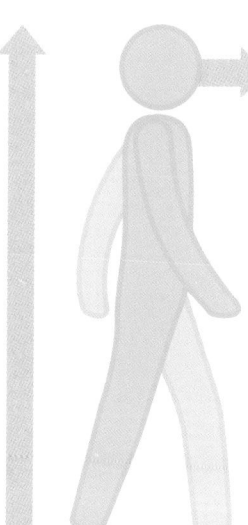

1 **Back upright,** leaning neither forwards or backwards.

2 **Eyes forward,** focused about 6 metres (20 ft) ahead of you.

3 **Chin parallel** with the ground to minimize neck strain.

4 **Shoulders relaxed.** Shrug once, and let your shoulders fall into a comfortable position.

5 **Stomach slightly pulled in** to brace the core muscles in your abdomen and lower back.

6 **Bottom slightly tucked in** to stop your back from arching.

7 **Phone and gadgets put away,** so you aren't tempted to walk staring down at your hand.

Walking with a good posture is easier on your body, and a less strained body makes for a less strained state of mind.

INCREASED ENERGY

20%

Feeling too tired to cope? Another 2008 American study reports that **walking regularly** can **increase energy levels** by 20% and decrease fatigue by 65%.

MINDFUL MOVEMENT
DE-STRESSING WITH YOGA AND TAI CHI

A popular recommendation when you're feeling stressed is to try a class that teaches meditative, low-impact exercise practices. If the idea appeals to you, research suggests it may indeed make you calmer.

When you're stressed, finding a regular time during the week to do a calming activity can really help. If you're looking for something that might fit the bill, consider yoga and tai chi classes. Both practices are popular and doctors sometimes recommend them to their stressed-out patients – but what does the science say?

Assessing the benefits
There are certainly health benefits to yoga and tai chi: both are low-impact forms of physical exercise, which is proven to be beneficial for stress management (see pp.152–153). Both are usually done in a class: if you seek out a friendly group, it can be a good way to widen your support network.

Medical research finds that yoga and tai chi, if practised regularly, also have several de-stressing effects on our biochemistry:

■ **Increasing** levels of mood-balancing neurotransmitters, such as dopamine and serotonin

> There are times when you just need to kind of **get moving** and work through the body.
>
> **Melanie Greenberg**
> American psychology professor and yoga expert

- **Releasing** pain-killing hormones called endorphins

- **Lowering** stress-provoked levels of brain chemicals such as noradrenaline and cortisol.

The evidence that regular practice of yoga and tai chi can indeed help regulate our stress response is mounting. A 2013 German meta-analysis, for instance, found some evidence that yoga helps people recover from depression, and a 2014 international meta-analysis reported evidence that tai chi aids stress management for many different population groups.

In general, the research on yoga and tai chi is cautiously optimistic: medical studies seem to support their benefits for stress relief – if you attend a class and find you feel better afterwards, then you are probably on to a good thing.

Safe practice

Deep breathing – which is central to yoga and tai chi – is generally relaxing, but one small warning: as a 2005 American study published in the *Journal of Alternative and Complementary Medicine* noted, over-breathing during yogic exercises can sometimes produce side effects such as dizziness, lightheadedness, or irritability – and can exacerbate an existing mental illness. Make sure you find a reliable teacher so that you don't overdo it, and seek medical advice if you suffer any uncomfortable effects.

Yoga and tai chi should be pleasurable, if mildly challenging, so practise safely and enjoy the de-stressing effects.

A BEGINNER'S GUIDE

Tai chi, which began as a defensive martial art, is strongly influenced by traditional Chinese culture and philosophy. Through flowing circular and spiral movements, you balance the flow of *qi* (vital energy) through the body, creating a healthy balance of active *yang* and receptive *yin*. Tai chi brings deep awareness to the breath, slowing our movements below the usual hasty pace of life to create a calmer state of mind and spirit.

Yoga originates in India, and in its traditional form it incorporates ethics, spirituality, meditation, and physical stretches. Contemporary, western yoga tends to focus on *asanas* (postures), *pranayama* (breathing), and *dyana* (meditation). Yoga's strong emphasis on breathing and mental focus generates a mood that is at once energized and relaxed.

Both practices encourage mindfulness (see pp.132–135), which research has shown to be a powerful stress-reliever – so if you'd like to combine some physical activity with your meditation, they're well worth a try.

HEALTHY BODY, HEALTHY MIND

Exercise is highly de-stressing (see pp.152–153), and it's always easier to face the challenges of life if you feel fit and confident in your body. The physical benefits of yoga and tai chi include:

- **Exercising** all the major muscle groups and joints.

- **Strengthening bone density,** reducing the chances of osteoporosis.

- **Improving the condition of joints,** balance, and coordination.

- **Promoting deep breathing,** which enhances lung capacity and improves circulation.

STRESS AND FOOD
EATING UNDER PRESSURE

Few of us feel good about ourselves if we eat unhealthily and gain weight. Under pressure, controlling our diet can be even more difficult, which can worsen the stress. How do we build a more positive relationship with food?

In cultures that associate beauty with being thin, food can become inherently stressful. A better understanding of our own impulses can help us to develop a more positive relationship with food, even when we're under stress.

Stress eating

There are sound biological reasons why, under stress, many of us are prone to overeating. Stress prompts the body to release the hormone cortisol, which stimulates appetite. The body has evolved to deal with physical threats such as avoiding predatory animals: cortisol prompts us to build up the body's food stores in preparation for fight or flight. This explains why we comfort eat: it's not greed, but the body's inherent response to stress.

Cortisol is also associated with wanting junk food. A 2001 American study found that "high cortisol reactors" – volunteers who released higher amounts of cortisol in response to a perceived threat – ate similar amounts to "low cortisol reactors" in calm circumstances, but ate significantly more sugar and fat when subjected to stress.

> **Stress** alone can cause us to **put on fat** by altering many metabolic functions.
>
> **Denise Cummins**
> American psychology professor

UNDER PRESSURE

80%

Under stress, some people eat more and some eat less, but according to 2013 American review, **4 in 5** people's eating habits change under stress. In tough times, the odds predict **healthy eating** will be a **challenge**, so take extra care over your food choices.

American exercise scientist Christine Maglione-Garves has also observed that cortisol increases the storage of belly fat: calorie for calorie, stressed people gain more weight.

A 2005 American study found that weight gain may be a way of turning off our stress response: lab rats kept in stressful conditions showed a drop in cortisol once they'd accumulated a certain amount of belly fat. What's more, a 2009 American study found that when monkeys were fed a high-calorie diet, monkeys living under greater stress gained more weight than the less stressed monkeys.

In short, if you're prone to feeling guilty or insecure because of your diet or body image, try to be kinder to yourself. Stress is likely a major contributor, and self-loathing only makes you feel worse. Your first step should be to reduce your stress by ceasing to blame yourself.

Should I diet?

Healthy eating is good for both our physical and psychological wellbeing, so if you'd like to shift to a more balanced diet, that's

THE SNACKING IMPULSE

Comfort eating is a **common reaction to stress**. In the 2017 stress survey by the American Psychological Association, around **1 in 4 women** and **1 in 5 men** said they engaged in stress eating.

26% ♀ women
18% ♂ men

probably a good idea: ask a doctor or a dietician to give you some pointers on how to get started.

However, it's wise to be sceptical of extreme diets that promise you rapid weight loss in a matter of weeks: multiple studies confirm that these are neither nutritious nor a stress-busting solution. Crash diets of this kind don't address the underlying causes of the weight gain and so their effects don't last.

Stress by numbers

The trouble with dieting is partly that counting calories can be, in itself, a stressful activity. A 2010 American study tested its subjects by restricting them to 1,200 calories a day for three weeks: those who were required to monitor their calories reported that they felt more stressed than those who ate less without monitoring their calories. However, simply eating less wasn't

🔍 FEELING HUNGRY?

The "Intuitive Eating" nutrition movement founded in the US by dieticians Evelyn Tribole and Elyse Resch advises that we distinguish between "stomach hunger" and "mouth hunger":

STOMACH HUNGER

A physical craving for food when we need to top up our calories. **Best satisfied** by wholesome food, consumed calmly, attentively, and steadily.

MOUTH HUNGER

A psychological craving to taste and chew. **Best satisfied** by small amounts of the more stimulating foods with a rich flavour or interesting texture.

Stress eating is more associated with "mouth hunger", so if you have to snack between meals, choose something small but tasty and pause to savour it properly. Most importantly, be sure to eat regular meals during times of stress.

stress-free: on the contrary, whether they counted calories or not, the participants who were on the restricted diet had elevated levels of the stress hormone cortisol.

For more effective solutions to stress-eating that will benefit both your physical and psychological wellbeing, see overleaf.

»

» Why crash diets fail

Evidence suggests that too much calorie restriction reprograms the brain to be more prone to binge eating. In an American study in 2010, some lab mice were given a restricted diet for a short period and then given access to as much food as they wanted. When subjected to stress, the mice that had been "dieting" consumed significantly more calories than the mice who had been allowed to eat freely. The scientists speculated that the strain of having their calories restricted had rewired their brains, making them more sensitive to stress and less able to control their reward-seeking behaviour – in this case, comfort eating.

This doesn't mean that if you've ever been on a diet you're doomed to endless weight gain. It does mean, though, that if you've gained some weight during a stressful period, a crash diet is likely to do you more harm than good. Tackle your stress levels first, and make healthy eating a longer-term, less guilt-ridden priority.

✓ BETTER SOLUTIONS

If you have been prone to comfort eating and you're less than pleased with your body shape as a result, what should you do? Research suggests that the best solution is to be kind to yourself: stress and food can be a challenging mix, but the more gently you treat yourself, the better your chances of a successful and healthy lifestyle change.

RESPECT YOUR HUNGER
and your feelings. Dieticians and nutrition therapists of the "Intuitive Eating" movement point out that fighting your feelings only strengthens your cravings. Eat when you're hungry, stop when you're full, and find new ways to comfort and nurture yourself that don't depend on snacking (see below).

BECOME MORE ACCEPTING
of your body image and try to reduce your perfectionism (pp.34–35, 68–69). A 2008 American study found that people with high levels of perfectionism, especially towards their own bodies, were most prone to alternating between dieting and bingeing, but a more self-tolerant attitude and greater faith in one's own efficacy (pp.18–19) made food less stressful to manage.

AVOID THE STRESS OF RIGID RESTRICTIONS.
A 2007 American review of weight programmes found that up to 64% of people who'd lost weight on a diet gained it back, and more, once their diet ended. It's more effective to focus on eating nutritious food over the long term.

TRY NEW WAYS OF RELAXING.
In a 2009 study in New Zealand, participants managed to lose a little weight without dieting: the group's methods included PMR (p.131), deep abdominal breathing (p.129), and yoga (p.157). Lowering your stress in this way can reduce the impulse to comfort eat.

CHOOSE A WAY OF EATING
that you're happy to stick with. As American psychologist and mindful eating expert Melanie Greenberg puts it, "Healthy living is something positive that can add pleasure and energy to your life". See opposite for some healthy options.

KNOW YOUR GI

All food boosts blood sugar, but high-GI foods boost it faster. The glycaemic index (GI) is a measure of how quickly a food is absorbed and metabolized. Under stress, we often crave a rapid shot of energy and tend to opt for high-GI snacks, but these create a blood sugar crash a few hours later that can leave us feeling worse. To help keep your mood steady, ensure your meal provides a healthy proportion of low-GI foods as part of a balanced diet:

50%
Vegetables, salad, fruit:
include low-GI choices such as broccoli, cabbage, salad leaves, peas, carrots, tomatoes, cherries, grapefruit, dried apricots, apples, pears, stawberries, and oranges

25%
Protein:
often low-GI, such as lean meat, fish, eggs, lentils, beans, and other legumes

25%
Carbohydrates:
low-GI choices are sweet potato, brown rice, and wholewheat pasta

STRESS-BUSTING FOODS

Prebiotic foods, which encourage the growth of "friendly" gut bacteria, can be good for your health – and according to research by Irish scientists John Cryan and Ted Dinan published in 2017, they also lower stress levels – at least in mice. Human trials are in the pipeline, but in the meantime, the recommended foods tend to be healthy, so try adding them to your menu as part of a balanced diet. Particularly good choices include:

✔ Artichokes
✔ Asparagus
✔ Bananas
✔ Chicory
✔ Garlic
✔ Leeks
✔ Milk
✔ Oats
✔ Onions
✔ Wheat

THE MEDITERRANEAN SOLUTION

The traditional Western diet – high in sugar, fatty meat, and processed food – is bad for our mental health: an Australian study published in 2015 found it can shrink the brain's hippocampus, which is associated with mood regulation. In a 2013 Spanish study, the traditional Mediterranean diet, supplemented with nuts, resulted in mentally healthier, less stressed subjects.

Try building your meals around:

Wholegrains rather than white bread, rice, or pasta

Fish, especially oily fish such as mackerel, which are rich in omega-3, a natural anti-depressant

Lean meat, preferably white meat like chicken

Olive oil for cooking and dressing

Fruit instead of cakes and sweets

Nuts, such as walnuts, hazlenuts, and almonds

If you're drinking alcohol, choose red wine

A GOOD NIGHT'S SLEEP
BEATING INSOMNIA

When life is busy, we may think sleep is wasted time, but in fact, it's crucial for our health. America's National Sleep Foundation notes that chronic insomnia – defined as trouble sleeping for at least three nights a week over a period of at least three months – is associated with a wide range of physical and mental health risks. Well-rested individuals gain more benefits from exercise, find it easier to regulate their emotions, and have lower anxiety and better cognitive functioning. A good night's sleep is clearly important, so if you've been lying awake, check your "sleep hygiene" (see opposite) and try some CBT techniques (see overleaf).

HOW COMMON?

1 in 3

According to a 1991 study by America's National Sleep Foundation **1 in 3 people have insomnia** at some point in their lives.

1 in 10

A 2002 study published in the international journal *Sleep Medicine Reviews* reported that **10–15%** of adults have **persistent sleep problems**.

Insomnia and stress can be a vicious circle: we lie awake because we're tense, and get more tense because we can't sleep. If you're struggling to get enough rest, CBT offers some techniques to help you.

Eight hours?

It's common to hear that eight hours is the perfect night's rest, but in fact, people vary in their individual needs (see below). A 2015 study published in *Sleep Health* advises we think of a sleep spectrum: you may fall on the higher or lower end. Be aware of your quality of sleep as well as quantity – six hours of sound sleep can be more restful than eight hours of fitful sleep. And we usually need more rest if we've built up a "sleep debt" from previous nights.

Sleep debt

As a 2007 Finnish study found, the effects of sleep deprivation are cumulative. One bad night will do you little harm, but three or four consecutive bad nights increases the stress hormone cortisol and raises your blood pressure: too much wakefulness creates a "sleep debt". Although it isn't easy to catch up with lost sleep, if you've had a few late nights – for instance, working long hours in order to make a deadline – you can solve the problem with some early nights. However, if you're having chronic trouble falling asleep, you may need a more intensive course of action (see overleaf). Even if you're busy, you'll be more productive if you get enough sleep. **»**

HOW MUCH SLEEP DO I NEED?

Most adults benefit from more sleep than they usually get. This chart shows the average number of hours most people need in order to function at their best.

Age	Hours of sleep per day				
Newborn baby (0-3 months)		11-13	**14-17**	18-19	
Infant (4-11 months)	10-11	**12-15**	16-18		
Toddler (1-2 years)	9-10	**11-14**	15-16		
Young child (3-5 years)	8-9	**10-13**	14		
Child (6-13 years)	7-8	**9-11**	12		
Teenager (14-17 years)	7	**8-10**	11		
Young adult (18-25 years)	6	**7-9**	10-11		
Adult (26-64 years)	6	**7-9**	10		
Older adult (65 and above)	5-6	**7-8**	9		

Too few hours   May be appropriate   Recommended range   Too many hours

SLEEP HYGIENE

If your sleep problem is mild, start by addressing your sleep hygiene:

- **Don't use your bed** for daytime activities such as reading or watching TV; that way, your body will know it's a place for sleep.

- **Take vigorous exercise** in the morning, or more relaxing exercise such as gentle yoga in the evening (pp.152–157).

- **Don't nap** during the day unless your sleepiness poses a risk to safety – if it does, try to limit your naps to under 30 minutes.

- **Avoid** alcohol, caffeine, chocolate, and nicotine after noon and spicy meals in the evening.

- **Keep your fluid intake** moderate near bedtime so that your bladder won't wake you during the night.

- **Make your bedroom** a pleasant and calming place, and ensure your bed is comfortable.

- **Have a peaceful** bedtime routine: for instance, switch off electronic devices, which can be over-stimulating, and read or listen to calming music instead.

This trains your body to expect nighttime to be relaxing, and breaks the association between your bed and insomnia. If following these tips doesn't seem to work, try adding Stimulus Control Therapy or Sleep Compression Therapy (overleaf).

»CBT for insomnia

The goal of CBT is to improve mood and reduce anxiety by altering thoughts and behaviours. CBT-I is dedicated to treating insomnia, and is recommended by the American Academy of Sleep Medicine. The principle is based on classical conditioning – put simply, insomnia trains us to associate bedtime with anxiety, and this is a habit we must unlearn. Sleep Compression Therapy and Stimulus Control Therapy (see opposite), coupled with good "sleep hygiene" (see p.163), have been found to help many insomnia sufferers.

Seeking help

If these strategies don't offer relief, consult your doctor: you might have a sleep disorder or underlying health condition that should be addressed. Sleeping pills tend to become less effective over time and can be addictive: a GP will usually only prescribe two to four weeks' worth. Instead, your doctor may refer you to a CBT or sleep therapy program that could prove helpful.

Beating sleeplessness can take time and determination, but with patience and the methods described on these pages, you should be able to get a proper night's rest.

BIRD SPOTTING

When are you at your best? According to American sleep researchers Michael Smolensky and Lynne Lamberg, people fall into the three groups shown below. Hummingbirds are the best at coping with the odd late night or early start, but even they need to pay a sleep debt. If you're an owl or a lark, it's particularly important to plan a schedule that ensures you get enough rest.

10% **are larks**, at their best in the early morning.

70% **are hummingbirds**, comfortable with being more flexible.

20% **are owls**, at their best late at night.

Q UNDERLYING ISSUES

Insomnia can stem from a variety of root causes – medical, psychological, and situational (such as jet lag or shift work). Consider your worst periods of wakefulness: they may give a clue to your biggest stressors, which can be the first step towards identifying long-term solutions.

- **Initial insomnia:** trouble falling asleep – frequently associated with anxiety (pp.204–207).

- **Middle insomnia:** waking up through the night – may be associated with medical illness, pain, or depression (pp.202–203).

- **Terminal insomnia:** waking too early – frequently associated with depression (pp.202–203).

COUNTING THE COST

30%

In America's National Health Interview Survey (NHIS) published in 2010, **30% of workers** said they regularly **don't get enough sleep**, which is associated with serious health issues.

$2,000

Tired people are **less productive**. A 2010 American study estimated that fatigue-related losses cost businesses **$2,000 per worker** per year.

✅ STIMULUS CONTROL THERAPY

According to a 1998 study published in the *Behavior Modification* journal and a 2006 study by the American Academy of Sleep Medicine, Stimulus Control Therapy is the most effective single treatment for chronic insomnia. In order to condition yourself to feel properly sleepy at bedtime, you need to make sure you only get into bed when you're feeling close to sleep already:

1 **Stay up** until you feel properly sleepy. Bear in mind that tired and sleepy are not the same: look out for yawning, heavy eyelids, and a nodding head.

2 **Don't clock-watch** – if there's a clock in the bedroom, hide or remove it if you can, and place your mobile phone out of reach.

3 **If you're still awake** after 15–20 minutes (use your best guess, not a clock), get up again. Leave your bedroom and do something boring or calming, such as reading or doing a relaxation technique. Avoid using any

electronic devices, including the TV, since these will make you even more wakeful.

4 **Stay up** until you begin to feel sleepy again, then go back to bed. Don't check what time it is.

5 **Repeat these steps** until you fall asleep.

6 **Rise at the same time** each day, regardless of how you slept. (Again, don't clock-watch – use a preset alarm on your phone.) This encourages your body to accept a regular routine and you should sleep better the following night.

✅ CALCULATE YOUR SLEEP EFFICIENCY

Insomniacs need to improve their sleep efficiency – that is, reduce the amount of hours spent in bed but awake. To calculate yours, the sum is:

$$\frac{\text{hours spent asleep}}{\text{hours spent in bed}} \times 100 = \text{sleep efficiency percentage}$$

For instance, if you spend six hours asleep and nine hours in bed, your sleep efficiency would be 67%. Sleep Compression Therapy advises that for insomniacs, the goal should be around 85%, so that nearly all your time in bed is spent asleep.

⬛ SLEEP COMPRESSION THERAPY

While many factors contribute to insomnia, low sleep efficiency (see below left) is one of the best areas you can control. Sleep Compression Therapy (SCT) trains your body to sleep by creating a "take it or leave it" pattern of behaviour: you compress your sleep time to a few hours, and even if you don't get enough sleep during that time, you still have to get out of bed at the same time each day. Your brain eventually learns that your time in bed is limited, so it has to make the most of it. To practise SCT:

1 Pick a length of time to sleep – less than you need, but slightly more than you are currently getting. The usual time is 6 hours.

2 Pick your wake-up time, and count back 6 hours to work out your bedtime. Make yourself stick to these times and avoid daytime naps.

3 After 5–10 days, you should find you sleep for the full 6 hours. Now make bedtime 30 minutes earlier.

4 After another 5–10 days, once you're sleeping 6.5 hours, make your bedtime another 30 minutes earlier. Continue the process until you're getting the sleep you need (see p.163).

THE SIMPLE LIFE
DECLUTTERING HOME AND HABITS

When life is stressful, it can be hard to keep on top of your living space. A cluttered environment, though, is likely to make you feel more stressed: clearing some of the clutter may be a step towards feeling better.

We live in a culture where it's all too easy to get overwhelmed by our stuff, and we aren't always good at getting rid of it. Sorting out the mess can lower our stress levels.

Clutter and the brain

Mess tends to affect our thinking. A set of studies at the University of Minnesota and published in 2013 asked volunteers to make various decisions after filling out dummy questionnaires in rooms that were either clear or cluttered:

- **Asked to donate** money to charity, 82% of subjects from the clean room did, as opposed to only 47% from the messy room.
- **Offered the choice** of a candy bar or an apple, the tidy-room participants were more likely to pick the healthier option.
- **Tested for creativity,** the messy-room participants came up with more inventive ideas.
- **Given a choice** between a new and a recognizable product, the tidy-room subjects preferred the familiar choice and the messy-room subjects the new one.

In short, untidiness may make us more creative, but it also makes us less responsible. If you're facing a stressful situation that calls for hard work to resolve it, a disorderly environment may discourage you.

When our environment is chaotic, it can also make it difficult for us to focus. Using fMRI brain scans, a 2011 American study at the Princeton University Neuroscience Institute discovered that people living and working in a visually busy environment found it more difficult to process information. Clutter is visual information, and having too much clutter in our sight lines overloads our attention – concentrating on anything becomes more stressful.

CAN'T BEAR TO GET RID OF IT?

75%

A 2012 American study found that 75% of middle-class families had garages they **couldn't park their cars in** – there was too much stuff…

11 million

In 2007, the *New York Times* reported that more than 11 million American households were **renting storage space** for excess stuff.

✔ HOW TO DECLUTTER?

Need to clear some stuff? Try some tips from professional organizers:

1 Out of sight, out of mind. With items you're not sure of, put them in a box out of sight. If at the end of the week or month you haven't thought about them, get rid of them without opening the box.

2 Start small but thorough. Pick one place to clear, such as a cupboard, clear it thoroughly, and don't stop until you've dropped everything off at the charity shop or recycling centre.

3 You are not your possessions. Don't tie your identity to your stuff: you are still you without it.

4 Treasure people, not stuff. Giving up an item associated with a person is not giving up your relationship with that person. You don't have to keep their every gift to be connected with them.

5 Have faith in the future. Holding onto objects "just in case" is a sign of anxiety; try to trust that you will be able to cope without them.

6 Distinguish between aspiration and actual use. Clothes you hope to fit into some day, books you haven't read – these are reminders of past dissatisfaction rather than a source of pleasure. Let them go.

7 Don't blame yourself for the mess: guilt is stressful, and makes it harder to get rid of things.

8 Forget perfectionism. If you expect your house to look like a magazine shoot, you'll only feel permanently stressed. Let reasonably tidy be good enough.

Why is it hard to declutter?

Some classic studies developed by Nobel Prize-winning Israeli-American psychologist Daniel Kahneman and his colleagues in the 1970s–90s may hold the key:

- **Prospect theory.** We feel losses more keenly than the reward we experience from equivalent gains: losing £5 causes us more pain than finding £5 gives us pleasure.
- **The endowment effect.** When something becomes ours, we value it more than we would an identical object that did not belong to us – even if we've only owned it for a few minutes.

No wonder parting with excess possessions can be difficult: our brains are built to resist the idea. A 2012 study at Yale University found that in hoarders – people driven to acquire objects and unable to dispose of anything, to the point where their homes become unsafe – getting rid of their own possessions actually lit up areas of the brain associated with physical pain. Clutter may be stressful, but so too is de-cluttering.

If you feel your stuff is getting on top of you, try some of the decluttering tips above. They can help you develop a more comfortable process for creating a low-stress environment. You don't need to get rid of everything – you may even be more creative if you keep some things – but a clearer environment can calm your mind.

STRONG ENOUGH

HOW TO MANAGE YOUR WILLPOWER

Have you noticed that when you're under strain, you're more likely to act on impulse or make rash decisions? Understanding how your willpower flags can help you stay sensible even when you're stressed and tired.

Stress triggers a "fight or flight" response, but in most stressful situations we shouldn't literally attack someone or run away from a problem. However, resisting this impulse can drain our willpower, which is not an infinite resource. Willpower can be built up, though, so long as we recognize what it is and how it can help.

Ego depletion

According to American psychologist Roy Baumeister, who pioneered the theory of ego depletion, resisting impulsive decisions and coping with stress requires energy. If our energy reserves get too low, we find it more difficult to stay resolute until we've rested – as numerous studies show:

- In Baumeister's 1998 experiment, subjects who were asked to resist a cookie and eat a radish gave up on an unsolvable puzzle after 8 minutes on average – whereas those who were allowed a cookie persisted for 19 minutes.
- According to a 2005 American study, people tended to drink more alcohol on days when they had to exercise high self-control.
- In a 2010 American study, impoverished shoppers who had to make tough decisions about what they could afford to buy were more likely to eat unhealthy snacks while they were shopping.

Self-control, like a muscle, gets tired: resisting temptation, pressing on despite frustration, and coping with stress all put willpower to the test. Stress can drain the energy on which healthy choices depend.

Keeping our strength up

If stress is depleting your energy but you want to maintain self-control, what can you do? There are a number of options:

✔ **Believe in your own strength.** A 2010 Stanford study of ego depletion found that if the researchers primed people with a questionnaire that subtly implied willpower is finite, they were more likely to show decreased willpower, while those given a less discouraging questionnaire did not. Baumeister noted that self-affirmation may benefit mildly depleted people, but seriously depleted people need a proper rest before taking on major challenges. If you're only feeling slightly stressed, though, a more empowered attitude can help.

✔ **Practise.** A 2010 study by American psychologist Mark Muraven studied people trying to quit smoking and found that subjects who spent two weeks performing small but regular acts of self-control were significantly more successful than subjects who hadn't.

✔ **Calm your mind.** A 2012 Swiss study suggested that "a brief period of mindfulness meditation may serve as a quick and efficient strategy to foster self-control" when you're feeling depleted (see pp132–135).

Stress can wear anyone down and it is more challenging to exercise self-control when times are tough – but through practice and pleasure you can help your willpower to endure.

EATING FOR WILLPOWER

Exercising self-control takes energy, which means it burns glucose – the sugar in our blood that is the body's main source of energy. To keep your willpower steady, try to eat more foods from the lower end of the glycaemic index (see p.161): studies show that low-GI foods keep your blood sugar steadier between meals. This protects you against periods when your willpower weakens – including the will to resist stress-induced snacking between meals.

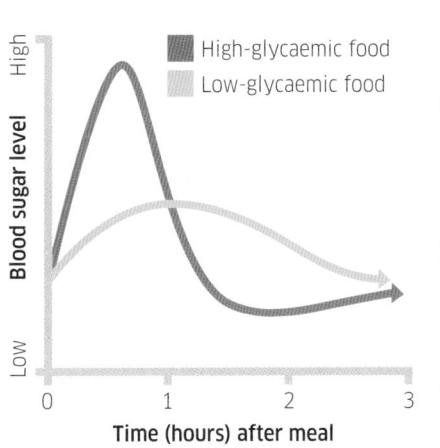

High-glycaemic food
Low-glycaemic food

Blood sugar level — High / Low

Time (hours) after meal

FEELING FEEBLE?

According to a 2011 report by the American Psychological Association, 27% of people say their **greatest obstacle to change** is a lack of willpower. If you feel guilty about being "weak-willed", you are not alone – and you're probably **not as weak as you think**.

🔍 LOW ON WILLPOWER?

The biggest triggers for failures of self-control, according to a 2011 American study, are these:

■ **A bad mood.** For example, "What's the point in quitting smoking? It's not as if anyone cares whether I'm healthy."

■ **Letting a minor indulgence** break your resolve, so you end up bingeing. "I'm meant to cut back on sugar, but now that the tub of ice-cream is open…"

■ **An overwhelming temptation.** "I said I'd cut back on my drinking, but it's a free bar and everyone else is drinking too."

■ **Having impaired self-control** due to alcohol or ego depletion, for example. "I've been good all week, but now I'm going to treat myself."

If you've made a resolution, be alert to these stumbling blocks, take note of your past triggers for loss of self-control, and plan for how you might control those impulses before you face them again. If the real problem is that stress has drained your willpower, giving in to temptation may offer a quick relief but won't make you feel better in the long run. It's better to try to identify the source of the stress and work on using your most effective coping strategies.

RESISTING OLD HABITS
STAYING FIRM UNDER PRESSURE

During stressful times, it's a lot more difficult to build positive habits. When stress is tempting you to give up on your plans for a healthy, well-managed life, you may need a more systematic approach.

Have you ever started an exercise regime or planned to spend less, only to return to your old ways when life got stressful? Stress drains our willpower and interferes with our judgement, making bad habits harder to control. There are well-studied neurological reasons for this: if you have habits to change, it's best to be prepared for the difficult times.

The goal-directed brain

When we're feeling relaxed or confident, it's usually easier to form good intentions. We decide that our lives will be better if we can achieve a particular goal – we know we'll have to make some changes to our usual behaviour to achieve it, but we feel the goal is worth the effort.

The trouble is, under the influence of stress hormones, we can quickly stop thinking that way. In a 2012 German study, researchers injected 69 volunteers with either a harmless placebo or stress hormones. During a series of tests in which the subjects could earn rewards, their brains

66 days

A 2009 UK study found that it takes an average of **66 days for a new behaviour** to become a habit. Stress can make change more difficult, so don't demand too much of yourself; instead, plan for the long haul.

were scanned. The placebo group's brains showed healthy activity in the pre-frontal lobes associated with goal-directed behaviour. The brains of the chemically stressed group, on the other hand, showed suppressed activity in the goal-directed regions, while the areas associated with habitual behaviour were unaffected. When your body is under stress, your biochemistry is working against you, making it more difficult to overcome bad habits and less likely to focus on achievements.

Overcoming resistance

These findings may sound like bad news if you're trying to shake a bad habit or you want to achieve a goal that requires some lifestyle changes. It's more difficult to change old patterns of behaviour when you're under stress, so you may need a little extra help to reach that goal or sustain that change.

Plan systematically and eliminate complications, and it may become easier to create positive new habits even during stressful periods.

⊘ REDUCE YOUR OPTIONS

According to a 2008 American study, having to make too many choices wears down our stamina and willpower, making it more difficult to stick to our resolutions. Try eliminating some unnecessary choices from your life.

For instance:

✔ Pick out a handful of outfits to wear to work each week: those are now your only choices.
✔ Have the same breakfast or lunch every day – assuming it's healthy and balanced – or, for more nutritional variety, have a Monday meal, a Tuesday meal, and so on.
✔ Make one day of the week your laundry day or vacuuming day.

Taking the stress out of routine decisions can make the bigger choices easier to handle.

⊘ CHOOSING YOUR GOALS

How you phrase your goal can make a difference. Psychologists identify a difference between a positive, acquisitional goal and a negative, inhibitional goal – see the two examples shown below. If you're planning to break a bad habit, try re-presenting your goal to yourself as a positive. By telling yourself that you're going to acquire habit-free days – that you'll be gaining rather than losing something – you are likely to find that making the change feels less stressful and more rewarding.

Inhibitional goal:
"I won't eat junk food."

Acquisitional goal:
"I'll achieve x number of days of healthy eating."

⊘ IF-THEN PLANNING

First described by American psychologist Peter Gollwitzer in 1999, "if-then" planning is a way of making our resolutions more concrete – see the two examples shown here. Research shows the "if-then" method can help with everything from greater use of public transport to less prejudiced thinking, so it's well worth a try.

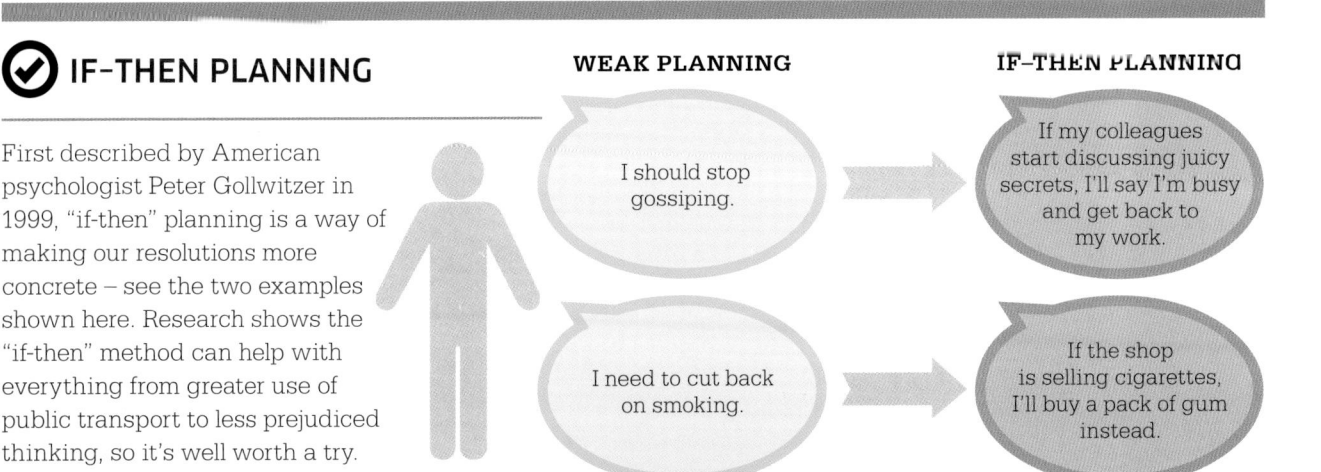

WEAK PLANNING

I should stop gossiping.

I need to cut back on smoking.

IF-THEN PLANNING

If my colleagues start discussing juicy secrets, I'll say I'm busy and get back to my work.

If the shop is selling cigarettes, I'll buy a pack of gum instead.

WHAT MAN ACTUALLY NEEDS IS NOT A TENSIONLESS STATE BUT THE STRIVING AND STRUGGLING FOR SOME GOAL WORTHY OF HIM

VIKTOR FRANKL, PSYCHIATRIST AND HOLOCAUST SURVIVOR

TOTAL IMMERSION
THE ART OF FINDING FLOW

If stress is the feeling that we cannot manage the tasks set before us, an effective antidote is flow: a state of profound and satisfying absorption that leaves us feeling confident and refreshed.

In the 1970s, Hungarian psychologist Mihály Csíkszentmihályi pioneered a truly stress-busting concept: in his words, "the process of total involvement with life I call flow". He defined flow as a combination of several factors:

- **Deep focus** on the present moment.
- **Action and awareness** merging together.
- **A lack of self-consciousness.**
- **A sense of personal control** over what you're doing.
- **A distortion of your time awareness** – for instance, time passing faster than you realize.
- **Autotelic experience** – that is, one which you find intrinsically rewarding.

In other words, flow is a state where we are so absorbed that the world and its pressures, for the moment at least, cease to matter.

Pushing yourself
In 1988, Csíkszentmihályi ran a study with 250 "high-flow" and "low-flow" teenagers. The low-flow teens spent more time on low-challenge activities such as socializing or watching television. The high-flow teens spent more time on active, challenging pursuits such as sports and hobbies; they tended to think their low-flow peers were having more fun, but it was the high-flow teens who had better self-esteem and greater long-term happiness.

Sometimes stress is so tiring that we just need to rest and relax – but another way to de-stress can be to

create a flow state, and for this, we need a challenge. Whether you find flow in your hobbies or adjust your working patterns to make them more rewarding, it's an excellent counterbalance to stress.

✎ MOOD DIARY

Looking for your flow? Try Csíkszentmihályi's Experience Sampling Method. Set your phone alarm to sound an alert at intervals through the day. When it beeps, stop to fill in a diary page on how you feel:

- **What was I doing** and who was I with?

- **On a scale of 1–10, how challenging** was the activity?

- **How skilled** did I feel? (1–10)

- **How absorbed** was I? (1–10)

- **How did I feel** – stressed / calm / happy / annoyed / lonely / confident / anxious / interested / engaged / proud / competent?

- **Did time pass** quickly / normally / slowly?

- **When I see myself** doing that activity, what kind of a person do I see myself as?

Repeat over several days, then look back for moments when you were absorbed in a challenge that made you feel engaged, interested, and good about yourself. That way you can identify what you really enjoy in life and might find de-stressing to pursue further.

✓ HOW DO WE CREATE FLOW?

According to Owen Schaffer, an American researcher on flow, creating a flow experience requires opportunity, action, and feedback. These create a positive loop in which we can remain happily absorbed. If you're under pressure and need a boost, look for activities that offer all three elements.

1 Opportunity
- ❯ We should know what to do.
- ❯ We should know how to do it.
- ❯ If it involves navigation, we should know where to go.

3 Feedback
- ❯ We should be able to tell how well we are doing.

2 Action
- ❯ The perceived level of challenge should be high.
- ❯ Our own perceived skill level should be high.
- ❯ We should be free from distractions.

✓ BRINGING FLOW INTO YOUR WORK

According to American psychologist Daniel Goleman, there are three main pathways we can use to encourage flow:

Find work that matches your skill set – just challenging enough to be engaging, but not overwhelming.

Do what you consider to be "good work" – work that you love, or that reflects your values (see pp.44–45).

Build your focus skills – for example, practise mindfulness meditations (see pp.132–135).

THE HUMAN SAFETY NET
FRIENDSHIP AND SUPPORT

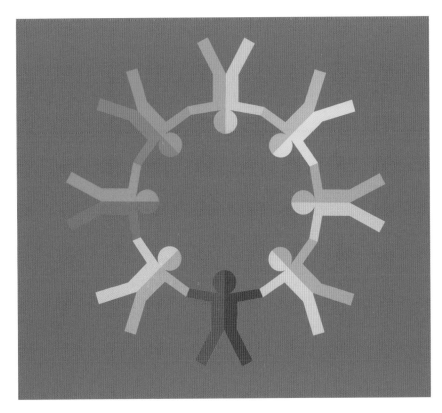

Humans are social beings; we need our social connections to maintain our mental and physical health. Having friends and supporters we can count on provides powerful protection against stress.

During difficult periods, especially if there are high demands on our time, we sometimes neglect our friendships. Yet trusted and loved companions are an extremely good buffer against stress.

Animal nature

Friendship lies deep in our evolutionary history as social creatures. Networks of mutual support and loyalty increase our chances of survival, and biologists have found numerous examples in the animal kingdom, where having strong social alliances results in greater resilience to stress and better physical health. Feeling safe when we have trustworthy companions is part of our nature.

A 2010 American meta-analysis found that people with a strong social support network had a 50% reduction in mortality from any cause, compared to those with weaker support. Social isolation or

Q THANKS FOR BEING THERE

A 2011 Canadian-American study tracked its volunteers' levels of the stress hormone cortisol over the course of several days, while they kept a detailed diary about any negative events they experienced. The results: when facing negative events alone, the volunteers' cortisol rose – but if they had their best friend with them, it held steady. With a trusted companion present, our bodies literally feel less threatened in the face of a stressor.

loneliness (see pp.190–191) was found to be on a par with other serious health risk factors, such as smoking and obesity.

I feel your pain

When a close friend is hurting, we literally experience their pain. A 2013 American study carried out brain scans while volunteers, their friends, or a stranger were "threatened" with mild electric shocks. Not surprisingly, the scans showed an elevated stress response when people were told that they themselves would receive a shock. Of note, however, was how they reacted when someone else was in line for the shock: when it was a stranger, the reaction was only mild, but when it was a friend, the brain scans showed that people reacted identically to how they did when they themselves were threatened with a shock.

The brain doesn't distinguish between a threat to a friend and a threat to us: we fully identify with our loved companions. This may make it stressful to watch a friend suffer, but when we're suffering ourselves, knowing that a friend shares our feelings can be a powerful comfort: we know we are not alone.

Giving back

Getting support from our friends can be tremendously comforting – but giving support can also lower our stress levels. A 2015 American study followed subjects over the course of 14 days and asked them to log both stressful events they'd experienced and moments when they'd acted helpfully towards

Q HOW DOES FRIENDSHIP HELP?

Psychologists offer two models of how social support helps us stay well and happy:

The Direct-Effects Hypothesis. Friendship directly promotes better emotional and physical health, no matter what our life circumstances.

The Buffering Hypothesis. Friendship is most powerful when we're stressed, helping us create psychological distance between ourselves and stressful events.

Which model you feel best applies to your social circle may be a matter of individual choice – but both models agree that, under pressure, trustworthy friends are what we need to feel better.

others. The result: people who engaged in "prosocial behaviours" – that is, kindness to others – were substantially buffered against the effects of stress.

It might seem like an extra burden to have to do favours for others when we're already feeling overwhelmed, but in fact, the prosocial behaviours that shielded

Q I NEED A HUG

If stress is really getting to you, ask a friend for a hug. Multiple studies have found that affectionate physical contact:

- **Reduces** our level of the stress hormone cortisol.
- **Stimulates** the vagus nerve in the brain, which slows the heart rate and lowers blood pressure.
- **Increases** the "cuddle hormone" oxytocin, making us feel more relaxed and trusting.
- **Activates** the release of the neurotransmitter dopamine in the brain's "reward centre", which provides a powerful sense of pleasure.

In short, science shows that a hug from a friend will do you both good.

the study's participants from stress could be very small – sometimes as little as holding open a door for someone. Even a small gesture of generosity or courtesy can lift your own mood and make stress seem less important. Overleaf, we'll look at ways to help you manage your social circle in order to get the best possible mutual support.

Q YOU AND YOUR GROUP

How many friends do we need? Having too many friends can heighten stress. According to biologists who study primate neurology, the number of close relationships we can manage is restricted by our memory capacity: the closer the relationship, the more demands it puts on the brain. Above a certain number, we can feel overloaded and lose track of important aspects of the relationship.

The five circles drawn here show the maximum number we can expect to manage at each level of friendship – though we can get by with fewer relationships if they're healthy, strong ones. If you're highly social but you're feeling stressed by your large circle, drifting apart from a few less-dear people may reduce the pressure.

1,500
People we only know by name: we don't know their personal details, such as whether or not they have children.

500
Casual acquaintances: we know them well enough to have a casual conversation, but we've shared only superficial details of our life.

50
Casual friends: we've shared some personal details, such as work or family situation, but they are not part of our closer circle of intimate supporters.

15
Fairly good friends: we know them very well and they'd offer support in times of crisis.

5
Close friends: they are aware of our most personal life experiences and provide ongoing, essential mutual support and caring.

❯❯ Choosing wisely

Having good friends to turn to is a tremendous comfort in difficult times, but it's wise to be alert to the possibility that some friends cause more stress than they relieve. If you have a friendship that seems to cause more drama and worry than relaxation and comfort, American psychiatry professor Irene Levine advises the following steps:

✔ **Think things through** in a quiet moment. Decisions taken in anger can backfire, so reflect if you want to end the relationship or just cool it down a bit.

✔ **In less close relationships,** work on drifting apart. Make excuses not to meet up until it's no longer expected of you.

✔ **If you have to make things explicit,** script out what you'd like to say in advance and

practise, so you can be sure you say what you mean. Try to avoid blame; people change, and the decision is your responsibility, so forget about recriminations.

This obviously doesn't mean you should reject friends just because they have problems – that would be unkind and would probably alienate the rest of your friends. But if you have the energy, you might consider

Q A SOOTHING COMMUNITY

If you're going through a difficult time, is any friend better than none? Actually, according to American researchers Nicholas Christakis and James Fowler, we're likely to pick up the moods of our friends through "emotional contagion". In a 2008 study they reported that:

1 mile

Having a **happy friend living within a mile of us** increases our probability of happiness by **25%**.

3 degrees

We can "catch" people's moods through **3 degrees of separation:**

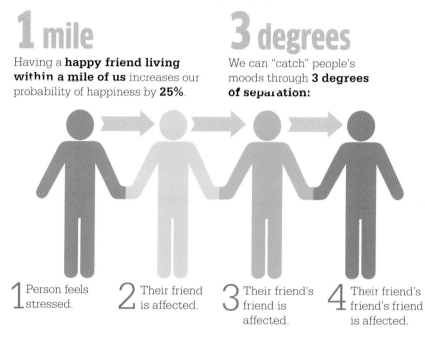

1 Person feels stressed.

2 Their friend is affected.

3 Their friend's friend is affected.

4 Their friend's friend's friend is affected.

If you're going through a particularly tough time, seeking out your calmest and most optimistic friends may do you more good than hanging out with the more negative ones. We're all subject to emotional contagion, so see if you can catch a confident mood.

trying to encourage your friends to be more positive (see pp.180–181).

Negative friendships can be a drain on your energy. If a friend has problems and you have the energy, consider encouraging them to be more positive. Positive friendships are crucial to your psychological health. With the right people in your life, your wellbeing is protected and you have a safe place to turn to if stress gets too much for you.

10 minutes

A 2010 American study found that as little as 10 minutes of **friendly conversation** boosts brain functions: even a quick chat over the phone makes you better able to tackle stressful problems.

? SPOTTING TOXIC FRIENDS

Good friends are reassuring, but a bad friend makes stress worse. American counsellor and relationship researcher Suzanne Degges-White identifies seven kinds of friend to watch out for:

1 **New acquaintances** who push for too much closeness too soon.

2 **Friends who only call you** when something goes wrong for them.

3 **Friends who don't take your preferences** into account when planning time together.

4 **Friends who only want to talk about themselves** and their own interests.

5 **Friends who constantly complain** that you aren't available or understanding enough.

6 **Friends who habitually compete** with you.

7 **Friends who are quick to borrow money** but slow to pay it back.

It's natural to want to support your friends, but you're likely to feel more relaxed and better able to manage stress if you save your energy for companions who give as well as take.

TALKING POSITIVE

THE BENEFITS OF AVOIDING COMPLAINTS

When we're under stress, it seems natural to "let off steam" by complaining about it. However, science shows that we're better off keeping our grumbling to a minimum.

Many people believe that "venting", "getting it off your chest", or "letting it out" are good ways to handle stress. In reality, too much complaining can cause more problems than it solves. So be aware of the neuroscience involved and cultivate positive habits even when under pressure.

The adaptable brain

To send important information from one part of the brain to another, our neurons (nerve cells) need to work together. Information is sent from one neuron to the next using the neurotransmitters (chemical messengers) that connect them, creating a neuronal pathway. Electrical signals that travel along the pathway are transmitting information from one brain area to another. The more we use a particular pathway, the stronger it becomes, and the easier it is to use that pathway to send infomation: this is how we learn. However, we can also build strong neuronal pathways for negative feelings and behaviours. The more we talk or think about a negative feeling, the more easily it comes to mind.

> **Venting anger** is an emotional expression … It sounds like a good idea, but it's dead **wrong**.
>
> Jeffrey Lohr
> American psychologist

✔ HOW TO PUT IT?

If you're talking to a close friend or partner about a stressful issue you're dealing with, try some of these phrases to put a more positive framing on the situation:

✔ This is going to call on me to be pretty persistent.

✔ It's going to be a big challenge.

✔ I'm going to have to put plenty of energy into this.

✔ I'll have to use a lot of ingenuity to sort this out.

✔ I'm going to have to show real grit while this lasts.

✔ I'm looking forward to this being finished.

This means that too much complaining can actually make us feel worse: when we constantly rehearse negative feelings, we reinforce the neuronal pathways that transmit those emotions. The brain gets better at processing them and may start creating negative moods even if there's no reason. With that in mind, it's sensible to keep your negative thoughts and talk to a minimum, and work on thinking and talking about positive emotions, thus strengthening your brain's happier pathways.

Keeping friends positive

If your friends are under pressure, it's quite possible you'll have to listen to them complaining even if you're trying not to. We tend to pick up other people's emotions, so you'll

⊙ POSITIVE COMPLAINING

American psychologist Robin Kowalski suggests there are two kinds of complaining: instrumental complaining – aimed at solving a practical problem, such as returning faulty goods – and expressive complaining, which is aimed at getting a response from people. The former is generally more positive, but if ever you're tempted to complain expressively, do it in moderation:

EXPRESSIVE COMPLAINING

Done **within reason,** it can **help us bond** with others.

Done with **little concern** for others' feelings, it can **alienate people** and isolate us.

Done too **habitually,** it becomes **self-reinforcing** and we **complain more**, further alienating others.

probably benefit if you can gently encourage them to be more positive. Some helpful tactics:

- **Model positive body language.** People unconsciously echo the stance of those they're with. Your stance can affect your mood, so project a more positive view and others may follow suit.

- **Give positive feedback.** If you have anything nice to say to people, say it: once their mood is lifted, they may stop complaining of their own volition.

- **Change the subject** to more positive topics.

- **Give as little response as possible** to excess negativity. Complainers want a response, so if you stick to neutral comments such as "Mmm" and "I see" but become more engaged when a more positive topic is introduced, you make it unrewarding to complain to you.

A little complaining is harmless, but in the long term, we tend to experience the moods we cultivate, so keep a reasonable proportion of your conversation positive, and your stress levels may drop.

FINDING A FUNNY SIDE
THE ROLE OF HUMOUR

Stress can seriously undermine our wellbeing – but laughter can be a powerful antidote. Enjoying the humorous moments in our lives can have a significant influence on how we experience stress.

I t might surprise many to discover that there is a great deal of science behind the benefits of laughter: a host of studies confirms that laughter does, both emotionally and physically, reduce our stress levels.

The biological benefits

Laughter has been found to trigger many physiological effects that lower stress. After a good laugh, your body naturally feels more relaxed: your blood pressure and heart rate drop, which leaves you feeling more tranquil. This occurs because laughing:

- **Reduces** the release of the stress hormone cortisol.
- **Releases endorphins** – neurotransmitters that are the brain's natural pain killers – which increases pain tolerance and boosts pleasure, optimism, and confidence.
- **Releases serotonin,** a neurotransmitter that helps to reduce anxiety and depression.

IS LAUGHTER THE BEST MEDICINE?

Stress can weaken our immune system (see pp.20–21), but laughter can help to restore and strengthen it. A 2003 American study showed participants a funny video and found that, compared to those who had viewed a non-humorous video, not only did their self reported stress levels drop, but over the next four days, their immune cell activity exhibited a significant boost.

- **Boosts the immune system** (see "Best medicine" opposite).

Laughing away the pain
In a 2011 British study, subjects who had laughed out loud at a comedy could – thanks to those endorphins – hold their hands in a freezing wine cooler for longer than subjects who had merely enjoyed the humour. If you're dealing with the stress of an illness or injury, watching something funny can be distracting and can also make the pain more tolerable.

Coping through laughter
Stress is often defined as the feeling that we are unable to cope with life's challenges, but laughter can cut our stressors down to size. In the US, a 2010 study showed subjects a series of potentially upsetting photographs and then asked them to reinterpret them in one of three ways:

- **Without humour:** for instance, a picture of a man gutting fish at a seafood plant could be described seriously: "He is lucky to have a good job".
- **With negative, disparaging humour:** "A fish factory is the ideal workplace for people with body odour".
- **With positive, good-natured humour:** "He always wanted to work with animals".

The results showed that the subjects who made positive jokes were significantly less affected by the photographs, including the far more distressing shots. Laughter, the researchers concluded, could be understood as a form of cognitive reappraisal (see pp.52–53), which is one of the most effective methods of reducing stress.

Laughing together
Laughter reinforces friendship. In 2000, American neuroscientist Robert Provine found that when people laugh in groups, only 10–20% of the laughs were in response to actual jokes, and even then, the jokes often weren't very funny – yet everyone was united by their hilarity. Just the presence of others made people find the situation more humorous. As Provine put it, "The critical stimulus for laugher is another person, not a joke". Laughing together bonds us, and social bonds are a powerful protector against stress (see pp.176–179).

Humour is personal
What we find funny is intensely personal. Numerous studies show that our mental and physical health improves when we feel in control of important aspects of our lives, and stress makes us feel less in control. Laughter is empowering: when we choose to laugh at the situation, we feel more in control, less hopeless, and more able to cope.

What we find to be funny is an important aspect of the beneficial effects of laughter. An American study published in 1996 found that post-surgical patients who were able to choose the humorous movies they watched required less pain medication than those who didn't watch movies. However, the patients who fared worst were those who had to watch "comedies" they didn't find funny.

BUILD YOUR LIBRARY
Humour expert and professor emeritus of psychiatry and behavioural sciences at Stanford University William Fry advises two steps to building a "laugh library":

1 For a few days, pay attention to what makes you laugh out loud. Laughter rather than perfect taste is the point here, so if it's corny puns or silly cartoons that get you giggling, embrace them.

2 Use your humour profile to start building up a library of books, films, comics, or whatever else makes you laugh. In times of stress, you can look to your personalized laugh library to help ease the load.

For laughter to be beneficial, we need to be exposed to the type of humour we find funny. Regardless of our particular sense of humour, laughing makes us feel better, mentally and physically, and draws us closer to others, which also reduces stress.

From the biochemical level to the cognitive one, laughter is an excellent de-stressor. In trying times, seeing the funny side of your situation – or even just laughing at something unrelated – can make you feel better.

WE CAN LAUGH TOGETHER. WE'RE GOING TO GET THROUGH THIS. WE'RE GOING TO BE OKAY

SOPHIE SCOTT, NEUROSCIENTIST AND STAND-UP COMIC

GET CREATIVE

BEATING STRESS WITH ARTS AND CRAFTS

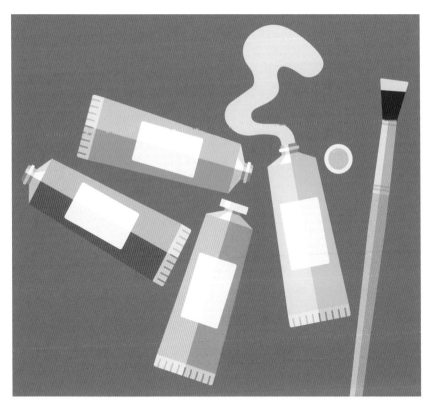

Are you an artistic or creative person? Whether the answer is yes or no, some creative experimentation might prove to be a good way to de-stress and make you more resilient, too.

A rtistic endeavour isn't exclusive to great painters: anyone who wants to pick up a crayon or crochet hook, chisel, or cello can enjoy the de-stressing benefits of creating something. When stress saps our joy in life, creative play can help to regain it.

Getting started

Many of us feel daunted at the idea of creative play. Perhaps we worry that we lack talent or that we're better at appreciating creativity than actually being creative. Fortunately, in order to experience the benefits of creativity, we don't need any special skills: just the act of creating – making something ourselves – is what helps. In a 2016 American study, subjects were given art supplies and told that they could make whatever image they chose. Three-quarters showed a marked drop in their cortisol levels after 45 minutes of artistic free play, even if they had no experience of making art – in fact,

Q GET COLOURING

Adult colouring books have enjoyed a surge of popularity in recent years, but the pictures you choose to colour can make a difference. A 2012 American study found that when people were given a mandala (a circular, spiritual symbol), a plaid pattern, or a blank piece of paper to fill in, the mandala group's anxiety levels dropped significantly more. If colouring to de-stress appeals to you, choose soothing images.

THE WINDOW OF TOLERANCE

In 2010, American psychiatrist Daniel Siegel proposed that our stress levels are bounded by a "window of tolerance" – that is, the optimal zone during a stressful experience when we are challenged rather than bored or agitated. For those of us prone to being overwhelmed by our feelings, creative play gives us a safe space in which to experiment and express emotion – which can expand our window of tolerance for stress.

Hypoarousal	Window of tolerance	Hyperarousal
› Withdrawn › Disengaged › Switched-off	› Engaged › Interested › Insightful	› Agitated › Flustered › Stressed

just under half were complete beginners. (However, among the remaining one-quarter, some people showed elevated cortisol levels. If trying to make art makes you feel more stressed, don't force yourself.)

A positive stressor

Creativity can reduce stress, but not just by being a relaxing activity. On the contrary, creative activity is a challenging, positive stress that necessitates increased brain activity. This positive or beneficial stress motivates us to keep going and strengthens our resilience – our ability to withstand stress in general. By exposing ourselves to challenges that are positively stressful, we are enlarging what American psychiatrist Daniel Siegel calls our "window of tolerance" (see above).

You may, of course, be naturally talented, but if you aren't, don't let that discourage you. Whether it's cake decorating or calligraphy, song-writing or welding, creative experimentation and expression can improve your stress-handling skills no matter what outlet you choose.

{ Creative activities can have a **healing** and **protective** effect on mental wellbeing ... boosting the immune system and **reducing stress**. }

Jill Leckey
British health scientist

A POSITIVE CYCLE

Creative activity can fuel what a 2016 study in New Zealand called an "upward spiral of wellbeing". Students kept diaries of their activities for 13 days; when they'd done something creative the day before, they showed a higher degree of "flourishing" – feeling well and capable rather than stressed and anxious – which in turn tended to make them feel even more creative.

CREATIVE SPIRAL

4 **Create** more.

3 **Feel** more energized and capable.

2 **Experience** engagement, enthusiasm, and happiness.

1 **Do** something creative.

The students' activities included song-writing, creative writing, knitting, crochet, cooking, painting, drawing, graphic and digital design, and musical performance. You can create your own upward spiral by choosing a creative activity that interests you.

THE POWER OF PETS

THE CALMING EFFECTS OF ANIMALS

Playing with a pet is one of the great pleasures in life, which is why it has a calming effect. Research confirms that having a companion animal – or playing with someone else's – can significantly lower our stress levels.

Owning a pet can improve quality of life and lower stress considerably, as many of us know from experience. If you don't have one yet, but feel able to take on the responsibility of caring for one, a pet can be a good way to help yourself feel calm, competent, and relaxed.

Calmer owners

Not only can time spent around a pet be relaxing, but pet ownership can be de-stressing even when you and your pet are apart. A 2002 American study subjected people to a stressful maths test and measured their heart rate and blood pressure. Those who owned a cat or dog:

- Had lower resting blood pressure and heart rate before the experiment began.
- Showed less agitated heart rates and lower blood pressure while performing the stressful task.
- Returned to their resting heart rates and blood pressure more quickly when the test was over.

> Ownership of a pet dog or cat can **ameliorate the effects** of potentially **stressful life-events**.
>
> **Deborah Wells**
> Irish psychologist

These effects were found even when the pet wasn't present; just owning a dog or cat was enough to make people calmer. When their pet was brought into the room, the effects were even more pronounced and the subjects made fewer mathematical errors, felt less stressed physically, and were better able to concentrate when solving the problems posed by the test.

Improved quality of life

The company of a pet can be relaxing in the short-term, but evidence also suggests that life in general can be healthier and calmer with an animal in it. A 2015 study in Australia and the US – where more than 60% of households own one or more pets – noted that owning an animal got people out into the community and provided them with opportunities to meet others: around 40% of the pet owners they surveyed had, through their pets, met people who provided them with social support. The effect was particularly pronounced with dogs – dog owners were three times as likely as other pet owners to have made supportive friends that way – but all pet owners felt benefits.

The pets had created what the researchers called "incidental social interaction" – an opportunity to meet people the subjects wouldn't otherwise have met, and an ice-breaking subject of mutual interest to discuss. By swapping anecdotes and advice about their pets, people were able to form valuable bonds with each other – and those bonds sometimes became stress-relieving friendships (see pp.176–179).

Time well spent

Even if we don't own an animal, just having contact with one can improve our wellbeing. In a 2011 Italian study, for instance, elderly people living in a care home were allowed to pet and play with dogs for 90 minutes a week: the experience was so beneficial that the amount of depressive symptoms among the residents dropped by 50% over six weeks, and their self-perceived quality of life was greatly improved.

If you don't have room in your life for a pet, stopping to play with a friend's pet can also help you to feel more relaxed. Either way, time spent with an animal is, from a stress-busting point of view, time well spent.

⊗ CAN'T SLEEP?

If stress is interfering with your sleep, a pet may not help: a 2014 British survey found that 54% of dog and cat owners reported they got less sleep than they'd like because their pets woke them early. If insomnia is a serious problem for you (see pp.162–165), perhaps consider other de-stressors before you commit to regular early-morning wake-ups from a friendly animal.

🔍 NOT JUST FURRY FRIENDS

We might think that only furry or fluffy animals are de-stressing, but science shows that's not the case. A 2003 Israeli experiment deliberately induced stress in arachnophobic volunteers by telling them they might have to hold a tarantula, and then gave some of them the chance to stroke a rabbit, a turtle, or a toy animal. The subjects who were given a real animal showed lowered stress levels than those with a toy, whether they petted the furry bunny or the hard-shelled turtle – even if they weren't particularly animal-lovers. Any animal can be de-stressing (except, perhaps, a tarantula).

🔍 THAT'S SO CUTE!

Facing a stressful challenge? A 2012 Japanese experiment found that people who were given a concentration test, then shown pictures of puppies and kittens and given another test, performed 10% better on the second test than the first. Researchers speculated that feeling more "caring" had made them more careful – an advantage when facing stressful tasks.

ALL ON YOUR OWN?

THE STRESS OF LONELINESS

Human beings are social creatures: we need to feel connected with each other, and if we don't, we become stressed. Research suggests that we have more control over loneliness than we might think.

Loneliness is a major stressor. A 2003 American study found that rejection lights up the same part of the brain that processes physical pain: feeling isolated from others literally hurts. Likewise, supportive relationships with friends or family have the ability to lessen pain. A large body of research associates loneliness with a heightened risk of both mental and physical illnesses. Tackling loneliness may be one of the best things you can do for your stress levels and your overall health.

Lonely but not alone

When you're lonely, it's easy to believe that you're not someone people would want to know. It may help your self-esteem to learn that feeling this way probably isn't an objective measure of your appeal. A 2000 American study found that undergraduate students who called themselves "lonely" were actually no different from their "non-lonely" peers in height, weight, academic achievements, attractiveness, or socioeconomic class – and more importantly, they had just as many social connections.

In other words, people in the same social situation can have very different emotional reactions to their circumstances. If we can cultivate more positive reactions, the stress of loneliness may decrease.

Becoming less lonely

How is it possible to feel lonely even when we're in a room full of people or when we have many friends? Research by American psychologist and social neuroscience expert John Cacioppo found that people who exhibit hypervigilance in brain regions responsible for detecting social threats – such as slights, rejections, or exclusions – are more likely to feel lonely in situations where others might not.

Cacioppo advises that lonely people should use cognitive behaviour techniques (see pp.52–

> People can live relatively **solitary lives** and **not feel lonely**, and conversely, they can live an ostensibly rich social life and feel lonely nevertheless.
>
> **Louise Hawkley and John Cacioppo**
> American psychologists

? USING SOCIAL MEDIA

Sometimes we're lonely because we live far away from the people we love most. In that situation, social networking sites may be our easiest option for regular contact – but do they leave us feeling more or less connected with others? According to American social psychologist Moira Burke, it depends how we use them:

Passive consumption – merely reading what others post – makes us feel less connected. Other people's lives often look more interesting than our own (at least on social media), which also makes us feel left out.

One-click communication – clicking "like", for instance – has little influence on how lonely or how connected we feel. There isn't much social exchange involved, so it doesn't have much emotional impact.

Broadcasting – posting announcements with no particular person in mind – makes us feel more lonely. We're not connecting with anyone, just hoping for a response which may or may not come.

Composed communication – sending a written message or chatting online – makes us feel less lonely, because it's a genuine social exchange.

Isolation is stressful, but if you live in circumstances where you can't always meet friends and family face to face, sometimes the Internet may be the most practical option for keeping in touch. In that case, "composed communication" makes the most of your contact with the people you love.

53) to challenge "maladaptive social cognition": for instance, if you catch yourself overreacting to a friend missing a phonecall, ask yourself whether that reaction is appropriate for the situation.

This cognitive re-appraisal not only makes us feel better, but improves our social skills too: as

American psychologist Guy Winch points out, loneliness can make us overly defensive, which can deter people from socializing with us. Reducing your hypervigilance can leave you feeling less stressed and easier to get along with, resulting in more social connections and feeling more enriched by them.

✓ BREAKING FREE

American psychologist and loneliness expert Guy Winch recommends three steps for breaking out of the stressful trap of loneliness:

1 **Take the initiative.** Get in contact with people you haven't seen for a while. If you feel isolated, find community events, volunteer groups, or other activities that give you the chance to meet people.

2 **Every day, reach out** to one potential contact, and don't take it personally if they happen to be slow to respond.

3 **Be optimistic and positive.** Fearing rejection is normal, but the more friendliness you display, the better your chances of connecting with people.

If you're used to feeling lonely, reaching out to others can be stressful, but persevere and you may well find that making contact soon becomes a pleasure.

THE ART OF GRIT
PERSISTENCE AND PASSION

Who do you want to be and what do you want out of life? Stress can make us feel overwhelmed and discouraged, but the psychological quality known as grit can carry us through.

The stress associated with life's challenges can feel overwhelming – but you are almost certainly stronger than you think. Research confirms that nearly everyone has the capacity for what psychologists call "grit": that is to say, the courage and strength of character to persevere despite problems and create the life you want.

Born with grit?

Is grit a matter of genetics? According to a 2016 British study, not entirely. The researchers found only moderate heritability; more important were qualities that we discuss throughout this book and which can be learned or cultivated: hopefulness, a willingness to use whatever coping strategies were most helpful, a belief in our control over our reaction to stress, a sense that life has meaning, and curiosity about what the future holds.

Staying open and positive is crucial when facing stress – and all of these qualities are attitudes we can all develop, no matter what genes we were born with.

> The gritty individual approaches **achievement** as a **marathon**; his or her advantage is **stamina**.
>
> **Angela Duckworth**
> American psychologist

Holding firm

Since positive qualities help us to cultivate grit, which ones are the most important to develop? A 2007 American study of how grit can help us to achieve our goals, despite setbacks and stress, produced some interesting conclusions:

1 Perseverance and intelligence both count. Even for intellectually demanding careers such as law or medicine, perseverance is at least as important as IQ – and both matter more than education.

2 Conscientiousness is the key trait in terms of the Big Five personality traits (see pp.30–31): gritty individuals are those who both finish the tasks at hand and stick industriously to their goals and ideals over the long term. If you have high neuroticism (that is, if you are easily distressed), you might assume you'd be less gritty, since distress feels discouraging. In fact, people with high neuroticism can be just as gritty as people whose neuroticism is low. In short, how deeply you feel stress matters less than how patient you can be in coping with that stress.

3 What do you want out of life? It helps to know. Those who have serious, long-term interests – that is, things they care about that give their life meaning (see pp.44–45) – are better able to be persistent despite challenges.

We can't live entirely free of stress – but with clear goals and grit, we can live as our best selves.

Q GETTING TOUGHER

Some good news for those who aspire to grit: according to a 2007 American study, we tend to have greater perseverence as we age (see pp.102-103). Life always presents us with setbacks and stressors, but when it comes to coping with them, it would appear that practice makes perfect: we can learn from our experience, and overcoming stress can leave us stronger.

Grit involves **passionate perseverance** toward long-term goals, especially **through obstacles** and **adversity**.

Dan Blalock
American psychologist

? HOW GRITTY DO YOU FEEL?

A grit scale used by psychologists can be a good way to consider your own habits: are you confident that you're getting the life you want despite your stressors, or do you need to make some changes? See whether you agree with these statements:

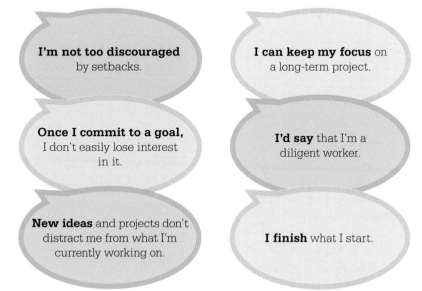

I'm not too discouraged by setbacks.

I can keep my focus on a long-term project.

Once I commit to a goal, I don't easily lose interest in it.

I'd say that I'm a diligent worker.

New ideas and projects don't distract me from what I'm currently working on.

I finish what I start.

Thinking about what really matters to you in life (see pp.44–45) and developing your prioritizing skills (see pp.146–147) will help you to better manage stress and be the person you choose to be.

CHAPTER 5

RESILIENCE AND RESOLUTION

FINDING SUPPORT AND BUILDING STRENGTH

I DON'T FEEL WELL

THE PHYSICAL SYMPTOMS OF STRESS

Stress can cause all sorts of unexpected physical problems. Sometimes your body is sending your brain a message, and the better you understand the message, the more effectively you will respond to it.

If stress becomes overwhelming, sometimes the first symptoms are physical. The body is a complex organism made up of interrelated systems, and stress may be experienced in unexpected ways (see chart opposite). It's never wise to self-diagnose – if in doubt, see a doctor – but if you're under a great deal of pressure and experiencing uncharacteristic physical symptoms, be aware that managing your stress might be the key to feeling better, mentally and physically.

Seek help

Stress may turn out to be the cause of your physical symptoms, but if so, that doesn't mean you should shrug them off as "just stress" and do nothing to treat them. The fact that your emotional state may be at the root of matters does not mean that your symptoms are imaginary: they are real, and deserve real attention. GPs, therapists, and good self-care can all make you feel much better.

 ## ALL IN THE HEAD

If a doctor told you that a physical symptom might be caused by stress, would you think, "They don't believe me; they're saying it's all in my head"? In reality, your every thought, feeling, and action is the result of brain activity, so pain from any source is indeed "all in your head", and real. What's important is that the problem, whatever the cause, is managed correctly, leaving you pain-free.

(?) GOT A HEADACHE?

The most common form of headache is a tension headache, which is a characteristic sign of stress. The typical tension headache is felt in the following places:

- Upper back
- Neck
- Base of the head
- Around or above the ears
- Hinge of the jaw
- Above the eyes

In the long term, exercise, regular sleep, and reducing your stress levels can help to prevent tension headaches. If you're prone to this type of headache, in the short term you might consider:

- ✔ Rest, dark, and quiet
- ✔ An ice pack (or heat pack if you prefer) on the source of the pain
- ✔ A warm shower, directing the jet of water over the sore muscles
- ✔ Massaging the tense spots
- ✔ The standard dose of an over-the-counter painkiller as early as possible after the pain starts

If these measures aren't helpful, consider consulting a doctor.

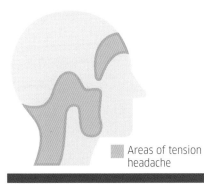
Areas of tension headache

COMMON STRESS COMPLAINTS

Exactly how your body reacts to stress – and the amount of stress required to trigger physical symptoms – is highly individual, but a 2013 list published in the *Harvard Review of Psychiatry* identifies problems to watch out for. If these sound familiar, mention stress as a possible contributor when you see your doctor.

Symptoms	What they mean
Sleep disturbance and fatigue	The sympathetic nervous system, which is activated by stress (pp.20–21), makes us wakeful – resulting in insomnia and sleep that is not refreshing (pp.162–165).
Frequent infections	Stress hormones such as cortisol can suppress the immune system (pp.54–55), so if you keep getting minor illnesses, such as coughs and colds, it may be a reflection of stress.
Asthma attacks or skin rash/eczema	When the immune system is suppressed, we can become hyper-sensitive to allergens. Stress also makes us more vulnerable to inflammation, which can also lead to skin rashes and eczema.
Pseudo-neurological symptoms	Stress-related hyperventilation (p.129) can cause symptoms that could easily be confused with problems with the nervous system. Common examples are dizziness, disorientation, blurred, clouded, or tunnel vision, flashing lights, memory loss, or fainting.
Chest pain	Chest pain may indicate a heart problem and shouldn't be ignored – but it could also be caused by stress-related muscle tension (see below) or anxiety or panic (pp.204–207).
Musculoskeletal pain	Under pressure, our muscles can become tense and sore because we're constantly on alert. This can lead to head, neck, and back pain.
Nausea/vomiting	Stress can cause the gut to become hyper-sensitive and trigger a similar reaction to the one experienced with food-poisoning or stomach flu.
Abdominal pain	Acute stress stimulates the gut to contract, which can cause diarrhoea and cramps.
Difficulty urinating	The sphincter muscles that hold our bladder sealed can be over-stimulated by stress, making it hard to relieve ourselves when we're too tense.

BIG BAD WOLF

OVERCOMING AN ABUSIVE CHILDHOOD

In our vulnerable early years, we need a sense of safety. If we've been unlucky enough to be raised around neglectful or frightening adults, we may need extra help to manage stress when we grow up.

Sadly, painful childhoods are all too common and can have serious, lasting consequences. A 2012 American study followed 6,000 maltreated children over a period of 16 years, and found significantly greater levels of mental illness, substance abuse, and suicide attempts. If your childhood was difficult, you may find that dealing with stress is particularly challenging, but it is possible to improve your coping skills.

The effects of early suffering

According to the 2012 study above, a stressful childhood environment can create "epigenetic" changes. To explain: our genes make us who we are – they determine all of our personal characteristics, such as eye colour, height, and temperament. Some genes are turned on or off at specific times, such as puberty or during pregnancy. Abuse or neglect can activate genes that make us

1 in 5

Abuse can feel isolating, but an influential American study in the late 1990s found that more than **1 in 5** people experienced childhood trauma.

> Maltreatment is a **chisel** that **shapes a brain** to contend with strife, but at the cost of **deep, enduring wounds**.
>
> **Martin H. Teicher**
> American psychiatrist

more prone to substance abuse, depression, anxiety, and risky behaviours such as unprotected sex or breaking the law – which can lead to yet more stressful situations. However, an abusive childhood does not necessarily mean you will have a stressful adulthood. You can do a great deal to help yourself.

Take care of your health
People who've been mistreated as children are more prone to illness in adulthood; a 2016 American study found that child abuse survivors tend to have reduced immunity. Treating your body kindly, starting with a good diet (see pp.158–161) and regular exercise (see pp.152–153), can help you to stay well.

Seek out support
Some abuse survivors are highly resilient, thanks to the supportive relationships that are crucial to our wellbeing. As American professor of pediatrics David Rubin observed in 2008, these survivors share three central concepts about themselves:

1 **I have people** around me who will help me.

2 **I am someone** people can like and love.

3 **I can find** ways to solve my problems.

It can be difficult to trust people if you grew up in a traumatic environment. Have compassion for yourself and accept the reality that trusting others may be challenging. Then work on communicating your needs to those around you, and together build bonds that feel secure.

Seek help
If your painful past is making it difficult to live the life you want, don't be ashamed to seek out the support you need. There are numerous options to consider:

■ **See a therapist.** Talk therapy, mindfulness, or spirituality are often helpful in building your coping skills and resilience.
■ **Find a local helpline** for abuse survivors.
■ **Look for survivors' groups** or advice sites online. Some are better than others, so trust your judgement and only stay when you feel welcome and safe.
■ **See your GP** if your past is overwhelming you. You might need more support in order to move forward.

You did not deserve to be mistreated as a child, and you shouldn't have to continue to suffer as an adult.

? STRONG FEELINGS

Childhood stress can cause us to "shut down" emotionally. With good therapeutic support, you may find your feelings begin to resurface. They can be surprisingly difficult to process. American psychologist Ellen McGrath identifies four common experiences:

■ **The trickle effect**
Feelings return slowly but steadily. Fairly manageable.

■ **Hit-and-run feelings**
An emotion overwhelms us, and we are so scared we run away from it. As it tends to come back again, good support from a therapist is needed to help us confront it.

■ **Tsunamis**
A previously repressed emotion smashes into us and we feel we're drowning – but when the emotional wave recedes, we find we're still alive and better for having let ourselves feel what we need to feel.

■ **Rollercoasters**
We know how we feel, but those feelings go up and down rapidly. Mindfulness (pp.132–135) and exercise (pp.152–153) can help us stay stable.

TAKING CARE

MENTAL ILLNESS FACTS AND FICTION

Mental illness can happen to anyone, no matter what their circumstances are. If stress is making you sick, understanding mental illness can help to eliminate the stigma you may feel and set you on the path to recovery.

In the past, people often held the false belief that mental illnesses were somehow a reflection of weakness or a character flaw – but research clearly shows that a mental illness really is an illness, just like any other illness. If you think stress might be making you sick, the information presented throughout this chapter can help you first to identify the mental illnesses most commonly associated with stress, and then to decide what steps to take to look after yourself. Never be afraid to seek medical advice: mental wellbeing is key to a happy, healthy, meaningful life.

What causes mental illness?

The causes are complicated, but broadly speaking, mental health problems have a "biopsychosocial" origin, which means that they are a combination of biology (such as genetics, hormones, and the brain's neurology), psychology (such as vulnerabilities and coping skills), and social hardships (such as poverty and isolation).

No one should expect to feel unwell forever. Improving your coping skills can aid recovery, as can medication and therapy (see pp.208–209). Doctors describe mental illnesses as interfering with "functioning": it's important to understand that this doesn't just mean meeting work and family commitments, but also includes the ability to enjoy life. If you appear to be all right from the outside but are suffering emotional pain, you should seek help.

Points to remember

Every illness has its own course of treatment, but there are some general principles when seeking help that apply to everyone:

✔ **It is important** that your doctor makes you feel heard and understood. If you feel you're not being taken seriously, go to a different doctor.

Q RISK FACTORS

A 2014 report for the British National Health Service identified particular risks factors for mental illness:

- **Living alone**
- **Poor physical health** – particularly people who suffer significant ongoing conditions such as asthma, cancer, diabetes, epilepsy, or high blood pressure
- **Unemployment**

However, anyone can have a mental illness at some point in their life, so if you do, don't feel ashamed: you are far from alone and deserve support.

HOW COMMON?

Mental illnesses are part of normal life: in 2014, the UK's National Health Service estimated that **1 in 6 adults** had a common **mental disorder**.

According to a 2015 national survey in America, almost **1 in 5 adults** currently experiences a mental disorder. If you suspect you have one too, don't assume it's unlikely.

- ✔ **The therapist** you work with should have in-depth knowledge and experience of treating your particular illness and be a good match for you personally (pp.208–209).
- ✔ **Mental illnesses** and traumas can lower your immune system and create physical symptoms (pp.196–197). If a doctor suggests your physical symptoms are caused by a mental health issue, that doesn't mean they're a figment of your imagination. If they are real enough to make you suffer, they are real enough to deserve respect and treatment.

Coping with a mental illness is extremely stressful, so make sure those who support you are the right people to help alleviate that stress.

Q DEBUNKING THE MYTHS

Misconceptions and myths can make life more stressful for those struggling with mental illness. A better understanding of the realities of mental illness should help you to confront it just like you would any other illness.

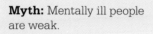

Myth: Mentally ill people are weak.

Reality: Even the strongest people can get sick. People struggling with mental illnesses can experience great distress, and may act in ways that seem strange to others; they may themselves feel embarrassed about this. It is important to remember that mental illness is not the patient's fault.

Myth: Mentally ill people can't live productive lives.

Reality: Mentally ill people can and do work, play an active role in their communities, and support their families. If an illness makes life harder, it may be a sign that a new approach or more support is needed, but there is no reason to assume a mentally ill person depends on the charity of others – most contribute fully to society.

Myth: Mentally ill people are violent and a threat to society.

Reality: Mentally ill people are no more violent than anyone else – in fact, they're more likely to be the victims of violence than to hurt others: a 2012 British survey found that people with mental illnesses were four times more likely to be attacked than people without. There is no need to fear someone just because they're dealing with a mental illness.

Myth: Mental illnesses are not treatable.

Reality: Mental illnesses don't go away on their own, so expecting someone to simply "get over it" is unreasonable and unfair. With support and timely, appropriate treatment, most people recover and lead the life they choose.

(For information on finding the right help, see pp.208–209.)

FACING THE BLACK DOG
LOW MOOD AND DEPRESSION

Sometimes stress is temporarily unpleasant – and sometimes it crosses the line into illness. If life starts to feel hopeless, you may need to consider whether your stress has resulted in clinical depression.

Clinical depression is more than feeling sad: it is a medical condition that saps your energy, interest, and joy in life, and can last months or even years. To quote a 2005 review in the *Annual Review of Clinical Psychology*, there is "a robust and causal association" between chronic stress and clinical depression. If you think stress has pushed you past your breaking point and you're depressed, it's vital that you seek help.

Depression versus low mood

What's the difference between being depressed and just feeling low? Depression has a known set of symptoms (see "Am I Depressed?" opposite), but be particularly alert to two warning signs:

- **Depression causes** sadness, but also anhedonia – a loss of pleasure in activities you previously enjoyed, such as seeing friends or doing hobbies.
- **Depression can sometimes** cause suicidal ideation – that is, wondering whether you'd rather be dead (see "The Worst-Case Scenarios", opposite).

You may have definite reasons for feeling stressed, such as serious work or relationship problems, but anhedonia and suicidal ideation are clear indicators of depression. Even if you're not sure if you're depressed, it's best to speak to a doctor about your feelings. And remember you are not alone: according to a 2017 World Health Organization report, more than 300 million people worldwide are living with depression.

HOW COMMON?

According to a 2005 international survey, at least 30% of men and 40% of women have at least **one episode of depression** in their lives.

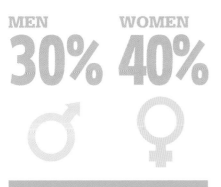

MEN **30%** ♂ WOMEN **40%** ♀

What causes depression?

According to the Stanford School of Medicine, around 50% of depression is genetic, and we are 2–3 times more likely to develop the condition if we had a depressed parent or sibling. Traumatic experiences early in life also make us more vulnerable.

Stress alone doesn't cause depression – but for a vulnerable individual, stress may play an important part in the development of the condition. Depression can become a chronic problem because with each episode, the amount of stress required to trigger depression decreases. Eventually, depression may arise "out of the blue", requiring no stress at all to trigger it.

If you are vulnerable to depression, it's important to recognize the power of stress and build your skills to manage stress more effectively.

The good news

Depression is highly treatable – a number of options are available:

❓ AM I DEPRESSED?

In the last two weeks, have you experienced any of the following:

■ Feeling low, hopeless, angry, or unhappy?

■ No longer enjoying things that used to give you pleasure?

■ Trouble with going to sleep or sleeping too much?

■ Trouble with appetite – eating too much or too little?

■ Having little energy?

■ Feeling worthless or a failure?

■ Trouble concentrating?

■ Being sluggish, or else fidgety and restless?

■ Feeling you might be better off dead? (See right, "Worst-case".)

Even if you've experienced only some of these issues, it's best to speak to your doctor.

■ **Anti-depressants.** There are many options and it's important to find the one that works best for each individual. Doctors may try several different prescriptions before finding the one that works best for you.

■ **CBT** (pp.52–53). A wide variety of studies have found that CBT can be as effective as medication, especially for mild depression.

■ **Other forms** of psychotherapy (pp.208–209).

■ **Exercise** (pp.152–153), especially if it's vigorous, can provide some

⚠ THE WORST-CASE SCENARIOS

Suicidal ideation (considering suicide) is one of the most dangerous symptoms of depression. Suicidal thoughts may be passive (considering or fantasizing about death) or active (making plans to end your life). Passive thoughts of suicide may include:

■ I wish I didn't have to wake up tomorrow morning.

■ Everyone would be better off without me.

■ My life is over.

■ If a car hit me tomorrow, that wouldn't be so bad.

■ If it wasn't for my loved ones, I could just end it all.

You may be depressed without having suicidal feelings, but if these phrases sound familiar, seek medical help immediately.

of the same benefits as anti-depressants. It doesn't replace them in severe depression, but it can make them work better.

Exactly what kind of treatment will help you most is likely to be a process of trial and error, and sometimes a combination of medications is necessary. Most importantly, it's essential you don't suffer in silence: stress can lead to depression even in the toughest people, and with the appropriate support, you can recover.

MANAGING FEARS

FOUR ANXIETY DISORDERS

Everyone is afraid sometimes, but if fear is taking over your life, you may be suffering from an anxiety disorder. Help is available – once you know what you're dealing with, you don't have to handle your anxiety alone.

Does your life feel more stressful and frightening than it should? It may be that you are suffering from an anxiety disorder – a condition in which your natural fear response has become excessive and is undermining your quality of life. Stress is challenging enough in ordinary circumstances, but anxiety disorders can make it feel impossible to manage. If you think your fears might be out of hand, make sure you seek medical advice: anxiety disorders seldom go away without treatment, but with good support, your life can feel back under your control.

Spotting the problem

Four of the most common anxiety disorders are generalized anxiety disorder, panic disorder, post-traumatic stress disorder, and social anxiety disorder.

All four are very distressing conditions, so if the symptoms described on the following pages sound familiar, be sure to seek out a supportive doctor for help and advice. **»**

> Anxiety is physiological but it can be **lessened** or worsened by the **ways you cope** with it.
>
> **Deborah Khoshaba**
> American psychologist

Q GENERALIZED ANXIETY DISORDER

Generalized anxiety disorder (GAD) is primarily characterized by out-of-control, intrusive anxiety that can make even minor, everyday stressors feel too big to handle. Key indicators:

- Excessive anxiety, more days than not, about several subjects, for at least six months.

- The anxiety is difficult to control.

- It is associated with at least three of the following (or at least one for children): restlessness or edginess; being easily tired; difficulty concentrating or mind going blank; irritability; muscle tension; trouble sleeping.

- It causes significant distress or makes daily life hard to manage.

- The symptoms are not better explained by other medical conditions, medication, or substance abuse.

- There is no other mental disorder to explain it.

GAD is distressing, but studies show it responds well to talk therapy, medication, or the two combined.

SPOT THE SYMPTOMS

GAD can masquerade as other problems: a 2002 German study found that almost **1 in 2** patients diagnosed with GAD had first complained of **physical symptoms**.

47.8%

Q PANIC DISORDER

Panic disorder is characterized by repeated, unprovoked panic attacks (see right). Under extreme stress, a single attack in response to an upsetting situation is not uncommon, and can happen to anyone, but seek medical advice if:

- You have repeated, unprovoked panic attacks.

- The fear of having a another panic attack is stopping you from going about your normal life – for instance, if you avoid certain places or situations you think might trigger an attack.

These are the key indicators of panic disorder, which can make life very difficult if left untreated, but which is known to respond well to treatment. Research suggests that talk therapy and medication are equally effective, so discuss with your doctor whether either or both options would suit you and your circumstances.

Surviving a panic attack

When a panic attack first strikes, you may feel like you're about to die. With a little foreknowledge, though, you can cope much better.

1 **Remind yourself that you are safe.** Panic attacks are frightening, but they are not fatal and they pass quickly.

2 **Eliminate distractions.** Sit down, cover your eyes, and focus on your breathing.

3 **Breathe slowly.** Holding your breath or hyperventilating will make things worse; instead, breathe slow and shallow, or take a deep breath and release it very gradually.

4 **Don't run away.** It's a natural desire, but fleeing the site of a panic attack can lead to you avoiding that place in future for fear of having another attack, which can become a serious problem. It's best to stay where you are and sit it out: it will pass.

HOW COMMON IS PANIC DISORDER?

Surveys across America and Europe estimate that between **1 in 50** and **1 in 20** people suffer from **panic disorder** at some point in their lives, but medical help can get repeated attacks under control.

2%-5%

POST-TRAUMATIC STRESS DISORDER

PTSD is an illness caused by a traumatic event – such as an assault, an accident, a difficult birth, or military combat – during which a person experienced intense fear, helplessness, or horror, and is unable to lower their stress levels to where they were before the trauma. Not everyone who is exposed to a traumatic event develops PTSD; a 2015 overview for the *British Medical Bulletin* reported that the two most decisive factors relate to the period immediately after the trauma:

- **Poor social support** (see pp.176–179).

- **Lacking a low-stress environment** in which to recover.

If you experience a traumatic event, prioritize finding a calm and supportive refuge rather than immediate counselling: a 2002 Dutch analysis found that psychological debriefing after a trauma made people more likely to develop PTSD. Initially it's best to take good care of yourself, surround yourself with supportive family and friends, and try to distract yourself with other positive activities. However, seek treatment if you experience several of these symptoms for more than a month:

- **Persistent thoughts,** images, dreams, illusions, flashbacks, or intense emotional distress in response to reminders of the event (including people and places).

- **The desire to avoid** discussion or reminders of the event.

- **At least two of the following:**
  - › Inability to recollect parts of the event.
  - › Persistent exaggerated ideas about the event's causes or consequences.
  - › Persistent negative beliefs about yourself, others, or the world.
  - › Loss of interest in usual or important activities.
  - › Feeling detached or estranged from others.
  - › Persistent inability to feel positive emotions.
  - › Anger, recklessness, self-harm, hypervigilance, jumpiness, poor concentration, or insomnia.

PTSD does not make you a coward; it is a real illness and can be treated. Trauma-focused CBT and a treatment known as Eye Movement Desensitization and Reprocessing (EMDR), administered by a trained expert, have been shown to have a good effect in reducing PTSD's symptoms.

WHO GETS PTSD?

7-8%

According to America's National Centre for PTSD, **10% of women** experience PTSD at some point in their lives, and **4% of men**. Research indicates the rate may be even higher among children.

SOCIAL ANXIETY DISORDER

Shyness is not a mental illness, but if the fear of social encounters stresses you to the point where it's difficult to work, socialize, or form relationships, you may have social anxiety disorder (SAD). Key features are:

- A persistent fear of situations in which you might be judged or rejected. (People from cultures with a strong emphasis on interdependence may also fear that they will embarrass the person they are talking to.)

- You know this fear is excessive but still avoid social situations or find them a miserable experience.

- This anxiety significantly affects your life and wellbeing.

A 2011 American study found that people with SAD (not to be confused with Seasonal Affective Disorder) had the most workplace problems of all the anxiety disorders, and were twice as likely to be unemployed. Medication and psychotherapy have been found to be effective treatment.

A WORD OF WARNING

26%

A 2013 American study found that 26% of people with anxiety disorders had thoughts of suicide. If that happens to you, **seek medical help immediately**.

What should I do?

Start by seeing your doctor, who will advise what treatments and therapies are available for anxiety disorders. While the strongest research evidence supports CBT (see pp.52–53), the best treatment is individualized for every person. Many studies suggest that combining medication and therapy gets the best results, so explore with your doctor what feels right to you. Good general self-care such as regular exercise, mindfulness, and social support are all important supplements to any course of treatment you pursue: the more you can reduce stress in your life, the more effective your treatment will be.

ANYTHING HOLDING YOU BACK?

Every anxiety disorder is associated with a particular fear, so depending on your condition, certain situations will be particularly stressful for you. Recognizing your symptoms and fears is the first step to identifying the help you need.

Condition	Symptoms	Fear
Generalized Anxiety Disorder	Excessive, uncontrolled, sustained anxiety that affects quality of life, and causes symptoms such as fatigue, headaches, stomach problems, restlessness, or muscle tension.	Fear of everyday stressors such as health or finances, but to an extreme and unwarranted degree for a period of at least six months.
Panic Disorder	Recurrent panic attacks (see p.205) that do not have another medical explanation.	During an attack: a fear of dying, having a heart attack or stroke, or losing your mind. Between attacks: a fear of places and situations that might trigger another one.
Post-Traumatic Stress Disorder	After a trauma, experiencing unwanted thoughts, images, and feelings, avoiding reminders, being constantly watchful, or feeling negative or disconnected from emotions.	Fear of re-living a traumatic event, or feeling that it is still happening.
Social Anxiety Disorder	Marked fear in social situations where there is a risk of being judged, leading to either serious distress or avoiding such situations.	Fear of being humiliated or embarrassed, to an excessive degree that interferes with your life and wellbeing.

SCREENING QUESTIONS

In trying to identify anxiety disorders, doctors have a set of standard screening questions. If you feel there's something wrong but you're not sure what, try anwering these four questions:

Would you call yourself **a worrier?** (Generalized Anxiety Disorder)

Do you have **waves of anxiety** that happen out of nowhere? (Panic Disorder)

Have you experienced **an upsetting event** that still haunts you? (Post-Traumatic Stress Disorder)

In situations where people can observe you, **do you worry about being judged?** (Social Anxiety Disorder)

A "yes" to one of these questions doesn't necessarily mean you have an anxiety disorder, but if you are finding life exceptionally stressful, ask your doctor for advice.

LIFEBOAT AHOY
COULD A THERAPIST HELP?

Sometimes we can cope on our own, or with help from loved ones, but if life is getting intolerably stressful, you might consider finding a good therapist to help you get your stress under control.

If stress is overwhelming you, it might be time to seek professional help. Psychologists, psychiatrists, clinical counsellors, social workers, and religious leaders can offer support and guidance as you work to manage your stress. When you're ready, sometimes just making the decision to ask for help can provide some relief.

> The object of therapy is to **gain relief** from symptoms and **improve quality of life**.
>
> **National Institute of Mental Health, America**

When to seek help
According to America's National Institute of Mental Health, common reasons for seeking therapy include:

- **Overwhelming sadness** or anxiety that won't go away.
- **Serious sleep issues** that are out of character for you.
- **Trouble concentrating** on work or everyday activities.
- **Potentially dangerous behaviour,** such as excessive drinking, drug abuse, or gambling.
- **Difficult situations,** such as family problems, bereavement, or pressure at work.
- **A desire to improve** your relationships and communication skills.
- **Feeling that you need to** understand yourself better.

If you feel you need therapy, respect that feeling and take prompt action to find the best person to provide that support.

Choosing the right person
It's important to find a therapist you can establish a good rapport with. According to Bruce Wampold, writing for the American Psychological Association, an effective therapist should:

- **Have strong interpersonal skills:** perceptiveness, warmth, and good communication.
- **Make a client feel** that the therapist is understanding and trusthworthy.
- **Form a professional relationship** with a clear, agreed-upon goal for the therapy.
- **Provide a sensible** and helpful explanation for the client's distress.
- **Offer a treatment plan** that matches the explanation.
- **Present the plan** in a convincing and encouraging way.

✅ WHERE TO LOOK?

Need some help with finding a therapist? Good places to ask for advice are:

- Doctors' referrals
- Website searches
- Local mental health associations
- Places of worship
- Word-of-mouth recommendations

- **Monitor a client's progress** with genuine concern for their wellbeing.
- **Be flexible** if a therapy plan isn't working out.
- **Facilitate** confronting difficult subjects in order to address the central problems.
- **Create a feeling** of hope for improvement.
- **Show awareness** of the client's particular character and context, such as their culture, religion, age, and motivations.
- **Be self-aware** and put aside their personal feelings.
- **Stay up to date** with the best research in the field relevant to the client's needs.
- **Constantly seek to improve** by listening to feedback.

✅ CAN YOU TELL ME?

America's National Institute of Mental Health advises asking a prospective therapist the questions below. Don't be shy: any reputable therapist will be perfectly happy to answer such questions. Unless you feel comfortable and confident, you're unlikely to have a beneficial experience.

What are your credentials and experience?

What are the goals of this therapy?

Do you have a speciality? (for instance, CBT, family therapy, trauma)

How many sessions do you expect to have with me?

Do you have experience in working with people like me?

Will there be homework?

What kind of therapy will we use? How does it work? What evidence is there to support it?

Do you prescribe medication? If not, and if I need medication, how will that be handled?

Are our sessions confidential? What do you do to assure that?

A poorly trained or unlicensed therapist can do a great deal of harm, so treat the first meeting as an interview (see above right) and make sure you feel comfortable. University training programs sometimes offer counselling at a discount: these are well supervised, and may be a sensible choice. Whichever route you take, see if there have been any complaints or negative feedback about your therapist: one or two bad ratings may just have been due to a personality clash – no therapist suits everyone – but if there are numerous complaints, take heed.

A therapist may need to raise some uncomfortable issues during your treatment, but if your discomfort is with the therapist themselves, find someone else. In order for you to feel better, your therapist must be someone you trust and who instills a sense of confidence.

HOLDING STEADY
LIVING A RESILIENT LIFE

Nobody, however strong or fortunate, lives a stress-free life, but even in times of adversity we can learn to manage stress and acquire resilience – and from there face the future with courage and optimism.

The tools described in this book help to build resilience – the capacity to recover quickly from the stresses of life. Stress provokes strong emotions, but resilience helps us to manage these and keep a sense of personal control. It is a life skill that almost everyone has the capacity to learn.

Staying strong

Finding ways of being resilient is a personal journey, but psychology offers key pointers to bear in mind:

✔ **Foster your relationships.** Make time to see loved ones and be ready to give and accept help: both are empowering.

✔ **Stay positive.** It's exhausting to search for the silver lining in every setback, but on a day-to-day basis, look for things to feel good about and enjoy them as much as you can.

✔ **Learn from experience.** Mistakes can teach us to make necessary changes. If we use good coping skills in the face of trauma or loss, we can build resilience even in dark moments.

✔ **Set positive, realistic goals.** Even a small achievement is something to celebrate.

✔ **Confront problems head-on.** Ignoring them lets them grow: if you gather your courage, identify the issues, and take constructive steps to tackle them, you're likely to feel a greater sense of control.

✔ **Cultivate faith in your own abilities.** Stress requires us to communicate our needs and find solutions; a resilient individual feels confident doing so.

✔ FOUR STEPS TO RESILIENCE

A useful path to identifying and building your resilience has been identified by American Cognitive Behavioural therapists Christine Padesky and Kathleen Mooney:

1 Search for your strengths. What positive beliefs, talents, abilities, and good qualities do you have that show you're a capable person? These needn't be qualities that only emerge in a crisis; look also for "hidden strengths" that show your resilience on ordinary days.

For example, "Even when I'm tired and fed up, I get my kids ready for school every day. I guess I'm persistent and responsible".

2 Construct a personal model of resilience (PMR). Write down the ordinary strengths you identified in step 1 and start creating a list of strategies that might help to promote your strengths. Think of images and metaphors that help build an identity you can be proud of.

"I'm a tough workhorse. I'll think about ways I can use my strength to make my job less stressful."

3 Think about how you might use your PMR to stay resilient in the situations that tend to cause you stress.

"The whole team is overworked. I'll make a point of being supportive to everyone."

4 When you experience setbacks or obstacles, start viewing them as opportunities to test your PMR and take pride in your successes.

"The boss was in a temper, but I stayed calm and checked in on everyone afterwards. I think it made us all feel better."

By using strengths-based CBT to develop a new self-identity as a capable person, you can make daily situations a "win-win": when things go your way, all is well, and when things are stressful, you'll be proud of your resilience.

✔ Love and care for yourself. Make time for rest, exercise, healthy food, and fun: these are ways of looking after yourself. And be sure to appreciate your strengths so that when things go well, you know you deserve it.

As American psychotherapist Amy Morin puts it, "Everyone has the ability to increase resilience to stress. It requires hard work and dedication, but over time, you can equip yourself to handle whatever life throws your way". We can never avoid stress entirely, but whenever we adapt in the face of adversity, manage our feelings, exercise good self-care, or recover from a period of pressure, we are both demonstrating and growing our resilience.

Q BUILD YOUR POSITIVITY

We can't expect to feel happy every minute of the day, but if we cultivate positive emotions such as pleasure, curiosity, affection, and optimism wherever we can, they help build resilience. A 2009 American study found positive emotions were strong predictors of wellbeing precisely because they make us more resilient, so enjoy life as much as you can: in the long term, as illustrated below, it will make you more stress-proof.

5 **Live a happier** and more successful life.

4 **Resilience increases.**

3 **Become better able** to build relationships and develop skills and resources.

2 **Feel less threatened** and stressed.

1 **Feel a positive emotion.**

I'M GOING TO CRY ABOUT IT, I'M GOING TO DRY MY EYES AND THEN I'M GOING BACK TO WORK

FRED JOHNSON, HURRICANE KATRINA SURVIVOR, INTERVIEWED BY PSYCHOLOGIST GARY STIX

SOURCES AND BIBLIOGRAPHY

While every effort has been made to ensure that the materials in this book are accurate, the publisher apologizes for any errors or omissions and would be grateful to be notified about any corrections.

Sources are given for main text, then panels. All links accessed May–July 2017.
APA: American Psychological Association.
Greater Good: The Greater Good Science Center at the University of California, Berkeley.
J.: *Journal of*

CHAPTER 1

12–13 I. M. Marks and R. M. Nesse, "Fear and fitness", *Ethology and Sociobiology* (1994); H. Selye, *The Stress of Life*, McGraw-Hill (1956). **14–15** K. McGonigal, in D. Schulte, "Science shows that stress has an upside", *The Washington Post* (2015); N. B. Schmidt et al, "Anxiety sensitivity", *J. Psychiatric Research* (2006); H. Murakami, *What I talk about when I talk about running*, Knopf (2008); APA (2017), "Stress in America: Coping With Change", Stress in America™ Survey. **16–17** K. McGonigal, cited in D. Grodsky, "Stress as a positive", TED Blog, 2013; D.Kaufer, cited in P. Jaret, "The Surprising Benefits of Stress", *Greater Good* (2015); E. D. Kirby et al, "Acute stress enhances adult rat hippocampal neurogenesis and activation of newborn neurons", *eLife* (2013); F. S. Dhabhar et al, "Stress-induced redistribution of immune cells", *Psychoneuroendocrinology* (2012); A. J. Crum et al "Rethinking stress", *J. Personality and Social Psychology* (2013); D. Kirby, cited in T. Bradberry, "How Successful People Stay Calm", talentsmart.com; J. P. Jamieson et al, "Improving Acute Stress Responses", *Current Directions in Psychological Science* (2013, first reported in 2012); APA (2015), "Stress in America: Stress Snapshot", Stress in America™ Survey. **18–19** B. P. F. Rutten et al, "Resilience in mental health", *Acta Psychiatrica Scandinavica* (2013); G. Donnaro, cited in G. Stix, "The Neuroscience of True Grit", *Scientific American* (2011); R. Dias et al, "Resilience of caregivers of people with dementia", *Trends in Psychiatry and Psychology* (2015). **20–21** G. S.

Everly and J. M. Lating, "The Anatomy and Physiology of the Human Stress Response", *A Clinical Guide to the Treatment of the Human Stress Response* (2013); W. B. Cannon, "The emergency function of the adrenal medulla", American J. Physiology Legacy Content Online; F. Hansen, "Fight or Flight vs Rest and Digest", adrenalfatiguesyndrome.com (2015); D. Goleman, "The Sweet Spot for Achievement", *Psychology Today* (2012); S. A. McLeod, "What is the stress response" (2010), *Simply Psychology*; P. J. Winklewski et al, "Stress Response, Brain Noradrenergic System and Cognition", *Advances in Experimental Medicine and Biology* (2017). **22–23** K. McGonigal, "How to make stress your friend", TED Talk (2013). **24–25** T. H. Holmes and R. H. Rahe, "The Social Readjustment Rating Scale", *J. Psychosomatic Research* (1967). **26–29** A. Wood Brooks, "Get Excited", *J. Experimental Psychology* (2014); E.K. Porensky and S. Wells-Di Gregorio, "Stress Management", Ohio State University; C. S. Carver and J. Connor-Smith, "Personality and Coping", *Annual Review of Psychology* (2010); R. Lazarus and S. Folkman, cited in S.M. Sincero, "Stress and Cognitive Appraisal", explorable.com; J.M. Grohol, "15 Common Defense Mechanisms", *Psych Central*. **30–31** L. R. Goldberg, "An Alternative 'Description of Personality'", *J. Personal and Social Psychology* (1990); O.P. John and S. Srivastava, "The Big-Five Trait Taxonomy", *Handbook of Personality*, The Guilford Press (1999). **32–33** S. E. Taylor et al, "Biobehavioral Responses To Stress In Females", *Psychological Review* (2000); L. Tomova et al, "Is stress affecting our ability to tune into others?", *Psychoneuroendocrinology* (2014); M. Ingalhalikar et al, "Sex differences in the structural connectome of the human brain", *Proceedings of the National Academy of Sciences of the United States of America* (2014), APA (2015), "Stress in America: Stress Snapshot", Stress in America™ Survey; APA (2010), "Stress in America Findings", Stress in America™ Survey. **34–35** K. G. Rice et al, "Meanings of Perfectionism", *J. Cognitive Psychotherapy* (2003); P. L. Hewitt, in E. Benson, "The many faces of perfectionism" *Monitor on Psychology*, APA (2003); R. C.

O'Connor and D. B. O'Connor, "Predicting hopelessness and psychological distress", *J. Counseling Psychology* (2003); J. Szymanski, "Perfectionism", *Expert Opinions*, International OCD Foundation; B. Brown, *The Gifts of Imperfection*, Hazelden Publishing (2010); "How to Overcome Perfectionism", AnxietyBC®; P. L. Hewitt and G. L. Flett, "Perfectionism and depression", *J. Social Behavior and Personality* (1990). **36–37** K. D. Neff and K. A Dahm, "Self-Compassion", in M. Robinson et al, *Handbook of Mindfulness and Self-Regulation*, Springer (2015). **38–39** P. Gilbert and C. Irons, "Focused therapies and compassionate mind training for shame and self-attacking", in P. Gilbert, *Compassion*, Routledge (2005); K. D. Neff and K. A Dahm (see 36–37 above); P. Gilbert, "Introducing compassion-focused therapy", *Advances in psychiatric treatment* (2009); H. Rockliff et al, "Heart rate variability and salivary cortisol responses to compassion-focused imagery", *Clinical Neuropsychiatry* (2008); K. Neff, "Exercise 2: Self-compassion break", self-compassion.org. **40–41** J. M. Smyth, "Written Emotional Expression", *J. Consulting and Clinical Psychology* (1998); K. J. Petrie et al, "Effect of Written Emotional Expression on Immune Function in Patients with HIV Infection", *Psychosomatic Medicine* (2004); P. M. Ullrich and S. K. Lutgendorf, "Journaling about stressful events", *Annals of Behavioral Medicine* (2002); J. W. Pennebaker, in B. Murray, "Writing to heal", *Monitor on Psychology*, APA (2002); J. W. Pennebaker and S. K. Beall, "Confronting a traumatic event", *J. Abnormal Psychology* (1986); J. W. Pennebaker and C. K. Chung (2011), cited in "James Pennebaker's Expressive Writing Paradigm", psychologyinaction.org. **42–43** M. H. Kernis. "Towards a Conceptualization of Optimal Self-Esteem", *Psychological Inquiry* (2003); R. Y. Erol and U. Orth, "Self-Esteem Development From Age 14 to 30 Years", *J. Personality and Social Psychology* (2011); G. Winch, "5 Ways to Boost Your Self-Esteem", *Psychology Today* (2016); N. Burton, "Building Confidence and Self-Esteem", *Psychology Today* (2012). **44–45** M. E. P. Seligman, "Pleasure, meaning, & eudaimonia", *Authentic*

Happiness (2002), University of Pennsylvania; D. A. Vella-Brodrick et al, "Three Ways to Be Happy", *Social Indicators Research* (2009, online 2008); V. Frankl, cited in "Viktor Frankl", The Pursuit of Happiness, Inc.; A. C. Parks and R. Biswas-Diener, in T. Kashdan and J. Ciarrochi, *Mindfulness, Acceptance, and Positive Psychology*, New Harbinger (2013); R. F. Baumeister, cited in E. Smith, "There's More to Life Than Being Happy" (2013), *The Atlantic*; C. Bailey and A. Madden, "What Makes Work Meaningful", *Sloan Management Review* (2016); L. George and C. L. Park (2016), cited in E. E. Smith and J. Aaker, "Pursue Meaning Instead of Happiness", *Science of Us*, nymag.com (2016). **46–47** J. Lamb et al, "Approach to bullying and victimization", *Canadian Family Physician* (2009); T. A. Field et al, "The New ABCs", *J. Mental Health Counseling* (2015); W. Hofmann et al, "Yes, But Are They Happy?", *J. Personality* (2014, online 2013); C. Pierce Keeton et al, "Sense of Control Predicts Depressive and Anxious Symptoms", *J. Family Psychology* (2008). **48–49** T. D. Borkovec (1983), cited in S. K. McGowan and E. Behar, "A Preliminary Investigation of Stimulus Control Training for Worry", *Behavior Modification* (2013); B. Verkuil, cited in J. Brownstein, "Planning 'Worry Time' May Help Ease Anxiety", livescience.com (2011); W. F. Doverspike, "How to Stop Obsessive Worry", Georgia Psychological Association (2008); L. Saulsman et al, "What? Me Worry!?!" (2015), Centre for Clinical Interventions; S. J. Gillihan, "5 reasons we worry", *Psychology Today* (2016). **50–51** W. James, cited in A. C. Ugural, *Living Better*, Eloquent Books (2009). **52–53** S. G. Hofmann et al, "The Efficacy of Cognitive Behavioral Therapy", *Cognitive Therapy and Research* (2012); F. Ghinassi, in C. Gregoire, "Work Stress", *Huffington Post* (2013); D. D. Burns, *Feeling Good*, William Morrow (1980). **54–55** "Know Your Stress To Manage Your Stress", Pattison Professional Counseling and Mediation Center (2014); B. Cullen et al, "Cognitive function and lifetime features of depression and bipolar disorder", *European Psychiatry* (2015).

CHAPTER 2

58–59 S. Cohen et al, "Socioeconomic status is associated with stress hormones", *Psychosomatic Medicine* (2006); R. V. Levine and A. Norenzayan, "The Pace of Life in 31 Countries", *J. Cross-Cultural Psychology* (1999); W. Ng et al, "Affluence, feelings of stress, and well-being", *Social Indicators Research* (2009, online 2008);

R. Veenhoven, "The Four Qualities of Life", *J. Happiness Studies* (2000); APA (2017), "Stress in America: Coping With Change", Stress in America™ Survey. **60–63** E. Ophir (2009), cited in T. Bradberry, "Multitasking Damages Your Brain and Career", forbes.com (2014); J. M. Kraushaar and D. C. Novak (2010), cited in A. M. Paul, "You'll Never Learn!", *Slate* (2013); L. Rosen, cited in J. Barshay, "How a 'tech break' can help students refocus", Hechinger Ed (2011); K. Lanaj, cited in S. Sleek, "The Psychological Toll of the Smartphone", Association for Psychological Science (2014); D. Derks et al, "Work-related smartphone use, psychological detachment and exhaustion", *J. Occupational Health and Psychology* (2014); R. Balding, cited in "People with smart phones fall victim to social networking stress", British Psychological Society (2012); E. A. Holman et al, "Media's role in broadcasting acute stress following the Boston Marathon bombings", *Proceedings of the National Academy of Sciences* (2013); APA (2017), "Stress in America: Coping With Change", Stress in America™ Survey; University of Cambridge, "Study shows some families have taken steps to avoid feeling overwhelmed by communications technologies", eng.cam.ac.uk (2011), reproduced under Creative Commons Attribution International License 4, with adaptation; R. Balding, cited in A. Kelly, "Student's phone study touches national nerve", *Worcester News* (2012); B. Wood et al, "Light level and duration of exposure determine the impact of self-luminous tablets on melatonin suppression", *Applied Ergonomics* (2013); M. Ritchel, "Attached to technology and paying a price", *The New York Times* (2010); D. Nelson, cited in W. K. Kleinman, "The stress factor of technology", newsok.com (2008); J. Suler, "The online disinhibition effect", *CyberPsychology & Behavior* (2004); A. G. Zimmerman, "Online Aggression", University of North Florida (2012). **64–65** D. Levitin, "Why the modern world is bad for your brain", *The Guardian* (2015); E. K. Miller, cited in J. Naish, "Is multi-tasking bad for your brain?", *Mail Online* (2009); E. M. Hallowell, cited in "The Power of Focus", *Tribal Business Journal*; D. Coviello et al, "Don't Spread Yourself Too Thin", *The National Bureau of Economic Research* (2010); G. Wilson, "The 'Infomania' Study" (2005); K. Foerde (2006), cited in A. Murphy Paul, "You'll never learn!", *Slate* (2013); G.D. Schott, "Doodling and the default network of the brain", *The Lancet* (2011); M. Karlesky and K. Isbister (2013), cited in M. Karlesky, "New widgets let you snap, crackle … and

think", livescience.com (2014); D. Meyer, cited in A. Murphy Paul, "You'll never learn!", *Slate* (2013); J. Andrade, "What does doodling do?", *Applied Cognitive Psychology* (2009); J. S. Rubinstein et al, "Executive Control of Cognitive Processes in Task Switching", *J. Experimental Psychology* (2001). **66–67** L. Bernstein, cited in R. Fox with H. Brown, *Creating a Purposeful Life*, Infinite Ideas (2012). **68–69** K. Murray, cited in J. Dodgson, "Body image problems linked to stress", abc.net.au (2009); C. C. Ross, "Why Do Women Hate Their Bodies?", *Psych Central* (2015); National Eating Disorders Association, cited in "Going to extremes", CNN; "Women's Body Image and BMI", rehabs.com; P. Diedrichs, cited in "Body image concerns more men than women", *The Guardian* (2012); S. T. Dunn (2004), cited in M. Dahl, "Six-pack stress", today.com; T. F. Cash et al, "Coping with body-image threats and challenges", *J. Psychosomatic Research* (2005); "New Plastic Surgery Statistics", American Society of Plastic Surgeons (2017). **70–73** J. Bowlby, cited in S. Johnson, *The Love Secret*, Little, Brown (2014); D. Saxbe and R. L. Repetti, "For Better or Worse?", *J. Personality and Social Psychology* (2010); L. A. Neff and B. R. Karney, "Stress and reactivity to daily relationship experiences", *J. Personality and Social Psychology* (2009); S. I. Powers, cited in L. Meyers, "Relationship conflicts stress men more than women", *Monitor on Psychology*, APA (2006); J. M. and J. Gottman, "How to keep love going strong", yesmagazine.org (2011); "Love and money", prnewswire.com (2015), B. R. Karney, "Keeping marriages healthy and why it's so difficult", *Psychological Science Agenda*, APA (2010); E. Lisitsa, "The Four Horsemen", The Gottman Institute (2013). **74–75** "Lack of sexual intimacy", National Healthy Marriage Resource Center; L. E. Savage, "Treating desire discrepancy in couples", goddesstherapy.com; B. W. McCarthy and E. J. McCarthy, *Rekindling Desire*, Routledge (2003); M. Weiner-Davis, "The Sex-Starved Marriage", psychotherapynetworker.org (2016); L. Brotto, cited in S. Auteri, "What you need to know about female sexual desire", American Association of Sexuality Educators, Counselors and Therapists (2014). **76–79** E. Stone (1985), cited in *Reader's Digest* (1989); K. H. Lagattuta et al, "Do you know how I feel?", *J. Experimental Child Psychology* (2012); H. T. Emery et al, "Maternal dispositional empathy and electrodermal reactivity", *J. Family Psychology* (2014); G. Dewar, "Parenting Stress", parentingscience.com (2016); D. M. Teti et al, "Maternal emotional availability at bedtime predicts infant sleep quality", *J. Family Psychology* (2010); S. Cronin et al, "Parents and Stress", University of Minnesota, *Children's Mental Health eReview* (2015); K. J. Joosen et al, "Maternal overreactive sympathetic nervous system responses to repeated infant crying", *Child Maltreatment* (2013); K. Zolten and N. Long, "Helping Children Cope With Stress", Center for Effective Parenting (2006); C. Carter, "Is Stress-Free Parenting Possible?", *Greater Good* (2011). **80–83** T. L. Lindquist et al, "Influence of lifestyle, coping and job stress on blood pressure", *Hypertension* (1997); "OSH Answers Fact Sheets: Workplace Stress", Canadian Centre for Occupational Health and Safety (2012); J. Ferrari, cited in D. Thompson, "The Procrastination Doom Loop", *The Atlantic* (2014); D. D. Burns, *Feeling Good*, William Morrow (1980); R. Eisenberger, "Learned Industriousness", classweb.uh.edu; P. Steel, "The Nature of Procrastination", *Psychological Bulletin* (2007); F. M. Sirois, "Procrastination and intentions to perform health behaviors", *Personality and Individual Differences* (2004); H. Gardner, "Leadership: A Master Class", youtube.com (2012), "A Passion for Work-Life Balance", Robert Half (2016); APA (2017), "Stress in America: Coping With Change", Stress in America™ Survey. **84–85** R. Bianchi et al, "Comparative symptomatology of burnout and depression", *J. Health Psychology* (2013); J. Montero-Marin et al, "Coping with stress and types of burnout", *PLoS ONE* (2014); P. Sheridan, cited in M. Ahmed, "One in three professionals 'is suffering from burnout'", *The Times* (2013); A. B. Bakker and E. Demerouti, "The Job Demands-Resources model", *J. Managerial Psychology* (2007); "Employee burnout common in nearly a third of UK companies", Robert Half (2013). **86–87** M. K. Gandhi, cited in N. Ramakrishnan, *Reading Gandhi in the Twenty-First Century* (2013). **88–89** K. Yarrow, in T. Klosowski, "How Stores Manipulate Your Senses So You Spend More Money", lifehacker.com (2013); E. W. Dunn et al, "Spending money on others promotes happiness", *Science* (2008); L. B. Aknin et al, "It's the Recipient That Counts", *PLoS ONE* (2011); M. A. Killingsworth and D. T. Gilbert, "A Wandering Mind Is an Unhappy Mind", *Science* (2010); T. Gilovich et al, "Waiting for Merlot", *Psychological Science* (2014); P. Raghubir and J. Srivastava, "The Denomination Effect", *J. Consumer Research* (2009); P. Brickman and D.T. Campbell (1971), cited in M. Binswanger, "Why Does Income Growth Fail to Make Us Happier?", Solothurn

University of Applied Science, Northwestern Switzerland (2003). **90–91** E. El Issa, "2016 American Household Credit Card Debt Study", nerdwallet.com; E. Y. Chou, cited in "Experiencing Financial Stress May Lead to Physical Pain", *Psychological Science* (2016); M. A. Skinner et al, "Financial Stress Predictors", *Cognitive Therapy and Research* (2004); R. L. Leahy, "Living with financial anxiety", psychotherapybrownbag.com (2009); APA (2017), "Stress in America: Coping With Change", Stress in America™ Survey; M. Amar et al, "Winning the Battle but Losing the War", *J. Marketing Research* (2011). **92–93** D. R. Ames and A. S. Wazlawek, "Pushing in the Dark", *Personality and Social Psychology Bulletin* (2014); V. M. Patrick and H. Hagtvedt (2012), cited in H. Grant Halvorson, "The Amazing Power of 'I Don't' vs. 'I Can't'", forbes.com (2013). **94–95** N. Pelusi, "The Right Way to Rock the Boat", *Psychology Today* (2016); G. A. Abed et al, "The Effect of Assertiveness Training Program on Improving Self-Esteem of Psychiatric Nurses", *J. Nursing Science* (2015); V. K. Bohns, cited in D. Ludden, "Ask and You Shall Receive", *Psychology Today* (2016). **96–97** S. Augustin (2009), cited in S. Whitaker, "The Effects of Population Density and Noise", *A Student of Psychology* (2014); E. C. Kim, "Nonsocial Transient Behavior", *Symbolic Interaction* (2012); R. S. Feldman (1985), cited in J. D. Meier, "Personal Space", sourceofinsight.com (2017); D. Elkin, "Protecting Your Personal Space", debelkin. com (2015). **98–99** R. S. Ulrich, "View though a window may influence recovery from surgery", American Association for the Advancement of Science (1984); O. Kardan, "Neighborhood greenspace and health in a large urban center", *Scientific Reports* (2015); N. M. Wells and G. W. Evans, "Nearby nature", *Environment and Behavior* (2003); B. Cimprich and D. L. Ronis, "An environmental intervention to restore attention in women with newly diagnosed breast cancer", *Cancer Nursing* (2003); B. J. Park (2010), cited in A. Alter, "How nature resets our minds and bodies", *The Atlantic* (2013); R. Kaplan and S. Kaplan, "The Restorative Benefits of Nature", *J. Environmental Psychology* (1995); P. Aspinall et al, "The urban brain", *British J. Sports Medicine* (2015, online 2013); G. N. Bratman et al, "Nature experience reduces rumination", *Proceedings of the National Academy of Sciences* (2015); M. Annerstedt et al "Inducing physiological stress recovery with sounds of nature in a virtual reality forest", *Physiology & Behavior* (2013); R. McCaffrey and P. Liehr,

"The Effect of Reflective Garden Walking on Adults With Increased Levels of Psychological Stress", *American Holistic Nurses Nurses Association* (2016). **100–101** M. L. Chanda and D. J. Levitin, "The neurochemistry of music", *Trends in Cognitive Sciences* (2013); S. Chafin et al, "Health can facilitate blood pressure recovery from stress", *British J. Health Psychology* (2004); E. Labbé et al, "Coping with Stress", *Applied Psychophysiology and Biofeedback* (2008); L. Brannon and J. Feist, "Health Psychology", Wadsworth Cengage Learning (2007); H. D. Thoreau, *Journals* IX (1857), cited in J. S. Cramer, "The Quotable Thoreau", Princeton (2011); T. Schäfer et al, "The sounds of safety", *Frontiers in Psychology* (2015); J. S. Verma and S. K. Khanna, "The Effect of Music on Salivary Cortisol", *J. Exercise Science and Physiotherapy* (2010); L. Bernardi et al, "Cardiovascular, cerebrovascular, and respiratory changes induced by different types of music", *Heart* (2006, online 2005); B. Bittman, cited in "How Playing Music Results in Breakthroughs for Inner City Youth", The National Association of Music Merchants (2009); D. Fancourt et al, "Singing modulates mood", *ecancermedicalscience* (2016); B. A. Bailey, "Effects of group singing and performance", *Psychology of Music* (2005); M. V. Thoma et al, "The Effect of Music on the Human Stress Response", *PLoS ONE* (2013). **102–103** R. Peters, "Ageing and the brain", *Postgraduate Medical Journal* (2006); R. Trouillet et al, "Impact of Age, and Cognitive and Coping Resources on Coping", *Canadian Journal on Aging* (2011); J. N. de Souza-Talarico et al, "Stress symptoms and coping strategies in healthy and elderly subjects", *Revista da Escola de Enfermagem da USP* (2009); C. M. Aldwin et al, "Age Differences in Stress, Coping, and Appraisal", *J. Gerontology* (1996); J. Pikhartova et al, "Is loneliness in later life a self-fulfilling prophecy?", *Aging & Mental Health* (2016, online 2105); R. Mushtaq et al, "Relationship between loneliness, psychiatric disorders and physical health", *J. Clinical & Diagnostic Research* (2014); J. Cacioppo, cited in I. Sample, "Loneliness twice as unhealthy as obesity for older people", *The Guardian* (2014); R. C. Atchley, cited in "Stages of Retirement", Families in Action. **104–105** "Key facts about carers and the people they care for", Carers Trust (2015); "Caregiving in the US 2015", National Alliance for Caregiving; M. M. Seltzer, cited in M. Diament, "Autism moms have stress similar to combat soldiers", *Disability Scoop* (2009); National Family Caregivers Association survey (2001), cited in "Caregiver statistics", Caregiver Action Network; "Facts about carers 2015", Carers UK; Alzheimer's Association®, "Caregiver stress", Alzheimer's and Dementia Caregiver Center. **106–107** APA (2006), "Forgiveness: a sampling of research results", Washington D.C., Office of International Affairs; F. Luskin and B. Bland, "Stanford–Northern Ireland Hope 1 Project", learningtoforgive.com (2000, 2010); J. Orloff, cited in S. Freedman and T. Zarifkar, "The Psychology of Interpersonal Forgiveness", *Spirituality in Clinical Practice* (2015). **108– 109** R. A. Emmons and M. E. McCullough, "Counting blessings versus burdens", *J. Personality and Social Psychology* (2003); A. M. Wood et al, "The role of gratitude in the development of social support, stress, and depression", *J. Research in Personality* (2008); A. M. Wood et al, "Gratitude influences sleep", *J. Psychosomatic Research* (2009); P. C. Watkins et al, "Taking care of business?", *J. Positive Psychology* (2008); N. M. Lambert and F. D. Finham, "Expressing gratitude to a partner", *Emotion* (2011); R. A. Emmons, "How Gratitude Can Help You Through Hard Times", *Greater Good* (2013); A. M. Gordon, "Five ways giving thanks can backfire", *Greater Good* (2013); S. Lyubomirsky, cited in J. Marsh, "Tips for keeping a gratitude journal", *Greater Good* (2011).

CHAPTER 3

112–113 T. J. Strauman et al, "Self-regulatory cognition and immune reactivity", *Brain, Behavior, and Immunity* (2004); S. R. Maddi, *Hardiness,* Springer (2013); J. D. Brown and K. L. McGill, "The cost of good fortune", *J. Personality and Social Psychology* (1989). **114–115** R. M. Nideffer, "Getting Into the Optimal Performance State", enhanced-performance.com; D. Greene, "11 Strategies for Audition and Performance Success", psi. donegreene.com; "America's Top Fears 2016", Chapman University; G. Ramirez and S. L. Beilock, "Writing about testing worries boosts exam performance", *Science* (2011, 2014). **116–117** M. H. Kernis and B. M. Goldman, "A multicomponent conceptualization of authenticity", *Advances in Experimental Social Psychology* (2006); A. L. Sillars et al, "Communication and conflict in marriage", *Communication Yearbook* (1983); R. M. Reznik et al, "Communication During Interpersonal Arguing", *Argumentation and Advocacy* (2010); K. A. Vertino, "Effective Interpersonal Communication", *Online J. Issues in Nursing* (2014); E. L. Deci and R. M. Ryan, "SDT",

selfdeterminationtheory.org. **118–119** N. Harrington, "Frustration Intolerance", *J. Rational-Emotive and Cognitive-Behavior Therapy* (2011); A. Lickerman, "How to Manage Frustration", *Psychology Today* (2012); N. Harrington, "The Frustration Discomfort Scale", *Clinical Psychology and Psychotherapy* (2005); M. E. Keough et al, "Anxiety Symptomatology", *Behavior Therapy* (2010). **120–121** D. A. Sbarra et al, "Divorce and Health", *Current Directions in Psychological Science* (2015); L. Kulik and E. Heine-Cohen, "Coping Resources, Perceived Stress and Adjustment to Divorce Among Israeli Women", *J. Social Psychology* (2011); D. A. Sbarra et al, "Divorce and Health", *Current Directions in Psychological Science* (2015). **122–123** M. K. Shea, "Getting Straight About Grief", *Depression and Anxiety* (2012). **124–125** S. Hayes, cited in R. Harris, "Embracing Your Demons", *Psychotherapy in Australia* (2006); K. Strosahl, in K. Kseib, "Pain is inevitable, but suffering is optional", *The Psychologist* (2016); S. Hayes, cited in J. Belmont, "Effective Use of Metaphors in the ACT Theory", belmontwellness.com; H. Brinkborgh et al, "Acceptance and commitment therapy for the treatment of stress among social workers", *Behaviour Research and Therapy* (2011). **126–127** K. Strosahl, in K. Kseib, "Pain is inevitable, but suffering is optional", *The Psychologist* (2016). **128–129** M. Mitchell, "Dr. Herbert Benson's Relaxation Response", *Psychology Today* (2013); A. Meuret, cited in S. Pappas, "To stave off panic, don't take a deep breath", livescience.com (2010); P. Philippot et al, "Respiratory feedback in the generation of emotion", *Cognition & Emotion* (2002), cited in R. P. Brown and P. L. Gerbarg, "Yoga breathing, meditation, and longevity", *Annals of the New York Academy of Sciences* (2009); J. J. Arch and M. G. Craske, "Mechanisms of mindfulness", *Behaviour Research and Therapy* (2006). **130–131** H. A. Hashim and H. H. A. Yusof, "The Effects of Progressive Muscle Relaxation and Autogenic Relaxation on Young Soccer Players' Mood States", *Asian J. Sports Medicine* (2011); P. N. Hui et al, "An Evaluation of Two Behavioral Rehabilitation Programs", *J. Alternative and Complementary Medicine* (2006); C. A. Puskarich et al, "Effects of progressive muscle relaxation training on seizure reduction", *Epilepsia* 33 (1992); A. Heenan and N. F. Troje, "Both Physical Exercise and Progressive Muscle Relaxation Reduce the Facing-the-Viewer Bias in Biological Motion Perception", *PloS ONE* (2014). **132–135** S. R. Bishop et al, "Mindfulness: A Proposed

Operational Definition", *Clinical Psychology: Science and Practice* (2004); J. Gu et al, "How do mindfulness-based therapy and mindfulness-based stress reduction improve mental health and wellbeing?", *Clinical Psychology Review* (2015); J. Kabat-Zinn and S. F. Santorelli, "Mindfulness-Based Stress Reduction (MSBR) Standards of Practice", The Center for Mindfulness in Medicine, Health Care, and Society, University of Massachusetts Medical School (2014); R. J. Davidson et al, "Alterations in brain and immune function produced by mindfulness meditation", *Psychosomatic Medicine* (2003); E. Goldstein, cited in J. Lin, "Mindfulness reduces stress, promotes resilience", *UCLA Today* (2009). **136–137** J. Frank "Stress management during the holidays", Clinical Psychology Associates of North Central Florida; G. Rubin "8 Tips to Beat Holiday Stress", gretchenrubin.com (2010); M. C. Daball and P. Kimpton, "How do I deal with seasonal affective disorder?", *The Guardian* (2015), APA (2008), "Financial Concerns Top List of Holiday Stressors for Women, Families with Children"; D. Cotterell, "Pathogenesis and management of seasonal affective disorder", *Progress in Neurology and Psychiatry* (2010); P. Regan and T. Orbuch cited in A. Ossola, "Why Are Holidays With Your Family So Stressful?", *Popular Science* (2015); K. Duckworth, cited in "Beat Back The Holiday Blues", National Alliance on Mental Illness (2008); P. Wiegartz, "10 Common Holiday Stresses", *Psychology Today* (2011). **138–139** L. Boschloo et al, "Heavy alcohol use", *Drug and Alcohol Dependence* (2011); A. Ostroumov et al, "Stress Increases Ethanol Self-Administration", *Neuron* (2016); A. Hassanbeigi et al, "The Relationship between Stress and Addiction", *Social and Behavioral Sciences* (2013); "Facts About Alcohol", National Council on Alcohol and Drug Dependence (2015). **140–141** A. Boyes, "Avoidance Coping", *Psychology Today* (2013). **142–143** D. L. Musselman (2001), cited in M. Wei, "The surprising psychology of the common cold", *Psychology Today* (2015); M. Schoen, *When Relaxation is Hazardous to Your Health*, Mind Body Health Books (2001); P. S. Chandra and G. Desai, "Denial as an experiential phenomenon in serious illness", *Indian J. Palliative Care* (2007); A. Vingerhoets, cited in E. Saner, "Sick on arrival", *The Guardian* (2007), M. Schoen, cited in S. Colino, "The Real Reason You Get Sick After A Stressful Period Has Ended", *Huffington Post* (2016).

CHAPTER 4

146–147 T. Ballard et al, "Departures from optimality when pursuing multiple approach or avoidance goals", *J. Applied Psychology* (2016); N. Liberman and Y. Trope, "The Psychology of Transcending the Here and Now", *Science* (2008); A. Winch et al, "Unique associations between anxiety, depression and motives for approach and avoidance goal pursuit", *Cognition and Emotion* (2015, online 2014); J. Szymanski, "The Real Curse of Being a Perfectionist", *CNBC* (2011). **148–149** C. A. Higgins et al, "Coping With Overload and Stress", *J. Marriage and Family* (2010); J. M. Patterson and H. I. McCubbin, "Gender Roles and Coping", *J. Marriage and Family* (1984); S. Behson, "How to Cope with Work-Family Conflict and Stress (part 2)", *Fathers, work and family* (2013); Bureau of Labor Statistics 2016, "Employment Characteristics of Families Summary", bls.gov (2017); G. W. Bird and A. Schnurman-Crook, "Professional Identity and Coping Behaviors in Dual-Career Couples", *Family Relations* (2005). **150–151** C. R. Martell, "Behavioral Activation Therapy", christophermartell.com; S. Dimidjian et al, "The Origins and Current Status of Behavioral Activation Treatments for Depression", *Annual Review of Clinical Psychology* (2011); "Choose Your Actions, Choose Your Mood", Harley Therapy (2014). **152–153** G. M. Cooney et al, "Exercise for depression", *Cochrane Database of Systematic Reviews* (2013); J. C. Smith, "Effects of emotional exposure on state anxiety after acute exercise", *Medicine and Science in Sports and Exercise* (2013); H. Guiney and L. Machado, "Benefits of regular aerobic exercise for executive functioning in healthy populations", *Psychonomic Bulletin & Review* (2013, online 2012); T. J. Schoenfeld et al, "Physical Exercise Prevents Stress-Induced Activation of Granule Neurons", *J. Neuroscience* (2013). **154–155** M. Teut et al, "Effectiveness of a mindfulness-based walking programme in reducing symptoms of stress", *European J. Integrative Medicine* (2012); R. L. McMillan et al, "Ode to positive constructive daydreaming", *Frontiers in Psychology* (2013); M. Opezzo and D. L. Schwartz, "Give Your Ideas Some Legs", *J. Experimental Psychology* (2014); R. Biswas-Diener, "Mindlessness Can Be Just as Productive as Mindfulness", *New Republic* (2014), M. G. Berman et al, "The Cognitive Benefits of Interacting With Nature", *Psychological Science* (2008), cited in A. Arbor, "Going outside–even in the cold–improves memory, attention", University of Michigan (2008); W. Bumgardner, "How to Get the Best Walking Posture", verywell.com (2017); T. W. Puetz, cited in S. Fahmy, "Low-intensity exercise reduces fatigue symptoms", University of Georgia (2008). **156–157** H. Cramer et al, "Yoga for depression", *Depression and Anxiety* (2013); F. Wang et al, "The Effects of Tai Chi on Depression, Anxiety, and Psychological Well-Being", *International J. Behavioral Medicine* (2014); R. P. Brown and P. L. Gerbarg, "Surdarshan Kriya Yogic Breathing in the Treatment of Stress, Anxiety, and Depression", *J. Alternative and Complementary Medicine* (2005); M. Greenberg, cited in A. Novotney, "Yoga as a practice tool", *Monitor on Psychology*, APA (2009). **158–161** E. Epel et al "Stress may add bite to appetite", *Psychoneuroendocrinology* (2001); C. A. Maglione-Garves et al, "Cortisol Connection", University of New Mexico; M. F. Dallman et al, "Chronic stress and comfort foods", *Brain, Behavior, and Immunity* (2005); C. A. Shively et al, "Social stress, visceral obesity, and coronary artery atherosclerosis", *American J. Primatology* (2009); A. J. Tomiyama et al, "Low Calorie Dieting Increases Cortisol", *Psychosomatic Medicine* (2010); D. E. Pankevich et al, "Caloric Restriction Experience Reprograms Stress", *J. Neuroscience* (2010); D. Cummins, "This is Why We're Fat and Sick", *Psychology Today* (2013); APA (2017), "Stress in America: Coping With Change", Stress in America™ Survey; *Intuitive Eating*, cited in M. Allison, "Lesson three – How does hunger feel?", *The Fat Nutritionist* (2011); A. S. Cain et al "Refining the Relationships of Perfectionism, Self-Efficacy, and Stress to Dieting and Binge Eating", *International J. Eating Disorders* (2008); T. Mann et al, "Medicare's search for effective obesity treatments", *American Psychologist*, APA (2007); M. Greenberg, "The 5 Best Ways to Manage Your Weight and Eating", *Psychology Today* (2011); A. J. Bradshaw et al, "Non-dieting interventions for overweight and obese women", *Public Health Nutrition* (2009); A. Burokas, cited in D. Ahlstrom, "Irish-based scientists find a way to beat stress by eating", *The Irish Times* (2017); F. N. Jacka et al, "Western diet is associated with a smaller hippocampus ", *BMC Medicine* (2015); A. Sánchez-Villegas et al, "Mediterranean dietary pattern and depression", *BMC Medicine* (2013). **162–163** National Sleep Foundation, "Insomnia & You"; M. Hirshkowitz et al, "NSF sleep time duration recommendations", *Sleep Health* (2015); P. Alhola and P. Polo-Kantola, "Sleep deprivation", *Neuropsychiatric Disease and Treatment* (2007); American Academy of Sleep Medicine, cited in S. Schutte-Rodin et al, "Clinical Guideline for the Evaluation and Management of Chronic Insomnia in Adults", *J. Clinical Sleep Medicine* (2008); NSF 1991 survey, cited in S. Ancoli-Israel and T. Roth, "Characteristics of insomnia in the United States", *Sleep* (1999); M. M. Ohayon, "Epidemiology of insomnia", *Sleep Medicine Reviews* (2002); M. Smolensky and L. Lamberg, *The Body Clock Guide to Better Health*, Holt (2001); NHIS 2010, cited in "Short Sleep Duration Among Workers", *Morbidity and Mortality Weekly Report*, Centers for Disease Control and Prevention (2012); M. R. Rosekind et al, "The cost of poor sleep", *J. Occupational and Environmental Medicine* (2010); B. Riedel et al, "A comparison of the efficacy of stimulus control for medicated and nonmedicated insomniacs", *Behavior Modification* (1998); T. Morgenthaler et al and the American Academy of Sleep Medicine, "Practice parameters for the psychological and behavioral treatment of insomnia", *Sleep* (2006). **166–167** K. D. Vohs, cited in "A messy desk encourages a creative mind?", *Monitor on Psychology*, APA (2013); S. McMains and S. Kastner, cited in E. Doland, "Scientists find physical clutter negatively affects your ability to focus", unclutterer.com (2011); D. Kahneman and A. Tversky (1979) and D. Kahneman (1990), cited in A. Castel, "Declutter NOW!", *Psychology Today* (2016); J. E. Arnold et al, *Life at Home in the 21st Century*", Cotsen Institute of Archeology Press, UCLA (2012); S. Gannon, "Hooked on Storage", *The New York Times* (2007); R. O. Frost and G. Steketee, *Stuff*, Houghton Mifflin Harcourt Publishing Company (2010). **168–169** R. F. Baumeister et al, "Ego Depletion", *J. Personality and Social Psychology* (1998); M. Muraven et al, "Daily fluctuations in self-control demands and alcohol intake", *Psychology of Addictive Behaviors* (2005); D. Spears, "Economic decision-making in poverty depletes behavioral control", Princeton University (2010); V. Job et al, "Ego Depletion–Is It All In Your Head?", *Psychological Science* (2010); M. Muraven, "Practicing Self-Control Lowers the Risk of Smoking Lapse", *Psychology of Addictive Behaviors* (2010); M. Friese et al, "Mindfulness meditation counteracts self-control depletion", *Consciousness and Cognition* (2012); D. J. A. Jenkins et al, "Glycemic index: implications in health and disease", *American J. Clinical Nutrition* (2002); APA (2011), "Stressed in America", Stress in America™ Survey; T. F. Heatherton and D. D. Wagner, "Cognitive Neuroscience of Self-Regulation

Failure", *Trends in Cognitive Sciences* (2011). **170–171** L. Schwabe et al, "Simultaneous Glucocorticoid and Noradrenergic Activity", *J. Neuroscience* (2012); P. Lally et al, "How habits are formed", *European J. Social Psychology* (2010); P. M. Gollwitzer and G. Oettingen (1999), in M. Gellman and J. R. Turner, *Encyclopedia of behavioural medicine*, Springer (2013); K. D. Vohs et al, "Making choices impairs subsequent self-control", *J. Personality and Social Psychology* (2008). **172–173** V. E. Frankl, *Man's Search for Meaning*, Simon and Schuster (1963). **174–175** M. and I. S. Csíkszentmihályi, *Optimal Experience*, Cambridge University Press (1988); R. Larson and M. Csíkszentmihályi, "The Experience Sampling Method", *Flow and the Foundations of Positive Psychology*, Springer (2014); O. Schaffer, "Crafting Fun User Experiences", Human Factors International (2013); D. Goleman, "How to Achieve a Flow State", linkedin.com (2013). **176–179** J. Holt-Lunstad et al, "Social Relationships and Mortality Risks", *PLoS Med* (2010); L. Beckes et al, "Familiarity promotes blurring of self and other in the neural representation of threat", *Social Cognitive and Affective Neuroscience* (2013); E. B. Raposa et al, "Prosocial Behaviour Mitigates the Negative Effects of Stress in Everyday Life", *Association for Psychological Science* (2016, online 2015); R. E. Adams et al, "The Presence of a Best Friend Buffers the Effects of Negative Experiences", *Developmental Psychology* (2011); M. Trudeau, "Human Connections Start With A Friendly Touch", npr.org (2010); R. I. M. Dunbar, "Do online social media cut through the constraints that limit the size of offline social networks?", The Royal Society Publishing (2016); J. H. Fowler and N. A. Christakis, "Dynamic spread of happiness in a large social network", *BMJ* (2008); S. Degges-White, "13 Red Flags of Potentially Toxic Friendships", *Psychology Today* (2015); O. Ybarra et al, "Friends (and Sometimes Enemies) With Cognitive Benefits" *Social Psychological and Personality Science* (2011, online 2010). **180–181** J. Lohr, cited in S. Boardman, "Conscious complaining", *Huffington Post* (2016); R. M. Kowalski, *Aversive Interpersonal Behaviors*, Springer (1997); B. Smyth, "Why We Complain and How to Make It More Effective", *NST Insights* (2016). **182–183** R. I. M. Dunbar et al, "Social laughter is correlated with an elevated pain threshold", *Proceedings of The Royal Society B* (2011); A. C. Samson and J. J. Gross, "Humour as emotion regulation", *Cognition and Emotion*

(2012, received 2010); R. Provine, "The Science of Laughter", *Psychology Today*, (2000); M. P. Bennett et al, "The Effect of Mirthful Laughter on Stress and Natural Killer Cell Activity", *Alternative Therapies in Health and Medicine* (2003); J. Rotton and M. Shats, "Effects of State Humor, Expectancies, and Choice on Postsurgical Mood and Self-Medication", *J. Applied Psychology* (1996); W. Fry, cited in P. Doskoch, "Happily Ever Laughter", *Psychology Today* (1996). **184–185** S. Scott, "Why we laugh", TED Talk (2015). **186–187** G. Kaimal et al, "Reduction of cortisol levels and participants' responses following art making", *J. the American Art Therapy Association* (2016); D. Siegel (2010), cited in C. Malchiodi, "Expressive arts therapy and windows of tolerance", *Psychology Today* (2016); R. van der Vennet and S. Serice, "Can coloring mandalas reduce anxiety?", *J. American Art Therapy Association* (2012); University of Otago, "Creative activities promote day-to-day wellbeing", *Science Daily* (2016); J. Leckey, 'The therapeutic effectiveness of creative activities on mental well-being', *J. Psychiatric and Mental Health Nursing* (2011). **188–189** K. Allen et al, "Cardiovascular reactivity and the presence of pets, friends and spouses", *Psychosomatic Medicine* (2002); L. Wood et al, "The Pet Factor", *PLoS One* (2015); F. Moretti et al, "Pet therapy in elderly patients with mental illness", *Psychogeriatrics* (2011); P. Donelly, "How pets make us MORE stressed", *Mail Online* (2014); S. Shiloh et al, "Reduction of state-anxiety by petting animals", *Anxiety, Stress and Coping* (2003); H. Nittono et al, "The Power of Kawaii", *PLoS One* (2012); D. Wells, "The value of pets for human health", *The Psychologist* (2011). **190–191** N. I. Eisenberger et al, "Does rejection hurt?", *Science* (2003); J. T. Cacioppo et al, "Lonely traits and concomitant physiological processes", *International J. Psychophysiology* (2000); L. C. Hawkley and J. T. Cacioppo, "Loneliness Matters", *Annals of Behavioral Medicine* (2010); G. Winch, cited in R. Marantz Henig, "Guess I'll Go Eat Worms", *The Archipelago* (2014); M. Burke and R. E. Kraut, "The Relationship Between Facebook Use and Well-Being", *J. Computer-Mediated Communication* (2016); G. Winch, "Why Loneliness Is a Trap and How to Break Free", *Psychology Today* (2013). **192–193** K. Rimfield et al, "True Grit and Genetics", *J. Personality and Social Psychology* (2016); A. L. Duckworth et al, "Grit", *J. Personality and Social Psychology* (2007); E. V. Blalock et al, "Stability amidst turmoil", *Psychiatry Research* (2015).

CHAPTER 5

196–197 K. Kozlowska, "Stress, Distress and Bodytalk", *Harvard Review of Psychiatry* (2013). **198–199** M. Jonson-Reid (2012), cited in A. M. Jackson and K. Deye, "Aspects of Abuse", *Current Problems in Pediatric and Adolescent Health Care* (2015); N. R. Nugent et al, "The Emerging Field of Epigenetics", *J. Pediatric Psychology* (2016); D. M. Rubin (2008), cited in Jackson and Deye (2015), above; E. McGrath, "Recovering from Trauma", *Psychology Today* (2001); M. H. Teicher (2000), cited in Jonson-Reid et al, "Child and adult outcomes of chronic child maltreatment", *Pediatrics* (2012). **200–201** S. McManus et al, "Mental health and wellbeing in England", *Adult Psychiatric Morbidity Survey*, NHS (2014); National Institute of Mental Health, "Any mental illness among U.S. adults", nimh.nih.gov (2015); K. Hughes et al, "Prevalence and risk of violence against adults with disabilities, *The Lancet* (2012). **202–203** C. Hammen, "Stress and depression", *Annual Review of Clinical Psychology* (2005); World Health Organization, "Depression: Let's talk", who.int (2017); D. F. Levinson and W. E. Nichols, "Major depression and genetics", *Genetics of Medicine*, Stanford Medicine. **204–207** H. U. Wittchen (2002), cited in H. Combs and J. Markman, "Anxiety Disorders in Primary Care", *Medical Clinics of North America* (2014); E. D. Paul et al, "The Deakin Graeff hypothesis", *Neuroscience and Biobehavioral Reviews* (2014); D. Khoshaba, "Are you living with chronic worry and fear?", *Psychology Today* (2012); N. Greenberg et al, "Latest developments in post-traumatic stress disorder", *British Medical Bulletin* (2015); A. A. Van Emmerik (2002), cited in Greenberg (2015), above; E. Moitra et al, "Occupational impairment and Social Anxiety Disorder in a sample of primary care patients", J. *Affective Disorders* (2011); J. Bomyea (2013), cited in Combs and Markman (2014), above. **208–209** National Institute for Mental Health, "Psychotherapies" (2016); B. E. Wampold, "Qualities and actions of effective therapists", *Continuing Education in Psychology*, APA Education Directorate. **210–211** A. Morin, "Are You Mentally Strong Enough to Combat Stress?", *Psychology Today* (2015); C. A. Padesky and K. A. Mooney, "Strengths-Based Cognitive-Behavioural Therapy", *Clinical Psychology and Psychotherapy* (2012); M. A. Cohn et al, "Happiness Unpacked", *Emotion* (2009). **212–213** F. Johnson, in G. Stix, "The neuroscience of true grit", *Scientific American* (2011).

INDEX